This book is a masterful com[bination of...] professional standards, and [...] supportive, and socially jus[t...] [...] and addressing problems of professional competence. Educators, supervisors, administrators, and policy makers will all find thought-provoking material and practical advice to guide effective and humane work.

—**Debora J. Bell, PhD,** Professor and Chair of Psychological Sciences, University of Missouri, Columbia, MO, United States; Fellow of the American Psychological Association

It is easy to tell trainees in our programs that they should feel welcome and that we care. The distinguished authors in this volume explore the much harder task of creating a culture that actualizes our commitment to *all* trainees, including those who struggle. The practical, ethical, legal, contextual, systemic, and theoretical considerations in this volume will be immensely useful to trainees and trainers at every level.

—**Mitchell M. Handelsman, PhD,** Professor and CU President's Teaching Scholar, University of Colorado Denver, Denver, CO, United States

In this book, recognized experts provide an excellent and comprehensive overview of the state of the field related to trainees with competence problems. However, what is truly groundbreaking is their explicit incorporation of communitarian and multicultural perspectives that provide an enhanced and compassionate context for the critical task of training future psychologists for lifelong professional competence and resilience.

—**Erica H. Wise, PhD,** Clinical Professor Emerita and Adjunct Professor, Department of Psychology & Neuroscience, University of North Carolina at Chapel Hill, Chapel Hill, NC, United States

Supporting Trainees
With Competence Problems

Supporting Trainees
With Competence Problems

A PRACTICAL GUIDE FOR PSYCHOLOGY TRAINERS

REBECCA A. SCHWARTZ-METTE
EVELYN A. HUNTER
NADINE J. KASLOW

Editors

 AMERICAN PSYCHOLOGICAL ASSOCIATION

Copyright © 2023 by the American Psychological Association. All rights reserved. Except as permitted under the United States Copyright Act of 1976, no part of this publication may be reproduced or distributed in any form or by any means, including, but not limited to, the process of scanning and digitization, or stored in a database or retrieval system, without the prior written permission of the publisher.

The opinions and statements published are the responsibility of the authors, and such opinions and statements do not necessarily represent the policies of the American Psychological Association.

Published by
American Psychological Association
750 First Street, NE
Washington, DC 20002
https://www.apa.org

Order Department
https://www.apa.org/pubs/books
order@apa.org

In the U.K., Europe, Africa, and the Middle East, copies may be ordered from Eurospan
https://www.eurospanbookstore.com/apa
info@eurospangroup.com

Typeset in Charter and Interstate by Circle Graphics, Inc., Reisterstown, MD

Printer: Gasch Printing, Odenton, MD
Cover Designer: Anthony Paular Design, Newbury Park, CA

Library of Congress Cataloging-in-Publication Data

Names: Schwartz-Mette, Rebecca A., editor. | American Psychological Association.
Title: Supporting trainees with competence problems : a practical guide for psychology trainers / edited by Rebecca A. Schwartz-Mette, Evelyn A. Hunter, and Nadine J. Kaslow.
Description: Washington, DC : American Psychological Association, [2023] | Includes bibliographical references and index.
Identifiers: LCCN 2022043522 (print) | LCCN 2022043523 (ebook) | ISBN 9781433840432 (paperback) | ISBN 9781433840449 (ebook)
Subjects: LCSH: Psychology--Study and teaching (Internship) | Clinical psychology.
Classification: LCC BF77 .S87 2023 (print) | LCC BF77 (ebook) | DDC 150.71--dc23/eng/20221212
LC record available at https://lccn.loc.gov/2022043522
LC ebook record available at https://lccn.loc.gov/2022043523

https://doi.org/10.1037/0000340-000

Printed in the United States of America

10 9 8 7 6 5 4 3 2 1

Contents

Contributors   *vii*

Introduction: Building a Supportive Culture for Trainees
Managing Competence Issues   3
Rebecca A. Schwartz-Mette, Evelyn A. Hunter, and Nadine J. Kaslow

1. Creating a Communitarian, Multiculturally Sensitive,
   and Socially Just Training Culture   9
   Mary Mendoza-Newman and Jennifer A. Erickson Cornish

2. Competencies in Health Service Psychology   25
   Lydia McGaffee, Cassandra Rasmussen, and Emil Rodolfa

3. Problems of Professional Competence   43
   Suzanne H. Lease and Catherine L. Grus

4. Systemic Perspectives on Trainees With Problems of
   Professional Competence   61
   Debra Mollen and Marlene G. Williams

5. Identification and Assessment of Problems of Professional
   Competence   79
   Salina M. Renninger and Consuelo E. Cavalieri

6. Remediation, Counseling Out, and Dismissal   99
   Rebecca A. Schwartz-Mette

7. **Trainee Confidentiality: The Hidden Challenge of Competence Problems**   125
Linda M. Forrest and Nancy S. Elman

8. **Ethical Issues in Working With Trainees With Problems of Professional Competence**   149
Jeffrey E. Barnett and W. Brad Johnson

9. **Legal Issues in Working With Trainees With Problems of Professional Competence**   171
Sanjay Shah and Sarah R. Fishel

10. **Building Program Policies in a Communitarian and Multiculturally Sensitive Training Culture**   193
Jennifer C. Veilleux and Meredith Scafe

11. **Troubleshooting Common Pitfalls**   213
Evelyn A. Hunter and Rebecca A. Schwartz-Mette

Appendix A: Key Terms   *231*
Appendix B: Cube Model for Competency Development   *237*
Appendix C: Competency Remediation Plan   *239*
Appendix D: Additional Resources for Readers   *243*
Index   *245*
About the Editors   *261*

Contributors

Jeffrey E. Barnett, PsyD, ABPP, Loyola University Maryland, Baltimore, MD, United States
Consuelo E. Cavalieri, PhD, University of St. Thomas, Minneapolis, MN, United States
Nancy S. Elman, PhD, University of Pittsburgh, Pittsburgh, PA, United States
Jennifer A. Erickson Cornish, PhD, ABPP, University of Denver, Denver, CO, United States
Sarah R. Fishel, MS, Esq., Drexel University, Philadelphia, PA, United States
Linda M. Forrest, PhD, University of Oregon, Eugene, OR, United States
Catherine L. Grus, PhD, American Psychological Association, Washington, DC, United States
Evelyn A. Hunter, PhD, Auburn University, Auburn, AL, United States
W. Brad Johnson, PhD, United States Naval Academy, Annapolis, MD, United States
Nadine J. Kaslow, PhD, ABPP, Emory University, Atlanta, GA, United States
Suzanne H. Lease, PhD, University of Memphis, Memphis, TN, United States
Lydia McGaffee, MA, California School of Professional Psychology, Alliant International University, Sacramento, CA, United States
Mary Mendoza-Newman, PhD, Stanford University, Counseling and Psychological Services, Stanford, CA, United States
Debra Mollen, PhD, Texas Woman's University, Denton, TX, United States
Cassandra Rasmussen, PsyD, University of Texas at Tyler Health Science Center, Tyler, TX, United States

Salina M. Renninger, PhD, University of St. Thomas, Minneapolis, MN, United States

Emil Rodolfa, PhD, California School of Professional Psychology, Alliant International University, Sacramento, CA, United States

Meredith Scafe, MSW, MA, University of Arkansas, Fayetteville, AR, United States

Rebecca A. Schwartz-Mette, PhD, University of Maine, Orono, ME, United States

Sanjay Shah, JD, PhD, Atlas Psychological Services, Atlanta, GA, United States

Jennifer C. Veilleux, PhD, University of Arkansas, Fayetteville, AR, United States

Marlene G. Williams, PhD, Texas Woman's University, Denton, TX, United States

Supporting Trainees
With Competence Problems

INTRODUCTION

Building a Supportive Culture for Trainees Managing Competence Issues

REBECCA A. SCHWARTZ-METTE, EVELYN A. HUNTER, AND NADINE J. KASLOW

Supporting trainees with competence problems is a near-universal experience for trainers. These situations can be incredibly stressful for all involved—trainees faced with difficult feedback and remediation, trainers who grapple with their dual responsibilities of educating and gatekeeping, and administrators and other stakeholders who may have less direct experience with trainees with problems of professional competence (TPPC) but who uphold academic standards and assist trainees in their educational experience. Moreover, situations involving problems of professional competence are rife with assessment, evaluation, relational, ethical, and legal challenges. As such, the stakes are high for trainers to manage these situations well.

Although excellent resources exist to guide trainees, trainers, and training program facilitators through these challenging situations, no centralized, comprehensive source of information was available. Given our commitment to this work, alongside and with our colleagues over the past several decades, we sought to bring the incredible depth and breadth of knowledge, experiences, and practical guidance together in this volume.

---

https://doi.org/10.1037/0000340-001
Supporting Trainees With Competence Problems: A Practical Guide for Psychology Trainers, R. A. Schwartz-Mette, E. A. Hunter, and N. J. Kaslow (Editors)
Copyright © 2023 by the American Psychological Association. All rights reserved.

THEMES IN THIS VOLUME

We have endeavored to infuse new energy into this area by expanding our existing conceptualizations of TPPC. Just as we expect our trainees to develop foundational and functional competencies toward becoming psychologists, we as trainers must develop, maintain, and extend our competence in supporting trainees who are struggling. In this vein, we briefly discuss several themes that informed the contributions to this book.

Embracing Communitarianism and Multiculturalism

This volume is an explicit challenge to historical models of training that are hierarchical, are top-down, and view trainers as the (only) experts. We encourage forward thinking that discusses opportunities for trainees and trainers to cocreate opportunities to tackle competence problems together. As such, we begin this book with attention to building a communitarian training culture, a paradigm shift toward a culture that infuses humility, reflective practice, collaboration, and supportive mentorship. In this context, we center the importance of multiculturalism (i.e., attention to diversity and intersectionality, equity, and inclusion) in the conceptualization and support of TPPC throughout this volume. Ignoring multiculturalism may inadvertently lead trainers to overpathologize the existence (or absence) of particular behaviors that are not reflective of majority culture as "problems," when they may accurately reflect cultural differences. Importantly, the assumption of this book is that we are working *toward* values of communitarianism and multiculturalism, with an acknowledgment that programs may have different points from which the facilitators begin their work to achieve those goals.

Adopting a Supportive, Proactive Approach

The authors in this volume highlight the importance of supportive, proactive approaches to addressing competence problems, as opposed to punitive, reactive approaches. Proactive approaches include creating training cultures that highlight the developmental course of competency building; creating appropriate policies for assessment and identification of competence problems; and engaging remediation practices that are growth-orienting and behaviorally based.

Taking a Systems Perspective

Although individual (e.g., trainee, trainer) influences in dealing with competence problems are important, the authors expand their perspectives to incorporate a systems view on competency, as individual, program, and societal culture can be highly impactful in these contexts. We avoid language and paradigms that directly or indirectly place competence problems squarely within trainees, particularly when competence issues may reflect systemic issues (including trainer competence issues). Systems perspectives engage a comprehensive approach to competence problems such that addressing issues involves consideration of the entire training system and potential impacts are better absorbed in the context of the training environment.

Focusing Across All Areas of Psychologists' Work

Competence problems can (and do!) appear across all training activities, including the mentorship relationship, clinical work, clinical supervision, research and publication, coursework, teaching, and supervision of undergraduate mentees. We include a broad focus in this volume so that the information contained within can be applied widely across contexts. We also endeavored to reference those individuals who teach, mentor, and/or clinically supervise as *trainers*, as opposed to using only the term *supervisors*. It is critical that we not limit our understanding or address competence concerns in the clinical area only.

Discussing Competence Across All Training Stages

As noted throughout this volume, competency building is necessarily developmental. As such, problems in professional competency develop across training stages and settings (i.e., new and advanced graduate students, interns, and postdoctoral residents). The chapters direct attention to commonalities as well as differences among training stages/settings, with an emphasis on providing an organizing framework for addressing what constitutes problems of professional competence and how differences in training stage necessitate adjustments to such definitions. Because of this broad focus, the term *trainee(s)* is used throughout, as opposed to *student(s)*, except where reference to individuals in student roles (e.g., graduate students) is appropriate.

Providing Information for All Stakeholders

Although the primary audience for this volume comprises training program facilitators (e.g., directors, supervisors, faculty), we aim to help a wide range of stakeholders. Typically, problems in professional competence ripple throughout systems and impact various stakeholders. As such, this volume is relevant for human resource supervisors and personnel, equal opportunity and Title IX officers, organizational counsel, disability and diversity service offices, and graduate and professional school administrators.

Attending to Ethical and Legal Considerations

Ethical and legal considerations appear, as relevant, throughout the volume. We also included stand-alone chapters dedicated to ethical and legal issues that cover these topics in greater depth. This "forest AND the trees" approach, we hope, helps to maintain a focus on ethics and legal issues as they apply to all aspects of the process when working with TPPC, as well as providing a more specific analysis of each that is not possible within each chapter.

Appreciating Dialectics

We know firsthand that TPPC situations require trainers to analyze and juggle multiple, and sometimes contradictory, ideas as they work to support struggling trainees. Like many concepts in psychology and ethics, competence issues are often murky and require that trainers balance competing goals. For example, we balance our roles as trainee supporter and gatekeeper. As another example, and as detailed extensively in Chapter 7, this volume ("Trainee Confidentiality: The Hidden Challenge of Competence Problems"), we value trainee privacy but may, in some circumstances, work to reduce secret-keeping surrounding TPPC in an effort to embrace communitarianism and preserve program culture.

Taking a Scholarly Approach That Is Practically Helpful

In addition to presenting a scholarly analysis of the existing literature, each chapter references and links to a variety of concrete, practical resources. Where possible, we reference various other locations that trainers may obtain consultation. Each chapter also presents various key challenges relevant to its domain. Finally, each author team assisted with generating a list of a series of common pitfalls that helped provide content for our final chapter of the volume (Chapter 11, "Troubleshooting Common Pitfalls").

A SNEAK PEEK: A ROAD MAP OF THE BOOK

In Chapter 1 ("Creating a Communitarian, Multiculturally Sensitive, and Socially Just Training Culture"), Mendoza-Newman and Erickson Cornish give us the lens through which we hope health service psychologists aim to prepare trainees for competence. The authors provide a rationale and practical strategies for creating a training culture that illuminates these values, and particularly so when supporting trainees with competence issues. McGaffee,

Rasmussen, and Rodolfa use Chapter 2 ("Competencies in Health Service Psychology") to help us precisely understand the competencies that are expected to develop in psychology trainees. This chapter provides a foundation for better conceptualizing the content of Chapter 3 ("Problems of Professional Competence"), by Lease and Grus. Mollen and Williams then underscore the central importance of taking a broad lens when conceptualizing competence issues in Chapter 4 ("Systemic Perspectives on Trainees With Problems of Professional Competence"). In Chapter 5 ("Identification and Assessment of Problems of Professional Competence"), Renninger and Cavalieri provide guidance with regard to the complex task of recognizing and evaluating competence problems. Schwartz-Mette continues detailing the processes involved in supporting TPPC to remediate, identifying alternate training options or, in rare cases, dismissal (Chapter 6, "Remediation, Counseling Out, and Dismissal").

In Chapter 7 ("Trainee Confidentiality: The Hidden Challenge of Competence Problems"), Forrest and Elman provide an in-depth and forward-thinking analysis of the challenges and possibilities with regard to confidentiality in TPPC situations. Next up are deep dives into ethical and legal considerations, respectively. Chapter 8 ("Ethical Issues in Working With Trainees With Problems of Professional Competence"), contributed by Barnett and Johnson, offers us extensive analysis of ethical issues in working with TPPC. Chapter 9 ("Legal Issues in Working With Trainees With Problems of Professional Competence"), contributed by Shah and Fishel, details the myriad legal considerations trainers should be aware of when taking action in this context. Chapter 10 ("Building Program Policies in a Communitarian and Multiculturally Sensitive Training Culture") brings us full circle, as Veilleux and Scafe help us practically visualize the creation, implementation, and maintenance of program policies that reflect our values and, ultimately, help us better support trainees. Finally, we (Hunter & Schwartz-Mette) crowdsourced from this impressive group of authors a variety of common challenges faced by trainers working with TPPC and present them in Chapter 11 ("Troubleshooting Common Pitfalls"). These challenges are exemplified in vignettes, each followed by brief analysis and practical guidance.

CONCLUSION

We appreciate your willingness to approach this challenging topic and your joining us to digest and reflect. We believe that the information in this volume will help you in your journey to competence in supporting TPPC. What is more, we hope that you recognize that no trainee or trainer is alone in this endeavor and that this book helps you situate yourself more securely in your competent community of colleagues. We certainly consider you a part of ours.

1
CREATING A COMMUNITARIAN, MULTICULTURALLY SENSITIVE, AND SOCIALLY JUST TRAINING CULTURE

MARY MENDOZA-NEWMAN AND JENNIFER A. ERICKSON CORNISH

Trainers can find the support of trainees with problems of professional competence (TPPC) to be a complex challenge. These trainers must consider that individual and diversity variables may intersect with contextual and ecological variables in a training situation. This intersection includes the context of the larger culture; the culture of the specific institution; and the intersection of the multiple and complicated identities of the trainers and trainees that includes historical experiences of shared/not shared identities, privileges, and marginalization (and sometimes all of these within the same individual). In addition, as Vasquez (1999) pointed out, trainees are always subordinate in the training hierarchy, so being mindful of the power differential is important and particularly crucial when trainees appear to be struggling. When trainers engage in the critical analysis of the dynamics of power and intersectionality as it relates to the supervisory relationship and to trainee competence, they encourage social awareness, transparency, trust, and ultimately relational safety in the supervisory relationship (Hernández & McDowell, 2010). Relational safety is foundational to a successful supervisory relationship; not only does it foster the personal and professional competencies of a trainee, but it

https://doi.org/10.1037/0000340-002
Supporting Trainees With Competence Problems: A Practical Guide for Psychology Trainers, R. A. Schwartz-Mette, E. A. Hunter, and N. J. Kaslow (Editors)
Copyright © 2023 by the American Psychological Association. All rights reserved.

also creates resilience and strength for managing competency concerns, both for the trainer and trainee, should they arise.

In this chapter, we discuss the necessity for training programs to create more communitarian, multiculturally sensitive, and socially just practices in the health service psychology (HSP) training culture. Doing so requires nothing less than a paradigm shift from an individualistic to a collectivistic approach that is cocreated by trainers and trainees. We consider important elements of such a paradigm shift, describe communitarian training in general, focus on multiculturally sensitive and socially just training as more than just an idea, outline inherent challenges, propose possible solutions/practical recommendations, and offer approaches to professional missteps. We conclude with eight key resources for readers and a brief summary of the main points described in the chapter.

COMMUNITARIAN TRAINING

Communitarian training requires a multiculturally sensitive and socially just approach, with an emphasis on decolonizing the supervisory relationship and proactively anticipating and responding to problems. A communitarian approach to problems with professional competence was originally proposed by Johnson et al. (2012) to move the field away from an individualistic approach that relied solely on self-awareness of professional competencies. This communitarian approach offered a more collectivistic perspective involving community support with the goal of promoting personal and professional competence. In place of psychologists completely self-monitoring their competence in some sort of superhuman way, a constellation consisting of colleagues, consultants, supervisors, and psychotherapists would serve as honest assessors and supporters of competence and competence problems. The competence constellation model (Johnson et al., 2013) was further expanded to include a necessary diversity of perspectives, including various identities, worldviews, cultural variables, and theoretical backgrounds, that expand beyond an inner core of primary mentors to a collegial community, collegial acquaintances, and ultimately a professional culture.

To create such an interdependent culture of communitarian ideals in the context of training, Johnson et al. (2013) recommended that psychologists are trained toward this paradigm shift early in their careers. From matriculating in a graduate program, to practicum placements, to internship, to postdoctoral fellowships, and beyond, psychologists would be encouraged to develop their own communitarian constellations, focused not just on their own development but also on the development of their peers and future professional colleagues. Presumably, educators and trainers would serve as role models, and the American Psychological Association's (APA's; 2017a) *Ethical Principles of Psychologists and Code of Conduct* (APA Ethics Code) and regulatory boards would infuse communitarian values (e.g., humility, reflective practice, compassion, self-care) and collegial engagement (e.g., mentorship, consultation, collaboration, mutual support, collegial assertiveness) into problems with professional competence. In such a communitarian training culture, trainees would learn about communitarian principles and behaviors that ultimately would provide them with a guide map when they are in need of personal and professional support from their competence constellation (Johnson et al., 2014). Ideally, a communitarian training culture integrates the need to develop professional competencies in trainees with the need to support trainees with competence problems while protecting the field and future consumers.

The competence constellation model expanded, in part, Forrest et al.'s (2008) ecological conceptualization of psychology trainees with competence problems. Previously, "impaired" trainees had been conceptualized as struggling from individual issues with no real consideration of systemic or contextual impacts on their performance and behaviors. The tendency to pathologize students (e.g., diagnosing them with various personality disorders) can certainly be tempting to psychologist trainers. However, Forrest et al. suggested that we view trainees with "problems of professional competence" (p. 183) as individuals and with consideration of their microsystem (interaction with peers, supervisors, advisors, and instructors), mesosystem (interactions among colleagues, peers, faculty, and supervisors), exosystem (licensure, accreditation, graduate school evaluation/remediation/dismissal policies), and macrosystem (cultural beliefs related to diversity identity variables and to being a psychologist). The Forrest et al. ecological approach to competency problem formulation recommends program policies that are consistent with professional standards, faculty who examine dominant cultural influences on an ongoing basis, clear and transparent communication and accountability, preventive curriculum and training experiences, ecologically based evaluation systems, and consideration of the developmental training sequence. Thus, for instance, when a trainee demonstrates one or more problems with professional competence, a multilevel approach that considers the ecological framework is most important. In other words, trainers seek not just to understand the problem but also to develop a transparent remediation plan rooted in context that gives the student a true chance to improve. See Chapter 4, this volume, for a discussion of systemic perspectives on conceptualizing competence issues.

MULTICULTURALLY SENSITIVE AND SOCIALLY JUST TRAINING: MORE THAN ONLY AN IDEA

Despite Johnson's work, the communitarian model remains more an ideal than a practice. The current framework remains stubbornly individualistic, characterized by ethnocentric ideals that discriminate and oppress. The United States has a long and tragic history of oppression, enslavement, colonization, racism, and exploitation. Our field of psychology itself has been no less influenced by the Euro American norms that have historically excluded and discriminated against minorities (Hays, 1996). When we neglect to critically examine how psychology has been used to uphold systems of oppression when conceptualizing trainee competency problems, we not only perpetuate such problematic realities but also contribute to ineffective strategies with the development of support plans for trainees with professional competence concerns. The failure to critically examine and incorporate context can damage trainees, especially systemically marginalized trainees. Students with competency problems, as well as other trainees, face unequal challenges. To actuate the change envisioned by Johnson and colleagues, trainers must continue efforts to dismantle the current framework, to decolonize the supervisory and power-inflected relationships, and to proactively anticipate and solve a variety of challenges. The move to a collectivistic and intersectional training and professional culture is also at the core of all feminist, multicultural, and social justice-based constructs. To truly incorporate a communitarian model, we must go beyond multiculturalism as just an idea to include action in the areas of diversity, equity, inclusion, intersectionality, social justice advocacy, and cultural humility; we must extend even further to include decolonization of mental health, training and supervision, liberation psychology, antiracism, and the denunciation and dismantling of White nationalism.

In 2017, the APA published the *Multicultural Guidelines: An Ecological Approach to Context, Identity, and Intersectionality* (APA Multicultural Guidelines; APA, 2017b). A communitarian approach to training aligns very well with the Multicultural Guidelines by expanding from the individual to the complexity and multiplicity of context and the dynamic interaction between all layers of the ecological system. The guidelines provide a helpful framework for how trainers conceptualize competency problems for students and trainees. These 10 overall guidelines can be used as a checklist when understanding and developing plans to address competency problems.

- Guideline 1: Recognize and understand the fluidity and intersection of identity.

- Guideline 2: Maintain an awareness of personal biases that influence perceptions and interactions with others.
- Guideline 3: Understand the role of language and communication.
- Guideline 4: Maintain an awareness of the social and physical environments of others.
- Guideline 5: Understand the historical and contemporary experiences with power, privilege, and oppression.
- Guideline 6: Promote culturally adaptive interventions and advocacy within and across systems.
- Guideline 7: Examine the profession's assumptions and practices within an international context.
- Guideline 8: Seek an awareness and understanding of how developmental stages and life transitions intersect with the larger biosociocultural context.
- Guideline 9: Conduct culturally appropriate and informed research, teaching, supervision, consultation, assessment, interpretation, and evaluation.
- Guideline 10: Take a strength-based approach.

DECOLONIZING SUPERVISION

The ongoing paradigm shift required to enact a communitarian model depends on decolonizing key relationships. Because training in health service psychology is provided through clinical supervision, explicit efforts to decolonize supervision practices strongly support a communitarian model. Decolonizing supervision practices rooted in White colonialism help break down the individualistic, Eurocentric, heterosexist, and racist mentality deeply embedded in the foundation of all aspects of psychology. These colonial ways of thinking maintain oppression, marginalization, and racial injustice, even in supervision. Such habits are contradictory to a communitarian model. Therefore, we must deconstruct colonized supervision practices to move closer to a communitarian model that takes us away from pathologizing an individual and toward an ecological framework that considers the intersection of an individual's complex identities and contexts. This action is particularly important when conceptualizing trainees with competence concerns. Where colonized supervision may fail to incorporate a multicultural, interdependent lens to take in a trainee's competence concerns, a decolonized supervision framework attends not only to the multiplicity of identities and context for the trainee in their conceptualization of the competency concerns but also to the interaction of the supervisor's own identities and the systems they represent. The primary goal is to assist the trainee in thriving and succeeding. This communitarian ethos promotes professional competence (Johnson et al., 2012).

As described by Falender (2021), decolonizing clinical supervision begins with an awareness of groups that are privileged as well as those that are marginalized. In other words, understanding the historical and current context of privilege and oppression is a necessary first step. Although certain graduate students in health service psychology programs may identify with privileged and/or marginalized groups, many are also basically colonized themselves through unpaid practicum positions, low internship and postdoctoral fellowship stipends, and unsustainable student loan debt that particularly affects Black and African American trainees, those from lower socioeconomic status backgrounds, and psychologists who received doctorates within the past 10 years (Wilcox et al., 2021). Decolonizing supervision means not just recognizing the power dynamics in the supervisory relationship but also actively working to improve the learning environment for students by identifying, challenging, and changing the values of a racist system. This work requires trainers to engage in a critical reflection and accountability of their role in an inequitable system that perpetuates discrimination, oppression, and power (Falender, 2021).

A supervisor's interpersonal engagement with a trainee is an important opportunity to initiate decolonizing work. This is relevant for all trainees, given that engagement with a trainee is critical to the process and outcome of supervision as well as to the outcomes for trainees with competence concerns. A culturally humble supervisor is acutely aware of themselves in relation to their supervisee and honest about their limitations. This observation includes the implicit and explicit acknowledgment of culture, social position, biases, and power—a context-aware, strength-based, collaborative, and transparent supervision model in which power dynamics and flaws are addressed through a supportive and safe supervision relationship. The incorporation of cultural humility into supervision is aligned with a communitarian model in that it embodies an interdependent framework rather than maintaining the supervisor as all-knowing. A communitarian model promotes the lifelong development and maintenance of professional competence through ongoing self-assessment and self-reflection through a constellation that provides regular feedback and consultation and that encourages connection and support. Cultural humility contributes to the development of a strong supervisory relationship through relational modeling.

In this approach, the supervisor attends to the supervisory relationship/alliance, assumes responsibility for assessing and repairing ruptures, acts as a role model by providing and receiving evaluation feedback, infuses multicultural conceptualizations in all aspects of their work including their perspective on professionalism, enforces ethical and legal standards, and manages supervisees with problematic competencies (Falender, 2021). In addition to providing supervision in the common clinical contexts, decolonizing supervision also involves engaging in immersive and experiential learning regarding privilege and oppression through working in communities in which marginalized clients have a voice and are provided with tools for change (Goodman et al., 2015).

METHODS FOR DECOLONIZING SUPERVISION

Multicultural feminist and relational cultural supervision models are two approaches that work well within a communitarian model and may be useful in considering supervision that incorporates cultural humility rather than colonization. Multicultural feminist supervision (Arczynski & Morrow, 2017; Nelson et al., 2006; Vasquez, 1999) may be used throughout the developmental training sequence. This blended approach seeks to integrate both feminist and multicultural supervision principles by addressing the limitations of each. Feminist supervision, grounded in a recognition of the power imbalance in relationships, was historically geared mostly to cisgender White heterosexual middle-class women whose worldviews were more like those of the dominant culture and excluded the experience of cultural and ethnic minorities (Hays, 1996). Multicultural supervision, on the other hand, has been informed by how culture and race influence the experience of people of color, yet it has generally neglected the experiences of gender and sexual identities. Both approaches inform the supervisor about the sociocultural factors and context that impact a trainee, acknowledge inequality and systemic oppression, call for social justice advocacy, and focus on power and responsibility in the supervisory relationship (E. N. Williams & Barber, 2004). Conceptualizing trainee competency problems from a multicultural feminist approach thus supports a communitarian training culture in that it extends beyond the trainee to integrate an interdependent framework.

Relational cultural supervision is another approach that incorporates the values of multicultural and feminist supervision and is well aligned with a communitarian approach to training. The emphasis is interpersonal and collectivism (Stargell et al., 2020) in promoting the professional growth of a trainee by providing a safe supervisory relationship that accounts for the trainee's unique lived experiences, including sociocultural factors, marginalized identities, and experiences with social injustice (T. R. Williams & Raney, 2020). Furthermore, relational cultural supervision examines cultural and sociopolitical forces that contribute to the power imbalance in the supervisory relationship, models mutual learning, and incorporates principles of relational cultural theory such as mutual empathy, relational authenticity, and mutual empowerment (Jordan, 2004) to foster personal and professional development of trainees and supervisors.

Communitarian and culturally humble supervision can be implemented in several ways. For example, at the onset of supervision, the supervisor can use the ADDRESSING model (Age and generational influences, Developmental or other Disability, Religion and spirituality, Ethnic and racial identity, Socioeconomic status, Sexual orientation, Indigenous heritage, National origin, and Gender Identity) as a guide (Hays, 1996) and a framework to share their own background of intersecting identities, and then encourage the supervisee to do the same, consistent with Standard 7.04, Student Disclosure of Personal Information, in the APA Ethics Code (APA, 2017a). Engaging in this exchange allows the supervisor to model and to encourage the supervisee to discuss identities in supervision and, furthermore, to promote a critical profession-wide competency (Individual and Cultural Diversity) in understanding how their own personal and cultural identities, history, attitudes, and biases affect their work with clients.

When supervisors lead with sharing and discussing identities in supervision, they model how to create safety and trust and promote empathy and respect in the supervisory relationship. A mutual understanding of what can be discussed in supervision, how to give and receive critical feedback, how to discuss differences, and how to engage in difficult dialogues must be addressed at the onset and throughout supervision. Supervisors must be committed to the development of their own multicultural competence to gain awareness and understanding of their biases and blind spots, have knowledge of their social location, have an awareness of their privilege, demonstrate accountability when they have committed a microaggression, process ruptures, and take responsibility for bringing up multicultural issues in supervision while never avoiding engaging in the discussion if a trainee brings up those issues.

Trainees with competency concerns often feel isolated in their struggles. A supervisor can share with a trainee certain experiences with clinical missteps or challenges, which models that vulnerabilities and areas of growth can be discussed and affirms the professional development process that we all go through. Furthermore, this process mitigates against the supervisor as all-knowing and empowers the trainee to increase their self-awareness and insight about their missteps and growth areas (T. R. Williams & Raney, 2020). The space that a trainer creates so a trainee can courageously bring up any concerns, given the inherent power differences, is an indicator of the strength and safety of the supervisory relationship. This modeling in the context of multicultural supervision normalizes the developmental process of psychology training and allows for a more open and integrated experience for trainees, especially when they struggle.

The preceding list of suggested ways to attend and nurture the supervisory relationship is not meant to be exhaustive. This shortlist of attitudes and behaviors provides a supervision competency framework consistent with APA's (2014) *Guidelines for Clinical Supervision in Health Service Psychology*. These guidelines provide supervision best practices, which is an advancement for the profession and training communities. This shift to competency-based supervision ensures that supervisors are competent, which is well aligned with a communitarian culture. Training communities have a collective responsibility not only to the professional development of their trainees but also to their supervisors. A communitarian model promotes lifelong development and maintenance of professional competence through ongoing self-assessment of competence and through a constellation of colleagues and peers that both provide regular feedback and consultation and that encourage connection and support. At a minimum, we recommend that supervisors engage in self-assessment of their supervision competencies by reviewing each domain of the guidelines.

Conversations about competency concerns are delicate and require care to avoid shaming the trainee. Therefore, establishing a robust supervisory relationship is paramount. The supervisory relationship requires ongoing nurturance and care to support the growth of trainees when things are going well, and when they are not. The duty to be responsive to a trainee is consistent with a communitarian approach (Johnson et al., 2013). A training culture of ethics and care creates a path to provide ongoing feedback, celebrate success, discuss concerns, foster self-reflective practice, gain insight, access support, integrate context and diversity, and cocreate solutions. This last point is important because it engages the trainee in a collaborative process that is at the core of communitarian values. A trainee will evolve in their professional development if the training community supports them in integrating the challenges along the way.

Vacha-Haase et al. (2019) described an approach to remediation plans based on healthy and safe training contexts that are competency based, ecosystemic, collaborative, and communitarian, yet also mindful of legal requirements. Vacha-Haase et al. incorporated issues of fairness and sought to balance privacy with limits of confidentiality, illustrating how to create and implement a remediation plan with objective and measurable outcomes and then evaluate trainee progress (see also Chapter 6, this volume).

CHALLENGES

The overarching challenge in building a communitarian training culture within health service psychology is that it takes place within a dominant culture that excludes non-White people of color and includes systemic racism and other biases. The majority (e.g., White, middle-class, heterosexual, Protestant people of northern European descent) may exert a considerable effort to maintain the status quo that filters to the institutions in which psychologists are trained. This effort may result in resistance to acknowledging or changing departmental policies and procedures or even in instituting much-needed diversity training to maintain and grow the multicultural competence of faculty and staff (Abrams, 2020). In addition, because the salaries of some faculty and staff may be dependent on tuition, the tendency to ignore or minimize the problem of increasing student loan debt is all too common.

The challenge of recruiting and retaining trainers and trainees with diverse identities is obviously complicated by such cultural and institutional biases that have long been inherent in departmental hiring practices. When, for instance, majority-White search committees can identify only with people who look and behave as they do, it is easy to overlook outstanding candidates. Although the psychology workforce is becoming more diverse, 84% of psychologists are White, as compared with 60% of the U.S. population (APA, 2020). When diverse candidates are hired, they may enter an environment that is unwelcoming and even toxic to them, yet is perceived as supportive by the majority others. Students of color not only frequently accrue large loan debt but also enter White-dominated educational spaces that may feel unwelcoming and lack multiculturally competent faculty and staff, which may lead to attrition; this further limits the lack of a diverse psychology workforce equipped to work with diverse communities (Gregus et al., 2020).

Within the supervisory relationship, power differentials and perhaps the unconscious desire to hold on to privilege (Hernández & McDowell, 2010) may prevent supervisors from acknowledging and noticing their cultural missteps or supervisees from bringing them up in supervision. On an even more fundamental level, supervisors may lack multicultural competence and/or supervisees may be better educated and trained in this area. Such a mismatch in multicultural competence between supervisor and supervisee leads to supervisee dissatisfaction with supervision and may result in a poor supervisory working alliance (Inman, 2006). Furthermore, supervisors who lack multicultural competence and/or cultural humility may perpetuate racial trauma of their supervisees by devaluing, minimizing, avoiding, questioning, or imposing majority as normative on the experiences of their supervisees of color (Society of Counseling Psychology, 2021). When the goal is to establish a communitarian training culture and to promote competency development, supervisors clearly must understand and respect the diversity of their trainees. Trainees cannot progress when basic survival becomes their focus.

Both trainers and trainees are challenged by implicit bias. In fact, the entire idea of a communitarian competence constellation was developed in part to address such bias. Implicit bias is unavoidable and pervasive (Holroyd et al., 2017). Even those with highly developed multicultural competence are prone to implicit bias. Such behavior, although generally unintentional, can be damaging and often leads to missteps with stereotyping, prejudices, discrimination, and even racist thoughts and behaviors. It is our ethical responsibility to not only be aware and respectful of differences but also to work to eliminate the effect of such biases. Otherwise, bias can derail any attempts to develop a communitarian culture in which trainees feel safe to develop competencies and challenge themselves to overcome difficulties.

On the most basic level, change is difficult! From the societal to the institutional to the personal, changing to a communitarian, multiculturally sensitive, and socially just training model is necessary for health service psychology to survive and thrive, but engaging in the hard work to do so will take a sustained and ongoing effort.

POSSIBLE SOLUTIONS AND PRACTICAL RECOMMENDATIONS

The Council of Chairs of Training Councils recently held a working conference over the span of 6 months to develop a series of toolkits for educators and trainers to support social responsiveness in HSP. Approximately 160 leaders from 15 training councils and 10 liaison groups, including students, participated in the workgroups to develop the Social Responsiveness in Health Service Psychology Education and Training Toolkit to prepare the next generation of socially responsive psychologists. This toolkit is revolutionary and timely in that it supports a communitarian and socially just training culture. We encourage the use of this toolkit when supporting the development of competence constellations for trainees, staff, and faculty. The toolkit includes the following nine training domains:

1. Diversifying health service psychology pipelines
2. Revisiting our program structures with increased shared governance
3. Liberating and transforming our curriculum across all levels of training
4. Moving toward socially responsive Health Service Psychology research training
5. Socially responsive ethics and professionalism
6. Social justice and advocacy
7. Socially responsive community engagement
8. Socially responsive evaluation of students, educators, and programs
9. Socially responsive lifelong learning

Licensure boards, accreditation, credentialing, and regulatory bodies need to engage in critical reflection of the ways in which they maintain systems of oppression and inequity with accreditation standards, the licensing processes, and when managing professional competence concerns. This reflection may begin by incorporating more diverse voices in leadership positions within such organizations, integrating communitarian and multicultural approaches by incorporating competence constellations into application procedures, and emphasizing prevention and the use of collegial support and engagement rather than intervention when concerns arise (Johnson et al., 2013).

Trainers need to be role models with their own competency constellations. This process requires a level of vulnerability and care in creating a trusted multisource network for psychological and professional feedback, evaluation, and assistance. This professional care team would assist via 360-degree evaluations, peer case reviews, role-plays, live or recorded performance ratings, and consumer surveys (Johnson et al., 2013). Learning is not a static accomplishment that ends with licensure; it is a constant process of lifelong learning and ethical responsibility. Continued development of competence in the profession-wide competencies ensures ethical practice and multicultural competence. Education and training institutions must provide ongoing training for faculty and staff that infuses diversity, equity, and inclusion in all areas (e.g., teaching, supervision, mentorship, research, consultation, clinical practice). Additional training required of faculty and staff are in the areas of human rights, ethics, social justice, and multiculturalism, as these are interrelated and inseparable in our global world.

Psychologists might consider advocacy related to the culture in general. If psychologists are too busy or too introverted, they might at least join county or state psychological associations and APA, which hire lobbyists to represent clients and the field. For example, advocacy is particularly needed with regard to unsustainable student loan debt. When students see supervisors who promote their career goals and advocate on their behalf, the supervisors can more easily promote a truly communitarian culture.

Training institutions need to engage in critical reflection to examine the systems that perpetuate racial injustice, oppression, and discriminatory practices. The Council of Chairs of Training Councils Social Responsiveness Toolkit offers helpful suggestions to ensure that programs have clear and transparent written policies that are antiracist, thorough, and fair and that maintain ethical principles, training standards, multicultural, and supervision guidelines. It is important to include trainees in such examinations of training cultures because they hold the least power; because they have a diversity of perspectives that must be heard, considered, and incorporated; and because trainers are responsible for the teaching and learning of future psychologists. Training institutions must develop diversity, equity, and inclusive due process guidelines that promote a communitarian model. This progress begins with ensuring that the policy is reviewed with trainees at the start of their training, holds trainers responsible for creating safety in their supervisory relationships to engage in mutual ongoing feedback, engages the trainee and their competence constellation in the development of their remediation plans, and offers fair and just hearing and appeals processes.

PROFESSIONAL MISSTEPS

Professional missteps are common and sometimes unavoidable. Missteps hold value in the learning opportunities they present and the reminder of role-modeling humility in the process of lifelong learning. For instance, two faculty members in a doctoral program cotaught a seminar on psychotherapy theoretical models to eight students. One of the students presented a case of a transgender individual who used they/them/their pronouns. During the presentation, one of the faculty members misgendered the individual several times, apologizing quickly but then moving on. The other faculty member failed to stop the seminar to address the misgendering while continuing to participate in other aspects of the presentation. Later, one of the students sent an email to the group expressing their pain and discomfort from the misgendering. Both seminar leaders wrote back to validate the concerns and to apologize. During the next seminar, considerable time was given to process this rupture. The leaders accepted responsibility for their mistakes and noted the courage of the student who raised the issue while acknowledging the power differential inherent in the seminar and pointing out that the seminar leaders (not the student) should have been responsible for addressing this immediately. Moreover, the leaders discussed aspects of their personal and professional journeys related to transgender and nonbinary issues and apologized for their behavior. The students expressed frustration with the leaders, shared aspects of their own journeys, and voiced their appreciation for the opportunity for everyone to learn from this difficult situation. Although the conversation was somewhat awkward and difficult, it led to mutual growth for the trainers and the trainees.

Of course, to have such a conversation, trusting relationships were required for everyone to feel that they could express their honest opinions and mistakes without fearing retribution. The seminar had already met for several semesters, previously setting norms that included an explicit focus on a balance of support and challenge along with the expectation that both leaders and students would be held accountable without being shamed. Although the rupture and the processing that followed was conducted via Zoom during the SARS-CoV-2 (COVID-19) pandemic, everyone had met the others in person previously, possibly leading to an easier establishment of trust.

When considering how to respond to this professional misstep, the faculty were guided in part by the APA (2017b) Multicultural Guidelines, outlined earlier in this chapter. Every guideline was helpful in this regard, particularly Guidelines 2 (the awareness of personal biases), 3 (the role of language and communication), 5 (understanding the historical and contemporary experiences with power, privilege, and oppression), and 9 (conducting culturally appropriate and informed research, teaching, supervision, etc.). In addition, Guideline 10 (a strength-based approach) allowed the faculty members to give themselves some grace toward their own mistakes.

This example also illustrates the way that modeling a competency struggle can help develop a communitarian culture. In honestly admitting their professional missteps, in using each other (and the courageous students) as part of a constellation of competency support, and by transparently discussing their plans for improving, the trainers hoped to encourage their students to consider a similar approach to their own competency issues. The successful processing of a hurtful professional misstep was aided by elements of courage by the student who voiced their concerns, vulnerability by everyone, disclosure by everyone in sharing how they were impacted by the rupture, and accountability by the supervisors to respond to and own their error. Clearly, professional missteps are universally condemned but universally experienced; addressing our growth edges with accurate self-assessment (and help from our constellation of competency support), openness, and humility is the only way to truly create a sustained, supportive, and healthy communitarian, multiculturally sensitive, and socially just training culture.

REFERENCES

Abrams, Z. (2020). APA calls for true system change in U.S. culture. *Monitor on Psychology, 51*, 20. https://www.apa.org/monitor/2020/09/systemic-change

American Psychological Association. (2014). *Guidelines for clinical supervision in health service psychology.* https://www.apa.org/about/policy/guidelines-supervision.pdf

American Psychological Association. (2017a). *Ethical principles of psychologists and code of conduct* (2002, amended effective June 1, 2010, and January 1, 2017). https://www.apa.org/ethics/code/ethics-code-2017.pdf

American Psychological Association. (2017b). *Multicultural guidelines: An ecological approach to context, identity, and intersectionality.* https://www.apa.org/about/policy/multicultural-guidelines.pdf

American Psychological Association. (2020). Psychology's workforce is becoming more diverse. *Monitor on Psychology, 51*(8), 19. https://www.apa.org/monitor/2020/11/datapoint-diverse

Arczynski, A. V., & Morrow, S. L. (2017). The complexities of power in feminist multicultural psychotherapy supervision. *Journal of Counseling Psychology, 64*(2), 192–205. https://doi.org/10.1037/cou0000179

Falender, C. (2021, May). *Decolonizing clinical supervision* [Conference presentation]. Decolonizing psychology training, Teachers College, Columbia University. https://www.tc.columbia.edu/media/conferences/decolonizing-psychology/pdfs/Decolonizing-Clinical-Supervision-Slides.pdf

Forrest, L., Shen-Miller, D. S., & Elman, N. S. (2008). Psychology trainees with competence problems: From individual to ecological conceptualizations. *Training and Education in Professional Psychology, 2*(4), 183–192. https://doi.org/10.1037/1931-3918.2.4.183

Goodman, R. D., Williams, J. M., Chung, R. C.-Y., Tallyrand, R. M., Douglass, A. M., McMahon, H. G., & Bemak, F. (2015). Decolonizing traditional pedagogies and practices in counseling and psychology education: A move towards social justice and action. In R. Goodman & P. Gorski (Eds.), *Decolonizing "multicultural" counseling through social justice* (pp. 147–164). Springer. https://doi.org/10.1007/978-1-4939-1283-4_11

Gregus, S. J., Stevens, K. T., Seivert, N. P., Tucker, R. P., & Callahan, J. L. (2020). Student perceptions of multicultural training program climate in clinical psychology doctoral programs. *Training and Education in Professional Psychology, 14*(4), 293–307. https://doi.org/10.1037/tep0000289

Hays, P. A. (1996). Addressing the complexities of culture and gender in counseling. *Journal of Counseling and Development, 74*(4), 332–338. https://doi.org/10.1002/j.1556-6676.1996.tb01876.x

Hernández, P., & McDowell, T. (2010). Intersectionality, power, and relational safety in context: Key concepts in clinical supervision. *Training and Education in Professional Psychology, 4*(1), 29–35. https://doi.org/10.1037/a0017064

Holroyd, J., Scaife, R., & Stafford, T. (2017). Responsibility for implicit bias. *Philosophy Compass, 12*(3), e12410. https://doi.org/10.1111/phc3.12410

Inman, A. G. (2006). Supervisor multicultural competence and its relation to supervisory process and outcome. *Journal of Marital and Family Therapy, 32*(1), 73–85. https://doi.org/10.1111/j.1752-0606.2006.tb01589.x

Johnson, W. B., Barnett, J. E., Elman, N. S., Forrest, L., & Kaslow, N. J. (2012). The competent community: Toward a vital reformulation of professional ethics. *American Psychologist, 67*(7), 557–569. https://doi.org/10.1037/a0027206

Johnson, W. B., Barnett, J. E., Elman, N. S., Forrest, L., & Kaslow, N. J. (2013). The competence constellation model: A communitarian approach to support professional competence. *Professional Psychology: Research and Practice, 44*(5), 343–354. https://doi.org/10.1037/a0033131

Johnson, W. B., Barnett, J. E., Elman, N. S., Forrest, L., Schwartz-Mette, R., & Kaslow, N. J. (2014). Preparing trainees for lifelong competence: Creating a communitarian training culture. *Training and Education in Professional Psychology, 8*(4), 211–220. https://doi.org/10.1037/tep0000048

Jordan, J. V. (2004). Relational learning in psychotherapy consultation and supervision. In M. Walker & W. B. Rosen (Eds.), *How connections heal: Stories from relational-cultural therapy* (pp. 22–30). Guilford.

Nelson, M. L., Gizara, S., Crombach Hope, A., Phelps, R., Steward, R., & Weitzman, L. (2006). A feminist multicultural perspective on supervision. *Journal of Multicultural Counseling and Development, 34*(2), 105–115. https://doi.org/10.1002/j.2161-1912.2006.tb00031.x

Society of Counseling Psychology, Division 17 [D17CounselingPsych]. (2021). *Anti-Black racial trauma in supervision: Strategies for healing and support* [Video]. YouTube. https://www.youtube.com/watch?v=KbGlA0czRoc

Stargell, N., Craigen, L., Bradley, N., Whisenhunt, J., Campbell, E., & Kress, V. E. (2020). Relational-cultural supervision: A humanistic approach to promoting vulnerability and counselor development. *The Journal of Humanistic Counseling, 59*(3), 188–200. https://doi.org/10.1002/johc.12144

Vacha-Haase, T., Elman, N. S., Forrest, L., Kallaugher, J., Lease, S. H., Veilleux, J. C., & Kaslow, N. J. (2019). Remediation plans for trainees with problems of professional competence. *Training and Education in Professional Psychology, 13*(4), 239–246. https://doi.org/10.1037/tep0000221

Vasquez, M. J. T. (1999). Trainee impairment: A response from a feminist/multicultural retired trainer. *The Counseling Psychologist, 27*(5), 687–692. https://doi.org/10.1177/0011000099275002

Wilcox, M. M., Barbaro-Kukade, L., Pietrantonio, K. R., Franks, D. N., & Davis, B. L. (2021). It takes money to make money: Inequity in psychology graduate student borrowing and financial stressors. *Training and Education in Professional Psychology, 15*(1), 2–17. https://doi.org/10.1037/tep0000294

Williams, E. N., & Barber, J. S. (2004, December). Power and responsibility in therapy: Integrating feminism and multiculturalism. *Journal of Multicultural Counseling and Development, 32*, 390–401.

Williams, T. R., & Raney, S. (2020). Relational cultural supervision enhances the professional development of postdoctoral residents of color in health service psychology. *Journal of Psychotherapy Integration, 30*(1), 140–146. https://doi.org/10.1037/int0000169

2 COMPETENCIES IN HEALTH SERVICE PSYCHOLOGY

LYDIA McGAFFEE, CASSANDRA RASMUSSEN, AND EMIL RODOLFA

Prior to establishing a communitarian, multiculturally sensitive, and socially just framework to support trainees with competence problems, psychologists and trainers must first clearly grasp the concept of professional competence in psychology. Within the past few decades, health service psychology (HSP) has put forth an extensive effort to establish competency standards to ensure the credible and ethical functioning of trainees and professionals. Competence among clinicians is necessary to uphold psychology's ethical obligation to the general public, yet it is also fundamental to establishing cohesion and credibility across the profession. Traditionally, *professional competency* has been defined as "the habitual and judicious use of communication, knowledge, technical skills, clinical reasoning, emotions, values, and reflection in daily practice for the benefit of the individual and community being served" (Epstein & Hundert, 2002, p. 226). In short, to be competent means to possess the ability to effectively employ professional skills, behavior, and interpersonal communication that proves one is capable of providing the requisite services of a psychologist. On a fundamental level, competency is "the cornerstone of psychologists' ethical obligation to the public" (Wise & Reuman, 2019, p. 129).

https://doi.org/10.1037/0000340-003
Supporting Trainees With Competence Problems: A Practical Guide for Psychology Trainers, R. A. Schwartz-Mette, E. A. Hunter, and N. J. Kaslow (Editors)
Copyright © 2023 by the American Psychological Association. All rights reserved.

A psychologist who neglects to ensure they are competent to practice puts at risk the very people who are served.

The American Psychological Association (APA; 2017), with its *Ethical Principles of Psychologists and Code of Conduct* (APA Ethics Code), and the Association of State and Provincial Psychology Boards (ASPPB) established codes that require competency to be primary in all facets of professional duties. These codes state that a professional must have "demonstrable competence" and refrain from "operating outside their realm of competence" (APA, 2017; Pope & Vasquez, 2016, Chapter 12). To accompany this, guidelines and standards such as the Commission on Accreditation (CoA) and its Standards of Accreditation (SoA; APA, 2019), have been created that guide the process and content of training, the evaluation of competence, and competent professional practices. These have been augmented by various models (discussed at length later) produced by researchers and theorists, which provide clear definition to what competent functioning entails. While competency is an ethical standard, its practical application and development is best understood through professional models and frameworks instead of ethical codes. As a dynamic process, competency is never static.

PROFESSIONAL VALUES AND COMPETENCY

To properly address the topic, it is necessary to first delineate the reasons why it is pertinent for health service psychologists to maintain competence throughout their lifespan as a practicing professional. The APA Ethics Code outlines competency as one of the first and primary obligations of psychologists (APA, 2017). Competency cannot be discussed without first addressing the reason for maintaining competence, the "why," which is directly related to the core values of HSP. To be competent, an individual must comprehend that the values on which a field agrees are paramount to their professional identity (Epstein & Hundert, 2002).

The "professional culture" of psychology emphasizes values as part of the standard of practice (Johnson et al., 2013). In other words, HSP's baseline practice should consist of a set of agreed-upon values. Others have defined foundational competencies as the constellation of the knowledge, skills, attitudes, and values that are considered the "rock" upon which all other competencies are built (Hatcher et al., 2013; Rodolfa et al., 2005). This rock is composed of stipulatory common values that ultimately unite the profession and provide guidance in times of disagreement and conflict (Eby et al., 2011; Johnson et al., 2013; Rodolfa & Schaffer, 2019). The APA Ethics Code is a contributing piece to the agreed-upon rock that serves as psychology's guiding principles.

In the General Principles section of the Ethics Code (APA, 2017), aspirational values are described as a guideline for the standards within which a psychologist should aim to operate. These principles include (a) Beneficence and Nonmaleficence: to act out of goodness and "do no harm"; (b) Fidelity and Responsibility: to establish a trusting relationship with those we serve; (c) Integrity: to hold oneself accountable for our professional practice; (d) Justice: to ensure that everyone has equitable ability to obtain and receive care; and (e) Respect for People's Rights and Dignity: to provide a continuously mindful practice focused on protecting individuals' rights and autonomy while respecting individuality, multiculturalism, and self-awareness of our role within the relationship. Each value can be easily connected to the importance of maintained competence throughout one's practice. The tenets of psychology warrant all professionals, including psychology trainees, to provide ethical, equitable, evidence-based, and fair treatment to all.

Competent practice relies on an enduring journey of self-awareness and continuing education with the goal of using assessments, interventions, consultations, and so forth, that are rooted in the latest research. The ethical treatment provided to the public can be built on a foundation of a trusting and honest relationship only if psychologists hold themselves accountable to maintain competence. If competence is not continually self-monitored, as well as assessed by others (i.e., faculty, supervisors, colleagues, licensing boards, board certification organization) and dutifully corrected when needed, a psychologist cannot honestly claim to be providing care in an ethical manner. In other words, to maintain competence is to maintain an ethical practice that upholds the values that the profession has agreed to when individual psychologists serve the public.

ARTICULATION OF COMPETENCIES

Competencies are dependent on habits of the mind, specifically in regard to attentiveness, critical curiosity, self-awareness, and present-mindedness (Epstein & Hundert, 2002). The practical side of competency is that it builds on the foundation of basic clinical skills, scientific knowledge, and moral development (Epstein & Hundert, 2002). Competency is strengthened by learning experiences focused on clinical skill development, scientific knowledge, and moral development and is the practical application of these elements. Competence is developmental, impermanent, and context dependent

(Epstein & Hundert, 2002), and its dynamic nature makes consistent self-assessment imperative.

Competency frameworks provide a baseline for identification and measurement of practice for trainees and professionals (Grus et al., 2016). Without tangible standards to follow, or a base measure, the appraisal of professional work becomes nebulous. By defining competency, and establishing essential components of competent functioning, behavioral anchors for each component can be practically established and assessed (Fouad et al., 2009). The articulation of benchmarks for competencies has provided not only training programs but also individual psychologists and credentialing organizations, a standard by which to assess professional work.

A profession's ability to clearly define core foundational and functional competencies delineates and separates it from other professions (Rodolfa et al., 2013). Yet the field of HSP has struggled to accomplish this, making it difficult to keep pace with other professions (Kaslow et al., 2009). The lack of cohesive competency standards across jurisdictions has also been a problem for the profession. This struggle to explicitly define competencies has placed HSP in jeopardy (Rodolfa et al., 2013).

Competency standards not only protect the profession, they strengthen it. Until recently, competency standards across the United States were not streamlined for regulatory bodies (Rodolfa et al., 2005), which presented a challenge for the maintenance of competent practice at the legal and professional level. The topic of competency development is important substantially because the behaviors and the work of each individual psychologist reflects on the profession as a whole. For credibility's sake, competence is vital to psychologists and psychology.

In an effort to reinforce professional standards, the Competencies Conference, organized by the Association of Psychology Postdoctoral and Internship Centers (APPIC) and the APA, served as the catalyst in 2002 for the establishment of a profession-wide competency (PWC) framework to define this concept (Kaslow et al., 2004; Nicholson Perry et al., 2017). Although this definition has helped to move from "good-enough" practice to behaviors anchored in clear domains of competency (Nicholson Perry et al., 2017), it has not completely solved the problem.

CORE FOUNDATIONAL AND FUNCTIONAL COMPETENCIES

The work achieved at the Competencies Conference serves as a foundation for enhancing the structure of competency standards within the field. From this conference emerged a direction that fueled the creation of concrete frameworks that provide definition and evaluation of professional work. These models are discussed in the upcoming section, and since their development during the past 2 decades, their positive effect can be seen in training programs.

The Competencies Cube

During the Competencies Conference, Rodolfa and colleagues (2005) articulated the domains of professional competencies. They generated a three-dimensional model of foundational and functional competencies superimposed against the professional developmental stages to provide a guide for understanding competencies at every level (Rodolfa et al., 2005). This competency cube is displayed in Figure 2.1.

Foundational competency domains are described as the primary parameters required for effective practice and are typically obtained during one's graduate education (Rodolfa et al., 2005). These competencies include (a) reflective practice–self-assessment, (b) scientific knowledge–methods, (c) relationship, (d) ethical–legal standards–policy, (e) individual–cultural diversity, and (f) interdisciplinary systems. These competencies provide a foundation for the work of all psychologists, regardless of specialty or setting.

Functional competencies are typical types of practices based on knowledge, skills, and attitudes/values, performed regularly by psychologists. These competencies include (a) assessment–diagnosis–case conceptualization, (b) intervention, (c) consultation, (d) research–evaluation, (e) supervision–teaching, and (f) management–administration. These competencies reflect the activities that psychologists engage in during their professional workday. As competencies do not exist in a vacuum, Rodolfa and colleagues (2005) hypothesized that each foundational competency influences each functional competency throughout the professional work life of a psychologist.

The third component of the competency cube—the developmental stages (Rodolfa et al., 2005)—addresses the sequence of practice that a psychologist experiences during their career, from training to independent practitioner. These stages of professional development include (a) graduate education/practicum, (b) internship, (c) postdoctoral training or residency, and (d) continued competency after licensure.

During graduate education, a trainee has many opportunities to display foundational knowledge, ethical values and professional values, and a growing skill base. Throughout internship and postdoctoral training, the trainee has consistent opportunities to exhibit their growing knowledge, developing

FIGURE 2.1. Competency Cube

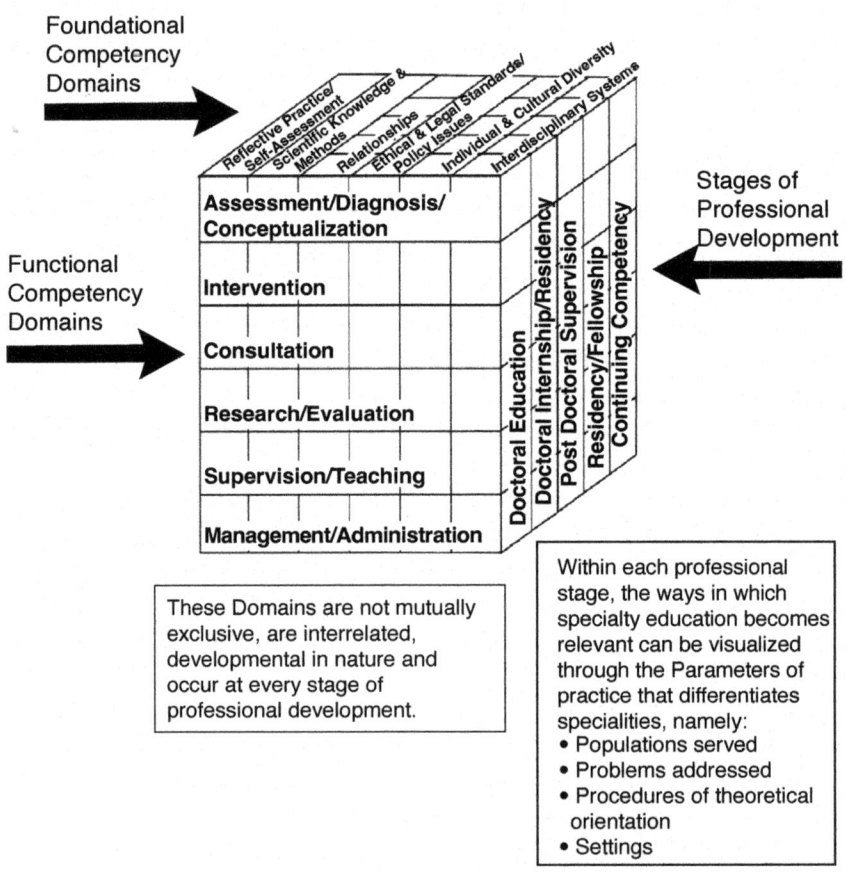

Note. From "A Cube Model for Competency Development: Implications for Psychology Educators and Regulators," by E. Rodolfa, R. Bent, E. Eisman, P. Nelson, L. Rehm, & P. Ritchie, 2005, *Professional Psychology: Research and Practice*, 36(4), p. 350 (https://doi.org/10.1037/0735-7028.36.4.347). Copyright 2005 by the American Psychological Association.

skills, and increasingly sophisticated and more nuanced attitudes to their supervisor. Eventually, the psychology trainee is ready to display their competence to members of a licensing board in order to become a psychologist capable of making independent practice decisions.

It is important to acknowledge that the assessment of competence is complex because as a psychologist advances across the phases of development, the baseline measure for specific competencies becomes more extensive. The competencies that are necessary for performance in the practicum setting will vary from those needed to function as an independent practitioner (Fouad et al., 2009). As the required functional and foundational competencies intersect with the professional development timeline, a progressive maturation of competence occurs as the trainee moves across the developmental stages (Rodolfa et al., 2005). As such, the types of competencies that are rated most important differ across the practicum, internship, and postdoctorate levels, with the growth in professional development reflecting higher expectations for depth of competence (Fouad et al., 2009).

Although these domains of foundational and functional competencies are all crucial, Grus and colleagues (2016) asserted that some competencies and professional behaviors are deemed "universally important" during each developmental stage (p. 201). For instance, they suggested that during the doctoral/academic level of training those competencies that are most formally addressed and assessed include ethical knowledge, ethical conduct, ethical decision making, and cultural diversity. As the trainee transitions to internships and postdoctoral training, the behaviors that are more prominently assessed include integrity, accountability, and interpersonal connectivity. Finally, as a psychologist advances into independent practice, the domains of functioning that become the most visible, and thus are deemed most critical for competent practice, include self-assessment, intervention techniques, ethical obligations, administrative management, and assessment (Grus et al., 2016).

Assessing Competence

To attain and convey a particular conduct, there must be a clear depiction of what that behavior looks like. The rise of the cube and other competency models have been advantageous in catalyzing standardized measures by which programs and professionals can appraise themselves. These models are needed to guide the implementation of a competency-based approach to training and to identify and evaluate trainee readiness and professional ability (Fouad et al., 2009).

The process of providing a definition for competency in the practice of psychology paves the way for appropriate and beneficial assessment, support, and correction. A deficit cannot be ascertained without an ideal by which to measure it. This process of assessment is vital to the continual improvement and strengthening of the profession as a whole and for its credibility. When competency is assessed, a baseline description must be present to determine when competence is absent. Part of the effort to bring unity to the profession is through the process of streamlining competency, instead of making it an individual pursuit in which competency is defined one way by one person and another way by someone else. The benchmarks system (Fouad et al., 2009) was developed to assist in the process of standardized identification of problems present within trainees and professionals. Assessment of competency should foster learning while inspiring confidence in the learner (Epstein & Hundert, 2002). Ascribing definition to an abstract concept allows for translation into pragmatic application and sets goals for clinicians at all levels of professional development.

At its core, competence is more than simply reaching a standard of good-enough practice; competence represents integrity and the pursuit of continual individual betterment that allows psychologists to provide the best possible care to those they serve. Adapting a competency-driven approach to practice, rooted in a values-based system, has the power to unify the profession by reflecting common values in competency. Identifying values and practicing in line with those values are actions at the center of what competency produces in the field of psychology (Wise & Reuman, 2019).

Competency-based training is the critical element in developing competent psychologists. For this reason, academic programs and training sites must describe training standards, define professional aspirations, describe the ethical tenets of the profession, and tangibly display their translation into everyday practice. Through the implementation of factors such as common assessment methods, guidelines for setting measurement approaches, and a shared approach to documentation of the maintenance of competence, the pursuit of effective training is being integrated into professional education (Eby et al., 2011). Using diverse training models and surrounding trainees with communal support and ongoing assessment are essential ways to convey the critical elements of competence and competent practice.

The beauty in the individuality of psychological practice is that no two psychologists will practice in the same manner; this is the art of the profession. Therefore, competency standards do not, and should not, necessitate that all psychologists be a cookie-cutter representation; rather, the standards promote the capable implementation of knowledge, skills, and attitudes in the service of clients. As each psychologist has something unique to offer, there is strength in creating community and allowing communal influence to promote competent assessment and reevaluation of practices.

Competence is enhanced by incorporating input from other psychologists. As iron sharpens iron, so one psychologist sharpens another—there is power in surrounding oneself with colleagues who promote integrity and can provide insight and instruction. A degree of silos within the field is inevitable, but common goals and a singular mission can increase collaboration and unity (Eby et al., 2011). Competency standards put words to the values that create the backbone of the field.

Three Current Competency Models

A further description of these models, which have been beneficial to the field, is now necessary. Although each of the models varies in its emphasis, they are all substantially similar in their content and guide training programs in the education of professionals. Thus, these models provide standards for the development of well-rounded psychologists and offer flexibility for the structure of training in individual programs.

The Benchmarks Model
In 2008, a group of psychologists met to better define and describe the competencies defined in the competency cube model. This model, described in a 2009 article by Fouad and colleagues, summarized the efforts of developing the first iteration of the benchmarks model, which added competencies to those already listed in the cube model. In 2013, a group of psychologists presented revisions to the benchmarks model in an attempt to simplify the model to six broad competencies in order to make it more usable (Hatcher et al., 2013). Hatcher and colleagues (2013) sought to emphasize flexibility in the development and use of this revised model.

Profession-Wide Competencies Model
The APA's CoA accredits at least 1,235 training programs in HSP. Of the noted 1,235 programs, 408 are academic, 652 are internship sites, and 175 are postdoctoral sites (APA, n.d.). One mission of the CoA is to ensure public safety within HSP (APA, 2019), as the CoA seeks to accredit programs that embody high professional standards. To provide guidance to programs, the CoA developed the PWC model, which simplified the cube and other psychology models of professional competence. Once this model was developed, the CoA was able to accredit programs by comparing the standards and operating procedures within academic and training institutions with the CoA's PWC model. Although the competency cube model was thorough, it was complex and difficult to implement in actual practice (Schaffer & Rodolfa, 2013); the more linear PWC model was easier for programs to pragmatically apply. By developing the PWC model, the CoA sought to ensure that the foundational and functional competencies are addressed at the appropriate level within a trainee's development as a psychologist. By providing the PWC model, the CoA instituted specific guidance for training programs that has limited the redundancy in an effort to clearly establish and define competency efforts (Molinari, 2012), thus strengthening the profession.

The Association of State and Provincial Psychology Boards Model

In the spirit of a culture of competency within professional psychology (Roberts et al., 2005), the ASPPB, which is the organization of the psychology licensing boards in the United States and Canada, developed a competency model that psychology regulators could use when deciding who has the competency to practice independently. Rodolfa and colleagues (2013) reported the results of the ASPPB Practice Analysis, which outlined specific competencies beyond the graduate school experience and sought to address the "lifespan" of a psychologist. They used, as a foundation, the competency cube (Rodolfa et al., 2005) and the initial benchmarks model (Fouad et al., 2009). This model was subsequently revised, refined, and finally focused on the point of licensure rather than a developmental continuum; the model is the basis for the Examination for Professional Practice Part 2–Skills licensing examination used by jurisdictions in the United States and Canada (ASPPB, 2017). Of note, the competencies of advocacy, management–administration, and teaching, which are listed in the benchmarks model, are not included in the ASPPB model, as typically these three behaviors are not specifically included in licensing laws.

Summary of the Current Competency Models

The current models in use by HSP were developed and structured differently but contain substantially the same competencies (see Table 2.1).

In an interesting commentary on the development of competency models, Hunsley and colleagues (2016) discussed the differences of practicing psychologists in their support and opposition of various competency models. Hunsley et al. expressed concern about the process of model development, speculating that the developed models have contradictory expectations that are simultaneously too high and too low, and the authors encouraged both regulators and trainers to further examine the process, development, and evolution of competency in psychology. Furthermore, Hunsley and colleagues supported Hatcher et al.'s (2013) comments about the importance of flexibility and creativity in the implementation of a competency model. Members of the profession were encouraged to maintain an open dialogue as the development of competency models continues, and the authors emphasized that competency models will "result in more competent psychologists and in a better served and protected public" (Hunsley et al., 2016, p. 918).

Program-Specific Competencies

The CoA (APA, 2019) incorporated program-specific competencies (PSC) as an augmentation to the PWC. PSC are specifically developed and taught by a

TABLE 2.1. Current Models of Competency

Models		
Benchmark	**CoA PWC**	**ASPPB**
Science[a]	Research	Scientific orientation
Scientific knowledge & methods		
Research & evaluation		
Application[b]	Assessment	Professional practice
Evidence-based practice	Intervention	Supervision
Assessment	Supervision	
Intervention		
Consultation		
Relational[a]	Communication & interpersonal skills	Relational
Relationships	Individual & cultural diversity	
Professionalism[a]	Professional values, attitudes, & behaviors	Professionalism
Values & attitudes		
Individual & cultural diversity		
Reflective practice/self-assessment/self-care		
Ethical & legal standards	Ethical & legal standards	Ethical practice
Systems[b]	Consultation & interprofessional/interdisciplinary	Collaboration
Interdisciplinary systems		Consultation
Management-administration		
Advocacy		
Education[b]		
Teaching		
Supervision		

Note. CoA = Commission on Accreditation; PWC = profession-wide competencies; ASPPB = Association of State and Provincial Psychology Boards.
[a]Foundational competencies. [b]Functional competencies.

program in addition to the PWC. PSC are taught at a program's discretion, and a program is not required to teach any competencies other than the PWC. In a precursor to PSC, Rodolfa and colleagues (2005) asserted that by dividing the competency cube's developmental domains, training programs that focused on areas of specialized practice can structure their training to meet their trainees' learning needs. Thus, when programs provide the flexibility for PSC, trainees at all developmental levels may prosper.

France et al. (2008) suggested that the expansion of the scope of practice of psychology has created an abundance of specializations, which complicates the understanding of core competencies that are expected for all practicing health service psychologists regardless of specialty. Nonetheless, specialty practice within HSP is gaining momentum (Neimeyer et al., 2012; Rodolfa et al., 2005; Silberbogen et al., 2018). For example, several specialties within HSP have sought to utilize the competency cube as a framework to enhance their understanding of the unique structure and qualities of their specialty within HSP practice (see Barlow, 2012; France et al., 2008; Jackson et al., 2012; Molinari, 2012; Rey-Casserly et al., 2012).

Molinari (2012) emphasized that it behooves the profession to continue to evolve the accreditation processes and other standards to enhance the competency and specialization of those practicing psychology because of the diverse populations that are treated today. France and colleagues (2008) attempted to guide facilitators of clinical health psychology training programs to understand the competencies needed for effective practice. However, they also noted that this endeavor may be challenging for some programs and asserted that flexibility is necessary to implement modifications that will best suit each program.

COMMUNITARIAN APPROACH TO COMPETENCY

During the 20th and 21st centuries, the profession of HSP has consistently grown and developed. Today, the scope of the practice of psychology is much broader than it was initially. As the scope of practice has increased, so too have the accountability concerns (Rodolfa et al., 2005). In consequence, the necessity for competence among psychologists has been continuously compounded. Several domains of practice need to be constantly assessed, in conjunction with the legal mandates that require consistent monitoring of professional work.

This responsibility can create a feeling of pressure for trainees and clinicians in all stages of their professional development. An additional challenge presents itself in the self-assessment of functioning, which often is inaccurate, and can be a weakness for many individuals (Johnson et al., 2013). Lilienfield and Basterfield (2020) highlighted many of the difficulties of reflective practice. Additionally, Schaffer and Rodolfa (2020) noted the critical importance of seeking to understand cognitive bias. Because of the complications of self-assessment, areas of incompetency can sometimes go unnoticed and unchecked, perpetuating a damaging cycle for trainers, trainees, and professionals alike. Thus, the individualistic nature of current competency standards can be overwhelming and foster feelings of isolation. Unification across the field is still needed to fuse efforts toward global competency and decrease individual pressures. Describing competency from a communitarian perspective catalyzes the pursuit of unity in the profession.

Communitarianism, which is a type of moral philosophy, asserts that individual dignity and the social dimension of human existence are interdependent (Etzioni, 1998). From this perspective, the ethical responsibility of an individual professional should be reinforced by the community that surrounds that individual (Johnson et al., 2014). In short, this communitarian approach encapsulates that ethics of care asserting interdependence and communal relationships are pivotal to emotional engagement and collegial care (Johnson et al., 2014). Wise and Reuman (2019) stated, "Competence is a dynamic set of skills and attributes that are context specific, ever evolving, and embedded in being connected to a community of others" (p. 130).

The communal piece of competency is lacking from the incorporation of competency training and standards in graduate programs, internships, postdoctoral residencies, and professional practice. By transitioning the full responsibility of competency from the individual to adding a component of communal obligation, and emphasizing the role of colleague care, a unifying bond across the profession could be created. Highlighting communal support over individualism would foster interdependence of clinicians and implement values of caring (Johnson et al., 2013). The act of surrounding oneself with supportive and attentive colleagues is one of the most prominent ways to guard against competency errors. Yet, for this approach to be prominent, this concept needs to be implemented from the beginning of training and continue through a psychologist's professional development (Johnson et al., 2013). This implementation would encourage the early-career psychologist, as well as the veteran, to continually consult and collaborate with colleagues.

Johnson and colleagues (2013) described "competence constellation" (Chapter 1, this volume) as the process of surrounding oneself with an assortment of professional relationships with the goal of reinforcing competent functioning. For this model of competency to be effective, this perspective would ideally be employed initially in training, through courses and intervention approaches; the role of trainees as "colleague" should be emphasized to reinforce this idea of community (Johnson et al., 2013). Furthermore, this process should be fostered in a cohort setting among trainees, and trainers need to model this concept, for true enrichment to ensue.

This perspective of communitarian competency counteracts the individualistic nature of the current ethical standards and strives to reduce feelings of isolation among clinicians (Wise & Reuman, 2019). As previously mentioned, the limited nature of self-assessment necessitates varied forms of feedback to compensate for the difficulty of self-insight and reflective practice (Lilienfeld & Basterfield, 2020; Wise & Reuman, 2019). Psychologists have attained a level of reflective practice through consultation groups and supervision; however, when clinicians move beyond their graduate programs and become comfortable in the profession, consultation-type interaction tends to wane (Wise & Reuman, 2019). In fact, most ethical disciplinary actions that are prompted by incompetent behavior occur when psychologists are mid-career (Wise & Reuman, 2019).

Although several factors may play a role in this pattern of deficiency, a large component may be the tendency for increased isolation and limited pursuit of colleague input when psychologists become established in their career. Communitarian competency aims to facilitate a change—to have the obligation of competency fall upon the profession as a whole by fostering supportive networks (Wise & Reuman, 2019). This is not to say that the individual should be absolved of responsibility for their own actions. Ultimately, the individual makes the decision to act. However, a communitarian perspective would assert that nurturing communal support, promoting colleague insight, and displaying a willingness to call out incompetent behavior could be largely beneficial in cultivating the competent function of psychologists, not only at the individual level but holistically as a profession.

COMPETENCY FROM A MULTICULTURAL PERSPECTIVE

The efficacy of peer support networks relies on certain things, including diversity, strength of the ties, emotional closeness, and intentionality in forming and nurturing these relationships (Johnson et al., 2013). Like all else in this profession, maintaining competence takes hard work and dedication. The need for diversity in relationships and the humility that is necessary to be receptive to insightful feedback elucidate another critical aspect of competency—multiculturalism.

Jones and colleagues (2013) suggested that being competent from a multicultural perspective involves beliefs and attitudes, knowledge, and skills. The abstract nature of multiculturalism, and its related competency, impacts the way in which it is interpreted, tracked, and documented within the professional context (Jones et al., 2013). Being able to articulate specific guidelines for competency in the realm of multiculturalism is necessary for general professional competency. The diverse nature of a psychologist's work demands a fundamental level of multiculturalism to obtain and continually foster competent functioning in all facets of practice.

The beliefs and attitudes component of multiculturalism is described as the ability to see beliefs and attitudes about others who are different (Jones et al., 2013). The process of becoming aware of values, biases, and assumptions that dominate the perception of the world is a significant element of the journey toward multicultural competency (Sue et al., 2019). Knowledge in multiculturalism means developing understanding of other cultures and involves the active attempt to understand the worldview of culturally diverse clients (Jones et al., 2013; Sue et al., 2019). Multicultural skills are embodied by the actual behaviors of the psychologist, the practical intervention strategies, and culturally sensitive approaches toward treatment—the functional competencies of practice (Jones et al., 2013; Kashima, 2014; Sue et al., 2019). All of these elements intersect to create a multicultural approach to being a competent psychologist. However, the multicultural perspective illuminates the reality that competence is an active, developmental, and ongoing process— one that is aspired toward rather than truly attained (Sue et al., 2019). The high level of self-awareness and perception that is necessary to strive for competence is daunting, further contributing to the notion that communal insight and support are vital to the psychologist; psychology as a profession; and, most important, the public that is served.

Beyond these three aspects of multiculturalism resides a fourth aspect that arguably is the most critical for psychologists to integrate. Advocacy and action are required of professionals to serve their clients to the utmost of their ability (Jones et al., 2013). Advocacy is the optimal step toward competence, as it incorporates the awareness of beliefs and knowledge along with skills and applies it toward change, thus facilitating action beyond an individual level (Jones et al., 2013). Inspiring action within the lives of others is at the heart of the profession, especially within a multicultural approach.

The concept of cultural humility—that is, a dispositional orientation that seeks to have an open attitudinal stance toward diverse clients—would assume openness and authenticity to be the primary factors in providing competent interventions for clients (Sue et al., 2019). Cultural humility is an indispensable component of the formation of competent action and learning. The process of learning and developing competence cannot manifest unless humility and openness are present, especially in regard to becoming aware of one's own shortcomings and biases. Competence demands insight. True insight cannot be attained without humble receptivity to acknowledging the individual areas of practice that require further development. With the help of colleagues and the support of remediation, competency can be dynamically improved in all areas.

SUMMARY

Competence is the effective application of knowledge, skills, and attitudes to provide service to vulnerable client populations. Competent practice protects both the recipients of service and the providers. By providing competent, multiculturally focused practice, psychologists uphold their ethical obligation to provide treatment based on the professional values of beneficence, fidelity, integrity, justice, and respect.

During the past few decades, the profession of psychology has worked diligently to develop models of competency. The cube model provided a foundation for subsequent models. The PWC model provides a framework for the education and training community. The benchmarks model offers its practical implementation, whereas the ASPPB model offers a structure for the licensure of competent psychologists. The lack of solidified competency standards for the profession has been a challenge; however, with the emergence of these frameworks, the pursuit of competency becomes more attainable and less abstract.

The foundational building blocks of competency development begin in graduate school and continue throughout licensed practice, a never-ending professional process. As it begins, competency development encompasses all aspects—academia, practicum training, internship, and postdoctoral residency experiences. To truly be competent, the psychologist must understand the importance of cultural humility and seek to bravely self-assess their knowledge, skills, and attitudes throughout their professional career. A psychologist's ongoing journey toward competent practice is epitomized by their dynamic engagement in their own learning process at both the individual and communitarian levels.

REFERENCES

American Psychological Association. (n.d.). *About APA accreditation.* https://www.accreditation.apa.org/about

American Psychological Association. (2017). *Ethical principles of psychologists and code of conduct* (2002, amended effective June 1, 2010, and January 1, 2017). https://www.apa.org/ethics/code/index.aspx

American Psychological Association, Commission on Accreditation. (2019). *Standards of accreditation for health service psychology and accreditation operating procedures.* https://www.apa.org/ed/accreditation/about/policies/standards-of-accreditation.pdf

Association of State and Provincial Psychology Boards. (2017). *2017 ASPPB competencies expected of psychologists at the point of licensure.* https://cdn.ymaws.com/www.asppb.net/resource/resmgr/eppp_2/2017_asppb_competencies_exp.pdf

Barlow, S. H. (2012). An application of the competency model to group-specialty practice. *Professional Psychology: Research and Practice, 43*(5), 442–451. https://doi.org/10.1037/a0029090

Eby, M., Chin, J., Rollock, D., Schwartz, J., & Worrell, F. (2011). Professional psychology training in the era of a thousand flowers: Dilemmas and challenges for the future. *Training and Education in Professional Psychology, 5*(2), 57–68. https://doi.org/10.1037/a0023462

Epstein, R. M., & Hundert, E. M. (2002). Defining and assessing professional competence. *JAMA, 287*(2), 226–235. https://doi.org/10.1001/jama.287.2.226

Etzioni, A. (1998). The responsive communitarian platform: Rights and responsibilities. In A. Etzioni (Ed.), *The essential communitarian reader* (pp. xxv–1). Rowman & Littlefield.

Fouad, N. A., Grus, C. L., Hatcher, R. L., Kaslow, N. J., Hutchings, P. S., Madson, M. B., Collins, F. L., Jr., & Crossman, R. E. (2009). Competency benchmarks: A model for understanding and measuring competence in professional psychology across training levels. *Training and Education in Professional Psychology, 3*(4, Suppl.), S5–S26. https://doi.org/10.1037/a0015832

France, C., Belar, C., Klonoff, K., Smith, T., Masters, K., Kerns, E., Larkin, T., Suchday, S., & Thorn, B. (2008). Application of the competency model to clinical health psychology. *Professional Psychology: Research and Practice, 39*(6), 573–580. https://doi.org/10.1037/0735-7028.39.6.573

Grus, C., Falender, C., Fouad, N., & Lavelle, A. (2016). A culture of competence: A survey of implementation of competence-based education and assessment. *Training and Education in Professional Psychology, 10*(4), 198–205. https://doi.org/10.1037/tep0000126

Hatcher, R., Fouad, N., Grus, C., Campbell, L., McCutcheon, S., & Leahy, K. (2013). Competency benchmarks: Practical steps toward a culture of competence. *Training and Education in Professional Psychology, 7*(2), 84–91. https://doi.org/10.1037/a0029401

Hunsley, J., Spivak, H., Schaffer, J., Cox, D., Caro, C., Rodolfa, E., & Greenberg, S. (2016). A competency framework for the practice of psychology: Procedures and implications. *Journal of Clinical Psychology, 72*(9), 908–918. https://doi.org/10.1002/jclp.22296

Jackson, Y., Wu, Y. P., Aylward, B. S., & Roberts, M. C. (2012). Application of the competency cube model to clinical child psychology. *Professional Psychology: Research and Practice, 43*(5), 432–441. https://doi.org/10.1037/a0030007

Johnson, W. B., Barnett, J. E., Elman, N. S., Forrest, L., & Kaslow, N. J. (2013). The competence constellation model: A communitarian approach to support professional competence. *Professional Psychology: Research and Practice, 44*(5), 343–354. https://doi.org/10.1037/a0033131

Johnson, W. B., Barnett, J. E., Elman, N. S., Forrest, L., Schwartz-Mette, R., & Kaslow, N. J. (2014). Preparing trainees for lifelong competence: Creating a communitarian training culture. *Training and Education in Professional Psychology, 8*(4), 211–220. https://doi.org/10.1037/tep0000048

Jones, J., Sander, J., & Booker, K. (2013). Multicultural competency building: Practical solutions for training and evaluating student progress. *Training and Education in Professional Psychology, 7*(1), 12–22. https://doi.org/10.1037/a0030880

Kashima, Y. (2014). How can you capture cultural dynamics? *Frontiers in Psychology, 5*, Article 995. https://doi.org/10.3389/fpsyg.2014.00995

Kaslow, N. J., Borden, K. A., Collins, F. L., Jr., Forrest, L., Illfelder-Kaye, J., Nelson, P. D., Rallo, J. S., Vasquez, M. J., & Willmuth, M. E. (2004). Competencies conference: Future directions in education and credentialing in professional psychology. *Journal of Clinical Psychology, 60*(7), 699–712. https://doi.org/10.1002/jclp.20016

Kaslow, N. J., Grus, C. L., Campbell, L. F., Fouad, N. A., Hatcher, R. L., & Rodolfa, E. R. (2009). Competency Assessment Toolkit for professional psychology. *Training and Education in Professional Psychology, 3*(4, Suppl.), S27–S45. https://doi.org/10.1037/a0015833

Lilienfield, S., & Basterfield, C. (2020). Reflective practice in clinical psychology: Reflections from basic psychological science. *Clinical Psychology: Science and Practice, 27*(4), Article e12352. https://doi.org/10.1111/cpsp.12352

Molinari, V. (2012). Application of the competency model to geropsychology. *Professional Psychology: Research and Practice, 43*(5), 403–409. https://doi.org/10.1037/a0026548

Neimeyer, G., Taylor, J., & Rozensky, R. (2012). The diminishing durability of knowledge in professional psychology: A Delphi Poll of specialties and proficiencies. *Professional Psychology: Research and Practice, 43*(4), 364–371. https://doi.org/10.1037/a0028698

Nicholson Perry, K., Donovan, M., Knight, R., & Shires, A. (2017). Addressing professional competency problems in clinical psychology trainees. *Australian Psychologist, 52*(2), 121–129. https://doi.org/10.1111/ap.12268

Pope, K. S., & Vasquez, M. (2016). *Ethics in psychotherapy and counseling* (5th ed.). John Wiley & Sons.

Rey-Casserly, C., Roper, B., & Bauer, R. (2012). Application of a competency model to clinical neuropsychology. *Professional Psychology: Research and Practice, 43*(5), 422–431. https://doi.org/10.1037/a0028721

Roberts, M. C., Borden, K., Christiansen, M. D., & Lopez, S. J. (2005). Fostering a culture shift: Assessment of competence in the education and careers of professional psychologists. *Professional Psychology: Research and Practice, 36*(4), 355–361. https://doi.org/10.1037/0735-7028.36.4.355

Rodolfa, E., Bent, R., Eisman, E., Nelson, P., Rehm, L., & Ritchie, P. (2005). A cube model for competency development: Implications for psychology educators and regulators. *Professional Psychology: Research and Practice, 36*(4), 347–354. https://doi.org/10.1037/0735-7028.36.4.347

Rodolfa, E., Greenberg, S., Hunsley, J., Smith-Zoeller, M., Cox, D., Sammons, M., Caro, C., & Spivak, H. (2013). A competency model for the practice of psychology. *Training and Education in Professional Psychology, 7*(2), 71–83. https://doi.org/10.1037/a0032415

Rodolfa, E., & Schaffer, J. (2019). Challenges to psychology education and training in the culture of competence. *American Psychologist, 74*(9), 1118–1128. https://doi.org/10.1037/amp0000513

Schaffer, J., & Rodolfa, E. (2013). A synthesis of competency initiatives in professional psychology: What's the next step. *Training and Education in Professional Psychology, 7*(2), 92–98. https://doi.org/10.1037/a0032038

Schaffer, J., & Rodolfa, E. (2020). Reflecting on reflective practice. *Clinical Psychology: Science and Practice, 27*(4), Article e12361. https://doi.org/10.1111/cpsp.12361

Silberbogen, A., Aosved, A., Cross, W., Cox, D., & Felleman, B. (2018). Postdoctoral training in health service psychology: Current perspectives in an evolving profession. *Training and Education in Professional Psychology, 12*(2), 66–73. https://doi.org/10.1037/tep0000182

Sue, D. W., Sue, D., Neville, H. A., & Smith, L. (2019). *Counseling the culturally diverse: Theory and practice* (8th ed.). John Wiley & Sons.

Wise, E. H., & Reuman, L. (2019). Promoting competent and life-long practice for psychologists: A communitarian perspective. *Professional Psychology: Research and Practice, 50*(2), 129–135. https://doi.org/10.1037/pro0000226

3 PROBLEMS OF PROFESSIONAL COMPETENCE

SUZANNE H. LEASE AND CATHERINE L. GRUS

What is meant by "problems of professional competence" (PPC)? The most common definition of PPC is "difficulty acquiring or maintaining developmentally appropriate levels of skill, functioning, attitudes, and/or ethical, professional, or interpersonal behavior across one or more settings" (Shen-Miller et al., 2015, p. 161). The understanding of PPC that one may have had initially ("I know it by its absence" or "I know it when I see it") is actually more involved. Several factors contribute to the challenge of comprehending and addressing PPC, and it is important to appreciate the complexities of PPC before trainers can effectively manage it.

First, trainers must determine in which competency domains the problems of PPC occur, as problems in certain competency clusters might be more straightforward to remedy than others. It is also crucial to understand the trajectory of the PPC. Is it competence that has not been gained or competence that has been lost during the training process? Has competence not been gained because of a developmental deficit that can be remedied or an intractable deficit that additional training will not be able to address? Where is the trainee in the educational process? Have they struggled with this same

---

https://doi.org/10.1037/0000340-004
Supporting Trainees With Competence Problems: A Practical Guide for Psychology Trainers, R. A. Schwartz-Mette, E. A. Hunter, and N. J. Kaslow (Editors)
Copyright © 2023 by the American Psychological Association. All rights reserved.

competency problem from the beginning, or is it a new concern? What accounts for competence that has been lost? Can competence be restored? Complicating factors are the intermingling of behavioral health concerns, interpersonal functioning, and cultural identities that can influence the recognition and remediation of problematic behaviors associated with many competence domains. Finally, trainers must consider the broad and long-term effects of trainees with PPC, because those effects are not limited to the trainees themselves. These effects include issues of gatekeeping and the social contract with the public and potential long-term effects on trainees who have been identified as having PPC, on their program peers, and on perceptions of the profession.

This chapter provides a comprehensive overview of PPC. First, terminology and approaches to describing competence problems are addressed. The subsequent section discusses the importance of considering whether the PPC are amenable to resolution or are entrenched and reviews central challenges in identifying and addressing competence problems. The chapter concludes with a discussion of long-term and broad impact considerations related to PPC.

TERMINOLOGY AND DESCRIBING COMPETENCE PROBLEMS

Trainees who are not meeting program expectations are now commonly referred to as trainees with problems of professional competence (TPPC); however, for many years the word *impairment* was routinely used. Falender et al. (2005) challenged that long-standing practice, noting that a principal concern with the term *impairment* is the overlap with the Americans With Disabilities Act of 1990 (ADA). In the ADA, *impairment* has a specific legal meaning and attendant requirements and thus should be used only in circumstances that truly fit the provisions of the ADA. To do otherwise creates legal risk to a psychology training program. Further, the term *impairment* confuses the reason(s) for the problem with the specific behavior(s) of concern. Elman and Forrest (2007) identified three components that should guide the terminology used to refer to trainees who are not meeting program expectations: noting a performance problem, relating the difficulty to a professional standard(s), and ensuring that the problem is defined in a manner consistent with the focus in health service psychology on competency-based education. This led to the now widespread practice of using the terminology *problems of professional competence*. Although the term's definition has been established, numerous challenges are associated with defining what is, or is not, PPC.

A key definitional consideration related to PPC is determining the specific nature of the competency domain(s) in which the problems are occurring. Interpersonal functioning is commonly reported as one of the most frequent domains in which competency problems are displayed (Forrest et al., 1999), whereas Kaslow et al. (2018) noted that PPC often manifest in the professionalism domain. Yet the professional competencies cover the range of activities in which professional psychologists engage. PPC can manifest in knowledge and skill deficits in classes and research teams as well as disrupted interpersonal interactions with classmates, trainers, and colleagues in assistantship and/or clinical placements.

The competency cube developed by Rodolfa et al. (2005) and discussed in Chapter 2 of this volume offers a framework to help structure how PPC are defined. The cube model divides competencies into two domains: foundational and functional. *Foundational* refers to those competencies that serve as the foundation for what psychologists do. PPC in the foundational domain can include behaviors that indicate poor professionalism, disrupted interpersonal relationships, low self-awareness, or challenges in recognizing and respecting individual and cultural diversity. The *functional* domain represents the competencies needed to perform the work of a psychologist. In the functional domain, PPC could manifest in the failure to demonstrate appropriate knowledge, skills, or attitudes in research or in clinical experiences. PPC can occur in both domains, and identifying the specific competencies that are not demonstrated at expected performance levels and the severity and impact of the deficits guides decisions about interventions (Kaslow et al., 2018). Efforts to remediate problems in functional competencies may be easier or more straightforward than those in foundational domains (Jacobs et al., 2011), but training programs must still evaluate and ensure competence in all domains.

Another key component in defining PPC is the understanding that competencies develop over time with training and follow an expected developmental trajectory (Kaslow et al., 2007), with trainees varying in their degree of competence. What might be termed a PPC for advanced trainees would not be considered such with trainees earlier in their programs. The competency cube contains a developmental axis, whereas the Competency Benchmarks (Fouad et al., 2009) and subsequent revision (Hatcher et al., 2013) provide trainers with clearly defined and measurable benchmarks for performance expectations at three levels: readiness for practicum, readiness for internship, and readiness for practice. These developmental benchmarks help to delineate the trajectory of competency development and are described further in a later section.

Contextualizing PPC

As noted earlier, the identification of PPC focuses on behavior and performance in comparison with expected levels rather than the reasons for those deficits (Elman & Forrest, 2007). Nevertheless, problems of competence can occur for various reasons, and differentiating among the factors that contribute to PPC is crucial for determining potential responses needed to assist trainees in gaining or regaining competence. These factors include understanding what precipitates PPC, determining whether the PPC reflects a slower-than-expected development of competence or competence that will not be attained, and considering broader factors that might influence the difficulties that are manifested.

Potential Sources of PPC

Although the cube model provides an excellent classification system for the domains of competence problems, Schwartz-Mette (2011) argued that there is not a similar organizational structure for the potential sources of PPC. She proposed the following categories for understanding the sources of competence problems that were not the result of a legally defined disability: (a) behavior problems ranging from tardiness in completion of tasks to substance use, (b) psychological problems including maladaptive personality traits or boundary issues, (c) situational stressors experienced by the trainee, and (d) developmental problems related to educational or experience deficiencies. Each source could account for problems with competence that had not yet been gained or competence that had been lost, but the source would guide trainers' approaches to developing potential remediation strategies. The next step following identification of the source, and one that is discussed in greater depth in Chapter 6 of this volume, is to develop interventions to remediate the problem that is informed by the causes of the trainees' PPC.

Kaslow et al. (2007) noted that PPC might occur because of situational factors or a lack of experience or education, but also as a result of problematic personality or interpersonal dynamics. The latter may result in trainees who are unable or unwilling to attain accepted minimal levels of competence on designated behaviors, fail to respond to feedback and make progress, lack self-awareness of their weaknesses, struggle with maintaining professional interactions, have problems with professionalism or interpersonal interactions that they have not addressed, or experience personal or mental health issues that affect their professional functioning. In their article, Kaslow and her colleagues (2007) included both the potential causes of PPC and descriptions of types of problematic behavior, underscoring the difficulty of disentangling descriptions of PPC from their sources.

In a study focused on trainees' reactions to peers with competency problems, Veilleux et al. (2012) grouped 16 competence problems into three factors indicative of the source of the PPC: trait characteristics reflective of long-term character deficits (e.g., lacking interpersonal or communication skills, self-awareness, or intellectual reasoning; immaturity), general distress (e.g., depression, anxiety, physical illness, major life changes), and chronic pathology (e.g., alcohol/drug abuse or dependence, personality disorders, anger management). This nomenclature shares certain characteristics with those of Schwartz-Mette (2011) and Kaslow et al. (2007) but includes some that might be addressed by legal definitions of disability (e.g., physical illness, depression) and does not include developmental deficits. The research sample of clinical psychology students viewed trait characteristics as more problematic than chronic psychopathology, which was more problematic than general distress. The participants viewed peers exhibiting trait character deficits as having more clinical impairment (defined in the study as compromised professional functioning but capable, or previously capable, of performing at acceptable standards) and lacking the ability to achieve competent functioning.

Developmental Versus Entrenched PPC
Although developmental or educational deficits may not be viewed as the most challenging sources of PPC, they are mentioned frequently as one explanation for failure to demonstrate expected levels of competence, and they must be addressed. Over the course of training, the developmental model proposes that trainees master increasingly demanding levels of competence within each domain. Thus, trainees might display competence across domains early in their training but later struggle with attaining competence at more advanced levels. Because trainees had been making acceptable progress earlier in their training, trainers might not immediately detect that the trainees have hit a stumbling block that requires extra focus.

For instance, beginning structured coursework in research design and statistics might be mastered, but students might struggle to translate that learning into conducting independent research projects (theses or dissertations). In the Competency Benchmarks form that provides behavioral examples of the essential components of competence across the levels (see Appendix D, Resources; American Psychological Association [APA], 2012), this might mean that trainees appropriately demonstrated the behaviors associated with readiness for practicum (e.g., writing literature reviews as part of courses, assisting faculty research) but not at the readiness for internship level (e.g., understanding research methods and techniques of data analysis).

The failure to display continuing competence from one level to another might signify lack of true mastery in the earlier phases that was not detected in the competency assessment or struggles with translating earlier concrete knowledge into abstract skills. This challenge in demonstrating the higher developmental level of competency could differ from the loss of an attained competency (i.e., diminished functioning); although at first glance, they might seem the same (e.g., the trainee previously demonstrated competency in scientific methods and now does not). However, concluding they are the same neglects the developmental trajectory of competencies. Although attempts to restore competency should be made in either case, differentiating between a developmental challenge to gaining competency and loss of competency because of emotional or physical health issues could shape those remediation attempts.

Although trainees might display developmental training deficits in the competencies, these deficits are often viewed in a different way than competency deficits that interfere with the ability to adequately provide services or perform the required tasks. This latter type of competency problem can be further categorized into those that can still be remediated and those in which trainees are determined to be unable to perform the expected duties of a professional psychologist (Schwartz-Mette, 2009; Vacha-Haase et al., 2004). The latter group is sometimes referred to as "lacking capacity" (Veilleux et al., 2012) or being "unsuitable," which Olkin and Gaughen (1991) defined as "those students whose personal limitations or problem behaviors are of such a nature or severity that they are deemed by educators to impede the students' ability to professional practice" (p. 279). Trainees who experience deficits but are viewed as capable of attaining competent functioning may be appropriate for remediation, whereas those who lack the capacity might need to be counseled out or dismissed from their training programs. The lacking capacity group is thought to be at greater risk for ethical misconduct (Johnson & Campbell, 2004).

As discussed, it is important to make a distinction among developmental competence deficits; competence that has been lost but can regained; and entrenched PPC such that trainees lack capacity (Schwartz-Mette, 2009; Vacha-Haase et al., 2004), as remediation pathways might differ based on the etiology of the deficit. However, even the use of this classification is not clear cut, because numerous behaviors might suggest "lacking capacity" and trainers cannot necessarily determine which personal limitations or behaviors can be corrected and which cannot without a period of attempted remediation. Although the majority of the competence problem literature focuses on

PPC in which trainees have lost a previous level of competence or are unable to demonstrate acceptable levels of competence rather than developmental training deficits, it is essential to keep the developmental framework of competence in mind.

Systems-Oriented Conceptualizations of PPC
Up to this point, our discussion of PPC has focused on the individual trainee. However, Elman et al. (1999) proposed that PPC occurs in the context of a larger training system, and focusing on the behavior of the individual trainee yields an incomplete picture (see also Chapter 4, this volume). Forrest et al. (2008) built upon the work of Bronfenbrenner's ecological model to broaden the focus to that of the larger training ecosystem. Envisioned as a series of expanding concentric circles, the smallest circle in the model is the individual or microsystem, which is embedded in the mesosystem that reflects the interactions of the individual with others in the training environment such as peers, faculty, and supervisors. The mesosystem is in turn embedded in the exosystem, which are the policies and regulations that guide education and training such as departmental policies, accreditation standards, and licensure requirements. These are all embedded in the largest circle, which is the macrosystem and accounts for the influence of concepts such as cultural norms about what makes a good psychologist, beliefs about the roles and responsibilities of gatekeepers for the profession, and cultural norms related to diversity characteristics and power. This model is useful in understanding the role of broader contexts in which PPC exist and serves as a reminder that remediation plans, although largely focused on the individual/microsystem level, should also consider how mes-, exo-, and macrosystem forces might be involved in the development, identification, and remediation of PPC.

Another "wide-lens" model uses the construct of the communitarian community to underscore the opportunities and obligations of those in the training environment and prevent PPC from developing or worsening (Johnson et al., 2014). Johnson and colleagues (2014) proposed a "communitarian training culture," discussed in Chapter 1 of this volume, in which care is a core value of the community and there is a shared sense of accountability for the well-being and professional competency of all in the community—that is, both trainers and trainees. By viewing competence as a collective responsibility, members of the community are empowered and expected to reach out to colleagues at the first sign of a PPC; this includes trainees reaching out to peers, trainers reaching out to other trainers, and trainers supporting trainees. Such early outreach could be helpful in mitigating the seriousness of PPC.

Complexities in Identifying and Addressing PPC

So far, we have suggested that by using the benchmark competencies and developmental trajectory, the identification of PPC should be relatively straightforward. Unfortunately, this is not always the case. Several factors contribute to the complexity of identifying and addressing PPC: the frequency with which PPC involves interpersonal and intrapersonal functioning, the intersection of PPC and diversity, and the way to work with isolated but serious violations of competence standards. Failure to understand and consider these complexities is likely to lead to an unsuccessful resolution of the PPC.

PPC Related to Interpersonal and Intrapersonal Functioning

Studies attempting to identify the types, sources, frequency, and severity of PPC vary widely in methodology, use of terminology (e.g., *impaired, unsuitable, problematic*), type and level of trainees (e.g., psychology, counselor education, social work, beginning vs. advanced), and research participants (e.g., faculty, supervisor, peers of trainees). Yet despite the diverse approaches, interpersonal (e.g., classroom behavior, limited self-awareness, poor judgment, unprofessional behavior) and intrapersonal (e.g., anxiety and depression, personality disorders, substance abuse) concerns are among the most frequently identified problems of professional competence requiring remediation or termination from a training program (Brear et al., 2008; Shen-Miller et al., 2011). PPC related to emotion regulation difficulties was the most frequently cited behavior by peers in psychology doctoral programs (Furr & Brown-Rice, 2018).

Unlike academic or skill deficits that correspond to the functional competency domains and are relatively easy to objectively define and assess, identifying and quantifying nonacademic aspects of PPC is challenging. Although certain interpersonal or intrapersonal behaviors are clear indicators of PPC necessitating remediation or even dismissal (e.g., substance use disorder, failing to comport with legal requirements), the most commonly identified indicators of PPC (e.g., problems in supervision, deficient interpersonal skills, inappropriate boundaries, professionalism deficits) are more challenging to recognize, define, and agree upon (Forrest et al., 1999; Rust et al., 2013). The ambiguity of some behavioral indicators of PPC makes it easier for trainers to minimize the severity of the concerns until they reach an extreme level, avoid addressing the PPC altogether, or be subject to their own unconscious bias in responding to the trainee. Hensley et al. (2003) noted the challenges presented by evaluator subjectivity when assessing personal qualities that negatively impact the professional domain. Common recommendations include developing defined program policies for addressing PPC that include explicit descriptions of core criteria related to personal functioning, describing trainee behavior in terms of compliance with the core competencies, and developing psychometrically sound instruments to aid in the measurement of competencies (Brear et al., 2008; Rust et al., 2013). The Benchmarks document assists with these tasks by providing behavioral anchors, although even those exemplar behaviors contain some level of subjectivity.

Intersection of Diversity and PPC
Individual and cultural diversity (ICD) is a core foundational competency, and certain studies have included lack of diversity awareness or respect as an important contributor to PPC in multiple other competency domains (e.g., interpersonal relations, clinical intervention). Trainees identifying as members of dominant cultural groups in the United States (e.g., U.S.-born, White, cisgender, male, heterosexual, middle- or upper-middle socioeconomic status, Christian) might not recognize how their identities shape their perceptions of those who are not members of these groups, potentially resulting in challenges in their hearing and working with clients or colleagues who have different experiences. PPC reflecting trainees' cultural encapsulation or attitudes that could be harmful to clients, future trainees, and colleagues must be addressed. Some trainees might raise objections to clients' behaviors or identities based on their personal beliefs and profess an inability or unwillingness to work with such clients. This raises the challenge of being respectful of trainees' personal beliefs while maintaining an allegiance to becoming competent to work with all clients, a central value of the profession.

The core competencies were developed to protect the public, and developing trainee competence cannot be selective, occurring in some areas or populations and not in others (BEA Virtual Working Group on Restrictions Affecting Diversity Training in Graduate Education, 2015). Training programs can balance competing demands between trainees' personal beliefs and professional responsibilities by creating a supportive training environment in which trainees are supported in their process of developing competency to work with diverse populations, trainees are respected for their right to have personal beliefs while developing diversity competencies, and trainers model how they engage in self-reflection as it relates to their own belief systems. Training programs also demonstrate a commitment to transparency in educational expectations, policies, and procedures by providing clear and available information about professional expectations to serve a diverse public and potential consequences if trainees do not develop these competencies. Finally, professional associations such as the APA should make a commitment to establishing and maintaining standards for professional competence to protect the public through policies such as an ethics code and establishing standards for education and training.

Just as trainees might struggle with cultural encapsulation and unexamined bias, there are trainers who are not as fully competent in ICD areas and do not attend to how their group membership and identities frame their evaluations of trainees and the power dynamics between trainers and trainees (Kaslow et al., 2007; Rust et al., 2013). If trainers are unaware of how cultural norms and values could intersect with the assessment of competence, they may identify trainees, especially diverse trainees, as having PPC when the issue is a function of the training system that is contributing to the concern or a lack of trainer multicultural competence (Shen-Miller et al., 2009). As Goodrich and Shin (2013) noted, current demographics suggest that it will be predominantly White training faculty and staff who are assessing students of color.

Shen-Miller et al. (2012) reported that existing conflicts around diversity among faculty (e.g., faculty holding color-blind vs. culture-attentive perspectives) increased the tension around identifying PPC in diverse trainees and complicated issues around gatekeeping, providing feedback, and supporting diverse students. Brown-Rice and Furr (2016) reported that more than one third of their sample of faculty trainers feared being seen as culturally insensitive or discriminatory when developing remediation plans for trainees from different cultural backgrounds. Past and potential conflict among faculty and fear could result in avoiding raising issues of diversity and competence when they should have been addressed or overidentifying PPC in diverse trainees. Working effectively with trainees with PPC requires that trainers possess the skills to engage in difficult conversations among themselves (Jacobs et al., 2011). Similarly, peers of TPPC noted challenges related to the intersection of diversity and PPC because of concerns about cultural competence or being perceived as biased (Shen-Miller et al., 2015). Having and adhering to formal evaluation and remediation procedures grounded in the behaviorally based Competency Benchmarks can reduce the likelihood of inappropriately evaluating culturally based behavior as PPC or that corrective actions will be viewed as discriminatory.

Egregious Violations of Competency
A final complexity centers on trainees who have demonstrated competence in most areas but who commit a single act that egregiously violates an important competency standard. Violating legal or ethical standards is the most common example. Ethical violations are not consistently included as categories of

problematic competence, although some authors (e.g., Olkin & Gaughen, 1991; Veilleux et al., 2012) included them in the list of problematic behaviors. However, Biaggio et al. (1983) reported that ethical violations were the single most important factor warranting dismissal from clinical psychology programs, and marriage and family therapy program directors identified ethical violations as their top concern among indicators of student problems of professional competence (Russell & Peterson, 2003). McCutcheon (2008) suggested that the profession generally favors remediation over punishment, even for licensed professionals, and that the developmental view of competency results in trainees being held to a different standard of behavior. He noted that training sites vary in the degree to which they tolerate failures of critical competencies and the subsequent consequences but that responses will often be based on the assessment of whether the behavior is part of an overall pattern or viewed as a mistake that is attributable to a correctable cause. Even so, certain behaviors are so egregious (e.g., sexual contact with clients, felony convictions, violations of university academic standards/institutional policy) that training programs might move immediately to dismissal without the option of remediation. This possibility should be explicitly stated in the training program's student handbook.

Broad Effects of TPPC

Although the primary focus when working with PPC remains on the individual trainees and their current struggles, PPC has ramifications for gatekeeping and protection of the public, working with current and future training sites, trainers, and other trainees in the program. PPC can reach across numerous system boundaries (e.g., practicum, classes, graduate assistantships, research labs, externship and internship training), increasing the challenges in addressing it. Attention to these broader systemic issues is a necessary aspect of ensuring professional competence.

Ethical and Legal Considerations

Trainers who have identified a TPPC often face an internal tension between optimism that the problem will dissipate over time or with the support of remediation and their ethical and moral responsibilities to the profession, the public, and the student should the remediation not prove successful. Functioning as a gatekeeper can be guided by considering ethical practices (Bodner, 2012). Specific ethical considerations include minimizing harm to trainees; giving trainees clear and timely feedback about problems of professional competence; and respecting cultural, individual, and role differences and understanding their interactions with decisions regarding trainee competency (see also Chapter 8, this volume). Trainers also have an obligation to consider the value of engaging in "forward feeding," particularly as relates to PPC that may be more challenging to detect and correct. Specifically, forward feeding refers to a process by which information is shared with future trainers about areas in which a trainee has experienced a PPC or is not fully meeting program benchmarks (Kaslow et al., 2018). This strategy can be particularly useful in situations where the PPC might get worse over time if undetected. Forward feeding requires balancing the demands for providing an accurate evaluation and the desire to support students as they apply for clinical placements and employment. McCutcheon (2008) posited that the relative separation between internship programs and students' graduate training programs and the importance of intern competence in light of changing requirements for postdoctoral experience prior to licensure heightens the need for effective communication and forward feeding between academic programs and clinical placements. Further, TPPC who are allowed to move to the next stage of training without addressing the concerns become the responsibility of the internship or postdoctoral trainers who feel "stuck" with the need to address the issue before the trainees begin independent practice with fewer opportunities for oversight (Johnson et al., 2008).

Gaubatz and Vera (2002) reported that gateslipping (i.e., allowing trainees with proficiency concerns to move through the program without addressing the concerns) was more likely to occur in programs that employed a higher number of adjunct faculty, where faculty perceived greater institutional pressure to not screen for or remediate TPPC, or when faculty were concerned about poor teaching evaluations resulting from screening or holding back a TPPC or being sued if they screened or dismissed a TPPC. Other characteristics of programs that are ineffective in managing PPC include a culture of avoidance, individualistic attitudes, and ignoring cultural and diversity factors or lacking competence in this area (Forrest et al., 2013). These program characteristics speak to the importance of attending to the training ecosystem and working with trainers who are more peripherally involved with the program, including at the administrative level, to convey the importance of helping trainees attain expected competence and supporting trainers who enforce standards of competence (see Chapter 4, this volume). Ideally, this attention to training environment should occur outside of a specific occurrence of PPC such that a shared value system can be developed over time. Hesitancy to address PPC may occur due to misperceptions about legal risk to programs if they remediate or dismiss a student. Gilfoyle (2008) offered a review of relevant legal risk management principles and steps that programs should take to mitigate legal risk (see also Chapter 9, this volume). Regardless of when PPC arises, when competence problems are determined to be significant or are shown to be unchanged by appropriate remediation, actions must be taken to protect the public and maintain the integrity of the field (see Chapter 6, this volume).

Effects of TPPC on Trainers and Other Trainees
Even though TPPC represent a small percentage of the total trainees in the program, when PPC is identified in trainees, significant trainer time and attention must be devoted to the process of addressing the competency issues (Brown-Rice & Furr, 2013; Kaslow et al., 2007; Rust et al., 2013). These demands have consequences for both training faculty and peers of the TPPC.

From the trainers' perspectives, addressing TPPC brings structural challenges (e.g., time demands related to extensive documentation and implementation of remediation plans, perceived lack of support from administration; Busseri et al., 2005; Forrest et al., 1999) and socioemotional challenges (e.g., reluctance to remediate an advanced student or one who is doing well in some areas in the program, difficulty balancing supportive mentor and gatekeeper roles, faculty disagreement regarding the trainee's PPC, emotional distress around dismissal; Busseri et al., 2005; Johnson et al., 2008). Furthermore, the level of trainer resources necessary for addressing PPC has the potential to affect more than just the trainers involved. As trainer time and energy is directed toward trainees with PPC, proficient students who are not experiencing any difficulty get commensurately less attention (Rose & Persutte-Manning, 2020), potentially resulting in, at best, a diminished educational experience and, at worst, their own learning gaps. These trainees might feel that they are left to sink or swim on their own, unsupported through their own struggles, and disillusioned with their program and perhaps the field at large. Their negative emotional reactions can spread to disrupted dynamics in the classroom and a diminished reputation for the program, potentially affecting both accreditation and recruitment efforts.

In addition to the indirect effect that TPPC might have on other trainees through the time demands on trainers, they can have a direct negative effect on the learning environment for their peers. Numerous authors (e.g., Forrest et al., 1999; Furr & Brown-Rice, 2018) have noted that trainees spend more time with their peers in a variety of contexts and are likely to be able to identify behavioral concerns among their peers that faculty might not observe. Trainees with peers exhibiting PPC may perceive that their peers "take up all the air in the room" with their own issues and exhaust peers by looking to them to provide support, but not reciprocating (Rose & Persutte-Manning, 2020). Veilleux et al. (2012) noted that trainees with peers who appeared to lack the ability to meet benchmark competence levels perceived challenges to their own learning, decreased faith in their program faculty, and a diminished value of their doctoral degrees if peers who were not competent were allowed to represent themselves as psychologists. Furr and Brown-Rice (2018) reported that trainees experienced disrupted learning environments and stress because of peers with PPC and resented those peers. This experience may lead to conflict within the trainee group that is challenging for all trainees (those with and without PPC) to navigate, and trainees may not know where to turn for trainer support (Rose & Persutte-Manning, 2020), especially if they are unsure if trainers are aware of the PPC. Trainers have the responsibility of supporting all the trainees with whom they work, so it is important to address PPC concerns as quickly as possible to help struggling students attain competency and reduce the detrimental effects of peers with PPC on proficient students (Rose & Persutte-Manning, 2020).

Finally, trainees who have been identified as experiencing PPC might be negatively impacted by that experience even after the problems have been successfully addressed. Limited research examined PPC from the trainees' perspectives, but most trainees have been academically successful throughout their entire educational history. Anecdotally, receiving feedback that their performance is not meeting acceptable standards, especially if the feedback is inconsistent with previous feedback or comes late in their training, can have devastating effects on their self-efficacy that last well after the remediation process is complete. Vacha-Haase et al. (2019) suggested that trainees might be embarrassed by their struggles, be concerned about negative "halo" perceptions among their trainers, and fear high levels of scrutiny for the duration of their training. Although these concerns can be ameliorated through the presence of clear policies and use of timely feedback or remediation plans that include trainee input, trainees might continue to be more cautious or reserved when interacting with trainers and stressed about potential delays in the completion of their programs (including financial stressors that could accompany delayed progress) or the effect of the PPC on internship match or attaining postdoctoral or employment positions (Kaslow et al., 2018).

CONCLUSION

Understanding PPC starts with a common definition that focuses on trainees' not meeting expected standards for the profession and the behaviors of relevance. However, trainers also need to consider the context(s) that lead to the development of the PPC to have a more complete understanding of pathways to remediate (or not). More complex PPC such as those related to inter- or intrapersonal functioning and those that intersect or involve dimensions of diversity are particularly challenging for trainers. Trainers also need to attend to broader implications, such as ethical and legal considerations and the impacts of a TPPC on the entire training ecosystem.

REFERENCES

American Psychological Association. (2012). *Revised competency benchmarks in professional psychology*. https://www.apa.org/ed/graduate/benchmarks-evaluation-system?tab=1

Americans With Disabilities Act of 1990, Pub. L. No. 101–336, 104 Stat. 328 (1990).

BEA Virtual Working Group on Restrictions Affecting Diversity Training in Graduate Education. (2015). Preparing professional psychologists to serve a diverse public: A core requirement in doctoral education and training a pedagogical statement. *Training and Education in Professional Psychology, 9*(4), 269–270. https://doi.org/10.1037/tep0000093

Biaggio, M. K., Gasparikova-Krasnec, M., & Bauer, L. (1983). Evaluation of clinical psychology graduate students: The problem of the unsuitable student. *Professional Practice of Psychology, 4*(1), 9–20.

Bodner, K. (2012). Ethical principles and standards that inform educational gatekeeping practices in psychology. *Ethics and Behavior, 22*(1), 60–74. https://doi.org/10.1080/10508422.2012.638827

Brear, P., Dorrian, J., & Luscri, G. (2008). Preparing our future counselling professionals: Gatekeeping and the implications for research. *Counselling & Psychotherapy Research, 8*(2), 93–101. https://doi.org/10.1080/14733140802007855

Brown-Rice, K. A., & Furr, S. (2013). Preservice counselors' knowledge of classmates' problems of professional competence. *Journal of Counseling and Development, 91*(2), 224–233. https://doi.org/10.1002/j.1556-6676.2013.00089.x

Brown-Rice, K., & Furr, S. (2016). Counselor educators and students with problems of professional competence: A survey and discussion. *The Professional Counselor, 6*(2), 134–146. https://doi.org/10.15241/kbr.6.2.134

Busseri, M. A., Tyler, J. D., & King, A. R. (2005). An exploratory examination of student dismissals and prompted resignations from clinical psychology PhD training programs: Does clinical competency matter? *Professional Psychology: Research and Practice, 36*(4), 441–445. https://doi.org/10.1037/0735-7028.36.4.441

Elman, N. S., & Forrest, L. (2007). From trainee impairment to professional competence problems: Seeking new terminology that facilitates effective action. *Professional Psychology: Research and Practice, 38*(5), 501–509. https://doi.org/10.1037/0735-7028.38.5.501

Elman, N., Forrest, L., Vacha-Haase, T., & Gizara, S. (1999). A systems perspective on trainee impairment: Continuing the dialogue. *The Counseling Psychologist, 27*(5), 712–721. https://doi.org/10.1177/0011000099275005

Falender, C. A., Collins, C. J., & Shafranske, E. P. (2005). Use of the term "impairment" in psychology supervision. *California Psychologist, 38*, 21–22.

Forrest, L., Elman, N., Gizara, S., & Vacha-Haase, T. (1999). Trainee impairment: A review of identification, remediation, dismissal, and legal issues. *The Counseling Psychologist*, *27*(5), 627–686. https://doi.org/10.1177/0011000099275001

Forrest, L., Elman, N. S., Huprich, S. K., Veilleux, J. C., Jacobs, S. C., & Kaslow, N. J. (2013). Training directors' perceptions of faculty behaviors when dealing with trainee competence problems: A mixed method pilot study. *Training and Education in Professional Psychology*, *7*(1), 23–32. https://doi.org/10.1037/a0032068

Forrest, L., Shen-Miller, D. S., & Elman, N. S. (2008). Psychology trainees with competence problems: From individual to ecological conceptualizations. *Training and Education in Professional Psychology*, *2*(4), 183–192. https://doi.org/10.1037/1931-3918.2.4.183

Fouad, N. A., Grus, C. L., Hatcher, R. L., Kaslow, N. J., Hutchings, P. S., Madson, M. B., Collins, F. L., Jr., & Crossman, R. E. (2009). Competency benchmarks: A model for understanding and measuring competence in professional psychology across training levels. *Training and Education in Professional Psychology*, *3*(4, Suppl.), S5–S26. https://doi.org/10.1037/a0015832

Furr, S., & Brown-Rice, K. (2018). Psychology doctoral students' perceptions of peers' problems of professional competency. *Training and Education in Professional Psychology*, *12*(2), 118–124. https://doi.org/10.1037/tep0000184

Gaubatz, M. D., & Vera, E. M. (2002). Do formalized gatekeeping procedures increase programs' follow-up with deficient trainees? *Counselor Education and Supervision*, *41*(4), 294–305. https://doi.org/10.1002/j.1556-6978.2002.tb01292.x

Gilfoyle, N. (2008). The legal exosystem: Risk management in addressing student competence problems in professional psychology training. *Training and Education in Professional Psychology*, *2*(4), 202–209. https://doi.org/10.1037/1931-3918.2.4.202

Goodrich, K. M., & Shin, R. Q. (2013). A culturally responsive intervention for addressing problematic behaviors in counseling students. *Counselor Education and Supervision*, *52*(1), 43–55. https://doi.org/10.1002/j.1556-6978.2013.00027.x

Hatcher, R., Fouad, N., Grus, C., Campbell, L., McCutcheon, S., & Leahy, K. (2013). Competency benchmarks: Practical steps toward a culture of competence. *Training and Education in Professional Psychology*, *7*(2), 84–91. https://doi.org/10.1037/a0029401

Hensley, L. G., Smith, S. L., & Thompson, R. W. (2003). Assessing competencies of counselors-in-training: Complexities in evaluating personal and professional development. *Counselor Education and Supervision*, *42*(3), 219–230. https://doi.org/10.1002/j.1556-6978.2003.tb01813.x

Jacobs, S. C., Huprich, S. K., Grus, C. L., Cage, E. A., Elman, N. S., Forrest, L., Schwartz-Mette, R., Shen-Miller, D. S., Van Sickle, K. S., & Kaslow, N. J. (2011). Trainees with professional competency problems: Preparing trainers for difficult but necessary conversations. *Training and Education in Professional Psychology*, *5*(3), 175–184. https://doi.org/10.1037/a0024656

Johnson, W. B., Barnett, J. E., Elman, N. S., Forrest, L., Schwartz-Mette, R., & Kaslow, N. J. (2014). Preparing trainees for lifelong competence: Creating a communitarian training culture. *Training and Education in Professional Psychology*, *8*(4), 211–220. https://doi.org/10.1037/tep0000048

Johnson, W. B., & Campbell, C. D. (2004). Character and fitness requirements for professional psychologists: Training directors' perspectives. *Professional Psychology: Research and Practice*, *35*(4), 405–411. https://doi.org/10.1037/0735-7028.35.4.405

Johnson, W. B., Elman, N. S., Forrest, L., Robiner, W. N., Rodolfa, E., & Schaffer, J. B. (2008). Addressing professional competence problems in trainees: Some ethical considerations. *Professional Psychology: Research and Practice, 39*(6), 589–599. https://doi.org/10.1037/a0014264

Kaslow, N. J., Grus, C. L., Allbaugh, L. J., Shen-Miller, D., Bodner, K. E., Veilleux, J., & Van Sickle, K. (2018). Trainees with competence problems in the professionalism domain. *Ethics & Behavior, 28*(6), 429–449. https://doi.org/10.1080/10508422.2018.1438897

Kaslow, N. J., Rubin, N., Forrest, L., Elman, N. S., Van Horne, B., Jacobs, S., Huprich, S., Benton, S., Pantesco, V., Dollinger, S., Grus, C. L., Behnke, S. H., Shen-Miller, D. S., Shealy, C. N., Mintz, L. B., Schwartz-Mette, R., Van Sickle, K., & Thorn, B. E. (2007). Recognizing, assessing, and intervening with problems of professional competence. *Professional Psychology: Research and Practice, 38*(5), 479–492. https://doi.org/10.1037/0735-7028.38.5.479

McCutcheon, S. (2008). Addressing problems of insufficient competence during the internship year. *Training and Education in Professional Psychology, 2*(4), 210–214. https://doi.org/10.1037/a0013535

Olkin, R., & Gaughen, S. (1991). Evaluation and dismissal of students in master's level clinical programs: Legal parameters and survey results. *Counselor Education and Supervision, 30*(4), 276–288. https://doi.org/10.1002/j.1556-6978.1991.tb01210.x

Rodolfa, E., Bent, R., Eisman, E., Nelson, P., Rehm, L., & Ritchie, P. (2005). A cube model for competency development: Implications for psychology educators and regulators. *Professional Psychology: Research and Practice, 36*(4), 347–354. https://doi.org/10.1037/0735-7028.36.4.347

Rose, J. S., & Persutte-Manning, S. (2020). Students with problems of professional competency and their impact on proficient students in counseling programs. *Journal of Counselor Preparation and Supervision, 13*(4). https://digitalcommons.sacredheart.edu/jcps/vol13/iss4/4

Russell, C. S., & Peterson, C. M. (2003). Student impairment and remediation in accredited marriage and family therapy programs. *Journal of Marital and Family Therapy, 29*(3), 329–337. https://doi.org/10.1111/j.1752-0606.2003.tb01210.x

Rust, J. P., Raskin, J. D., & Hill, M. S. (2013). Problems of professional competence among counselor trainees: Programmatic issues and guidelines. *Counselor Education and Supervision, 52*(1), 30–42. https://doi.org/10.1002/j.1556-6978.2013.00026.x

Schwartz-Mette, R. A. (2009). Challenges in addressing graduate student impairment in academic professional psychology programs. *Ethics & Behavior, 19*(2), 91–102. https://doi.org/10.1080/10508420902768973

Schwartz-Mette, R. A. (2011). Out with impairment, in with professional competence problems: Response to commentary by Collins, Falender, and Shafranske. *Ethics & Behavior, 21*(5), 431–434. https://doi.org/10.1080/10508422.2011.604551

Shen-Miller, D. S., Forrest, L., & Burt, M. (2012). Contextual influences on faculty diversity conceptualizations when working with trainee competence problems. *The Counseling Psychologist, 40*(8), 1181–1219. https://doi.org/10.1177/0011000011431832

Shen-Miller, D. S., Forrest, L., & Elman, N. S. (2009). Training directors' conceptualizations of the intersections of diversity and trainee competence problems: A preliminary analysis. *The Counseling Psychologist, 37*(4), 482–518. https://doi.org/10.1177/0011000008316656

Shen-Miller, D. S., Grus, C. L., Van Sickle, K., Schwartz-Mette, R., Cage, E., Elman, N. S., Jacobs, S. C., & Kaslow, N. J. (2011). Trainees experiences with peers having competence problems: A national survey. *Training and Education in Professional Psychology*, *5*(2), 112–121. https://doi.org/10.1037/a0023824

Shen-Miller, D. S., Schwartz-Mette, R., Van Sickle, K., Jacobs, S. C., Grus, C. L., Hunter, E., & Forrest, L. (2015). Professional competence problems in training: A qualitative investigation of trainee perspectives. *Training and Education in Professional Psychology*, *9*(2), 161–169. https://doi.org/10.1037/tep0000072

Vacha-Haase, T., Davenport, D. S., & Kerewsky, S. D. (2004). Problematic students: Gatekeeping practices of academic professional psychology programs. *Professional Psychology: Research and Practice*, *35*(2), 115–122. https://doi.org/10.1037/0735-7028.35.2.115

Vacha-Haase, T., Elman, N. S., Forrest, L., Kallaugher, J., Lease, S. H., Veilleux, J. C., & Kaslow, N. J. (2019). Remediation plans for trainees with problems of professional competence. *Training and Education in Professional Psychology*, *13*(4), 239–246. https://doi.org/10.1037/tep0000221

Veilleux, J. C., January, A. M., VanderVeen, J. W., Reddy, L. F., & Klonoff, E. A. (2012). Differentiating amongst characteristics associated with problems of professional competence: Perceptions of graduate student peers. *Training and Education in Professional Psychology*, *6*(2), 113–121. https://doi.org/10.1037/a0028337

4

SYSTEMIC PERSPECTIVES ON TRAINEES WITH PROBLEMS OF PROFESSIONAL COMPETENCE

DEBRA MOLLEN AND MARLENE G. WILLIAMS

Three key bodies of scholarship inform our understanding of and approach to this chapter. After sharing a fictitious case vignette, we review the literature on competence, particularly its conceptualization and application to health service psychology. Second, we explore the growing scholarship on addressing trainees who have been identified as having problems of professional competence. We centralize diversity and systems, particularly as they inform our understanding of competence and the issues that arise in the identification and addressing of trainees with competence problems. We close our chapter by revisiting our case example and making systemic, multiculturally based recommendations for scholars, trainers, and supervisors when interacting with trainees identified as having problems attaining competence.

CASE VIGNETTE

Alex is a biracial (Asian American and White), nonbinary (they/them) 26-year-old 3rd-year doctoral trainee in an American Psychological Association– (APA–) accredited counseling psychology program in a midwestern state.

https://doi.org/10.1037/0000340-005
Supporting Trainees With Competence Problems: A Practical Guide for Psychology Trainers, R. A. Schwartz-Mette, E. A. Hunter, and N. J. Kaslow (Editors)
Copyright © 2023 by the American Psychological Association. All rights reserved.

During their first 2 years, they made steady progress and formed strong connections with two members of their cohort and their doctoral faculty mentor, Dr. Hill, a 38-year-old Black queer female faculty member (she/her). In their 3rd year, Alex began seeing clients in their first training experience at the program's in-house clinic.

At their midsemester review, the clinic's director, a 53-year-old White heterosexual man (he/him), Dr. Stanton, tells Alex he is concerned that three of Alex's first few clients prematurely discontinued therapy with them after two sessions each. Dr. Stanton notes that Alex's physical presentation is more informal and "flamboyant" than trainees and staff typically dress at the site and wonders whether that might be contributing to their clients' discomfort with them. Alex is distressed by Dr. Stanton's feedback and begins to withdraw, arrive late to meetings, and slip in their coursework. Dr. Stanton reaches out to Dr. Hill with his concerns about Alex. Dr. Hill, surprised by the feedback, discusses Alex in the next core faculty meeting. Other faculty members and Alex's close cohort friends share their observations and worry about Alex with the program director, Dr. Rosenberg.

During Alex's annual student review at the end of the academic year, they are placed on a formal remediation plan that includes sessions with a therapist to help address their distress as well as expectations for improved professionalism in the ensuing academic year. When Alex meets with Dr. Rosenberg to discuss and sign the remediation plan, they ask what specifically is meant by "professionalism." Dr. Rosenberg notes the importance of professional attire, grooming, and appearance and on-time arrival for meetings and classes. Alex expresses concern about finding a therapist unfamiliar and unaffiliated with the program and about paying for treatment.

This case vignette illustrates the many complexities associated with identifying and remediating professional competence problems. Before considering larger issues, take a moment to reflect: What feelings emerged as you read this vignette? What assumptions did you make about any of the people? What other information would you need to understand and respond to this case? How might you conceptualize the emergent issues for each person? How do the issues that Dr. Stanton identified affect Alex, their peers, the rest of the faculty members, the staff and clients of the training clinic, and the broader training community?

COMPETENCE

Although the development of competency benchmarks and the identification of professional competence problems among trainees have received increased attention, the importance of competence, particularly as a guidepost for practice, has been an enduring focus of professional ethics (APA, 2017). As an ethical standard, the attention to competence has been largely broad and ill-defined, such that psychologists consulting the APA's (2017) *Ethical Principles of Psychologists and Code of Conduct* (APA Ethics Code) may find the language regarding competence unspecific, lacking in utility, and tautological; for example, Standard 2.01(a), Boundaries of Competence, specifies that "psychologists provide services, teach, and conduct research with populations and in areas only within the boundaries of their competence, based on their education, training, supervised experience, consultation, study, or professional experience." Those consulting the APA Ethics Code for guidance may rightfully wonder what level and type of education, training, and experience are suitable for ensuring minimal acceptable levels for competent practice.

Barnett et al. (2007) stressed that competence should be understood flexibly and continually and noted that designating minimal acceptable levels of competence is challenging. They conceptualized competence as inclusive of "knowledge; skills; and the attitudes, values, and judgment needed to effectively implement and use them" (p. 510). Many psychologists who have contributed to the literature on trainees with issues of professional competence have used a definition in the medical literature: "professional competence is the habitual and judicious use of communication, knowledge, technical skills, clinical reasoning, emotions, values, and reflection in daily practice for the benefit of the individual and community being served" (Epstein & Hundert, 2002, p. 226). We draw from both definitions, noting their commonalities (emphasis on knowledge, skills, and values) while appreciating Barnett et al.'s (2007) attention to attitudes and judgment and Epstein and Hundert's (2002) inclusion of reasoning, emotion, and reflection. Some authors conflate competence with competency. We distinguish between these, conceptualizing competencies as the building blocks of competence that are synthesized through the intentional application of an integrated deep structure, including attention to purposefulness, timing, motivation, selection, and sequencing (Ridley et al., 2011).

A significant development in the conceptualization and application of competence, particularly in guiding trainers tasked with its assessment and evaluation, occurred with the publication of the Competency Benchmarks (Fouad et al., 2009) and the revised subsequent iteration (Hatcher et al., 2013). The original Competency Benchmarks consisted of 15 core functional and foundational competencies, organized across developmental levels of readiness: for practicum internship, and entry into professional practice. The subsequent iteration (Hatcher et al., 2013) consolidated the original foundational and functional competencies into three clusters each (Professionalism,

Science, and Relationships for the foundational competencies and Application, Education, and Systems for the functional competencies).

Although existing models and frameworks for gauging, establishing, and assessing competence have provided vital structure, we mention several cautionary notes, particularly for trainers, supervisors, and educators, in determining students' competence, consistent with our focus on systemic considerations in this chapter. First, as Nicholson Perry et al. (2017) noted, supervisors assessing competence must themselves be competent to do so. Given the biases inherent in accurately assessing our own abilities, such as the tendency for poor performers to inflate their own skills, trainers imbued with the responsibility to educate and gatekeep the next generation of psychologists may not necessarily be competent themselves. The tendency for poorly performing people to overestimate their own abilities—the Dunning–Kruger effect—has been well established in a wide array of domains, including in evaluating one's racial- and gender-based egalitarianism (West & Eaton, 2019). Second, Rodolfa and Schaffer (2019) stressed that psychologists are not impervious to their own biases and to views impacting the evaluation and assessment of trainee competence. Indeed, Koch and colleagues (2018) asked doctoral students to assess faculty multicultural competence and found that some students reported that their trainers invalidated students and exhibited diminished competence, cultural insensitivity, and defensiveness.

TRAINEES WITH PROBLEMS OF PROFESSIONAL COMPETENCE

Historically and until recently, trainees who had been identified as having difficulty in achieving competence were described as "impaired" (e.g., Gizara & Forrest, 2004), which is similar to language describing people with disabilities. Elman and Forrest (2007) offered a thoughtful review of terminology, identified important updates in language, and provided guidance for new ways to conceptualize trainees with struggles in achieving competence. They advocated terminology that was neither too limited nor wide, that indicated a problem with trainees' performance, that emphasized professional standards, and that was inclusive and centering of competence. Moreover, scholars have discussed the need to avoid incorrect use of the term "impaired" so as not to inadvertently invoke protections under the Americans With Disabilities Act of 1990 (C. Collins et al., 2011; Falender et al., 2009; Schwartz-Mette, 2011).

Many researchers have heeded their call, using iterations of Elman and Forrest's (2007) suggestions of "problematic professional competence" (p. 508), ensuring adherence to their direction to use person-first language (i.e., trainees with professional competence problems). We resonate with Shen-Miller et al.'s (2011) definition based on Elman and Forrest's guidance: Trainees with problems of professional competence (TPPC) are "those whose performance, behavior, and/or attitudes do not meet ethical or professional standards that should be expected given their stage of training" (p. 113). Shen-Miller and colleagues (2015) later offered that problems of professional competence "include difficulty acquiring or maintaining developmentally appropriate levels of skill, functioning, attitudes, and/or ethical, professional, or interpersonal behavior in functional or foundational domains in one or more settings" (p. 162), centering trainees' problems with professional competence squarely in the Competency Benchmarks (Fouad et al., 2009; Hatcher et al., 2013). Forrest et al. (2008) suggested the use of "identified" as a modifier ("trainees identified with problems of professional competence"; p. 183) to note the role social construction serves for trainer designating trainees with difficulties attaining competence.

Systemic Issues With TPPC

Researchers have highlighted many systemic issues that arise within programs for both trainers and trainees. Lack of cultural competence among faculty can contribute to biased trainee evaluations (i.e., microaggressions and stereotypes) and unclear programmatic policies that increase tension and frustration during the trainee evaluation process (Shen-Miller et al., 2015). Marginalized students are negatively impacted by biased evaluations based on stereotypes and consequently may not get the support they need to succeed in the program (Constantine & Sue, 2007; Kissil et al., 2013; Ng & Smith, 2009). In this section, we review the specific diversity issues in addressing TPPC experienced by training faculty and trainees.

Diversity Issues in Addressing TPPC

A lack of cultural responsiveness in trainee evaluation procedures likely contributes to the lower enrollment rates of students of color (APA, 2017; Shen-Miller et al., 2012) and less satisfaction with graduate training programs among marginalized students (Maton et al., 2011; Tram et al., 2022). Policies and procedures for evaluation and remediation have not historically taken into the consideration the trainers' and trainees' cultural contexts (Vasquez, 1999). The lack of focus on diversity may contribute to biased evaluations of competence for trainees with marginalized identities that are centered on identity-based assumptions that negatively influence trainers and marginalized trainees (Shen-Miller et al., 2009; Sue et al., 2009). Of note, feminist multicultural approaches to training consider power differentials and cultural contexts (Killian, 2001; Vasquez, 1999).

Remediation often engenders feelings of anger, confusion, and shame, with some trainees reporting that trainers exerted power over them during the evaluation process (Kallaugher & Mollen, 2017). Although research is nascent, a more balanced approach that considers power dynamics in addressing TPPC is needed. Further, there are added considerations to addressing TPPC regarding diversity factors (Shen-Miller et al., 2009, 2012). Marginalized graduate students, in particular, experience unique, often overlooked barriers at multiple levels of training that affect their performance evaluation and overall academic experience (Sue et al., 2009).

Challenges for Trainers
Scholars and trainers have focused more on trainees' than trainers' cultural competence, including the effect on their evaluation of trainee competence (Shen-Miller et al., 2012). Certain research has identified barriers that trainers experience regarding contextual factors (Shen-Miller et al., 2012) and how trainers conceptualize diversity and TPPC issues (Shen-Miller et al., 2009). Trainers often are unsure about how to address diversity, and some may avoid, minimize, or overlook diversity factors and biases that influence their evaluations of trainees. Trainers may be fearful of being negatively perceived by their colleagues and trainees, having their own multicultural competence challenged and fear of litigation or retaliation from students as consequences of addressing diversity issues related to TPPC concerns (Shen-Miller et al., 2009, 2012, 2015).

Faculty vary on their personal and programmatic perceptions of and commitments to diversity, which may instigate additional concerns when TPPC with diversity issues arise (Shen-Miller et al., 2009, 2012). Shen-Miller et al. (2009) found that training directors voiced fears of behaving in a culturally inappropriate way or abusing their power when working with students with marginalized identities. They also reported concerns about how trainees react to remediation. Trainers vary regarding their awareness and integration of cultural identities (i.e., race, ethnicity, gender, sexual orientation, social class) in their conceptualizations of TPPC issues. Most trainers tended to focus more on race/ethnicity and less on gender, to not address identity at all, or to distinguish race/ethnicity from the student as separate components (Shen-Miller et al., 2009, 2012). Trainers did not capture the intersections of students' unique social location as both racially/ethnically marginalized and in subordinated positions as graduate students attending an academic institution (Shen-Miller et al., 2009). Faculty also seemed to differ in their perceptions of diversity and definitions of competence, further complicating the TPPC process. Shen-Miller et al. (2012) found that faculty's perceptions of multicultural training values and their obligations in supporting diverse student trainees varied. Faculty also differed in their level of commitment to having an ongoing conversation about diversity related to TPPC.

Avoiding ongoing considerations of diversity in TPPC can lead to over- or underidentifying TPPC (e.g., underidentifying it in White students, overidentifying it in students of color; Shen-Miller et al., 2012). Thus, trainers may be more reluctant to acknowledge TPPC issues with trainees because of the fear of being perceived as biased, and their lack of awareness of their own biases may lead them to overidentify TPPC among marginalized students. In sum, as a result of not integrating cultural context into their TPPC processes, training directors had difficulty attributing responsibility of trainees and trainers, understanding cultural context, and operationalizing program policies. Shen-Miller et al. (2012) provided recommendations that included applying existing models of racial and ethnic development to assessment of trainee competence, developing empirically supported mechanisms of remediation, initiating difficult and uncomfortable conversations about their diversity-related frustrations and concerns, and suggesting that noted trainers address diversity tensions before TPPC concerns arise.

Trainee Challenges

Training programs' failure to consider marginalized students' unique social locations and contexts of trainees' experiences negatively impacts evaluation procedures. Marginalized trainees, including students of color, international students, and transgender and gender-diverse students, experience issues on individual (e.g., microaggressions and lack of inclusivity) and systemic (e.g., campus-wide and programmatic policies that do not account for diverse perspectives or student safety) levels that affect their training experiences (Goldberg et al., 2019; Maton et al., 2011; Ng & Smith, 2009; Shavers & Moore, 2019). Socialization and fostering professionalism often lack acknowledgment of how cultural context and institutional climate influence students' performance in graduate work (Gardner, 2008, 2010; Tram et al., 2022). Trainers who address issues of competence often fail to consider cultural variance in expressions of and adjustments to Westernized professionalism among diverse trainees (Tram et al., 2022).

Trainees who do not identify with the dominant culture are overlooked or silenced when programs use a strictly Westernized definition of professionalism to address TPPC issues. Ng and Smith (2009) found that international trainees reported language barriers, institutional discrimination, difficulty with Western approaches to mental health, and difficulty in clinical courses. The authors encouraged training faculty to consider the ways that international trainees must translate their cultural expressions to fit into Eurocentric ideals of professionalism. Transgender and nonbinary students often lack safe spaces on campus (Knutson et al., 2022), are misgendered by faculty, and are negatively impacted on multiple levels within the academic system (i.e., the institution, graduate faculty, students; Gardner, 2010; Goldberg et al., 2019). Black students commonly experience supervisors' racial microaggressions that contribute to negative assumptions about their competence (Constantine & Sue, 2007) and imposter syndrome (Moxley, 2020). Faculty contribute to the imposter syndrome by adding pressures to meet the expectations of White academia and failing to be inclusive or considering the experiences of Black students. Black and Asian women graduate students in particular have reported unique barriers at intersections of their marginalized identities that may affect their graduate work and be overlooked by faculty trainers (Crumb et al., 2020; Leigh et al., 2021; Shavers & Moore, 2019). Research about marginalized students reveals a lack of consideration for their experiences and acculturation issues in and outside of their training programs.

Impact on evaluations of TPPC. Trainees' experiences of microaggressions reveal the way that faculty's bias can impact evaluation (Constantine & Sue, 2007; Kissil et al., 2013; Ng & Smith, 2009; Sue et al., 2009). Constantine and Sue (2007) found that trainers were more likely to consider internal attributions to be personal flaws when evaluating the professional competence of trainees of color. For example, Black trainees reported that supervisors made assumptions about their competence embedded in their racial bias toward them, expressed fears of being viewed as racist for providing feedback, and primarily focused on clinical weakness in trainee evaluations. Surveying trainees' perceptions of faculty multicultural competence, Koch et al. (2018) found that faculty perceived as lacking cultural competence are more likely to lack cultural sensitivity and make assumptions about others (including trainees) that negatively impaired their relationships with trainees. Students identified specific attributes indicative of faculty multicultural competence, including faculty being nonjudgmental and having cultural awareness. Kissil et al. (2013) found that supervisors' perceived lack of cultural competence influenced foreign-born trainees' self-efficacy more than trainee acculturation status, demonstrating that a lack of faculty multicultural competence can also affect trainee performance. The authors emphasized the importance of contextualizing TPPC concerns and cautioned trainers not to make personal attributions about a student's competence based on one's own negative perceptions of non-Westernized ideals of professional competence (Kissil et al., 2013; Ng & Smith, 2009). Marginalized students' adverse experiences during the remediation process highlight the need for faculty to demonstrate their cultural sensitivity and awareness.

DISCRETE VIEWS OF TRAINEES IDENTIFIED WITH PROBLEMS OF PROFESSIONAL COMPETENCE

Researchers have studied those trainees identified as struggling to achieve professional competence. They have found that generally some trainees have struggled to attain, although the rates have varied depending on the individuals surveyed (i.e., trainers such as faculty and clinical supervisors or trainees themselves). Of note, to date, scholars have almost exclusively relied on looking at the issue of competence problems from singular lenses, studying trainers; those who are peers of trainees identified as having problems of professional competence; and, more recently, those trainees who themselves were identified as having problems of professional competence who were placed on formal remediation plans in their programs. However, when querying students, faculty, and clinical supervisors, several researchers noted systemic implications of their findings. Later, we explore in more detail the tendency to study trainees identified with problems of professional competence in a piecemeal manner, including its potential limits juxtaposed against recent suggestions for cultivating communitarian approaches to treatment.

Peers' Experiences

Shen-Miller and his colleagues (2011) conducted a national survey of trainees whose peers were thought to have competence problems. Participants included trainees in both master's and doctoral counseling, clinical, and school psychology programs, including those on internship. Nearly half of the participants reported knowing a peer with professional competence problem, such as problems with professional behavior, interpersonal problems, clinical or academic skills, and mental health problems. Trainees identified programmatic characteristics and dynamics, such as avoidance and denial and programs' omission of attention to issues of competence and interpersonal functioning, as moderate contributory factors that affected their experiences with peers who had competence problems. They reported that consulting and chatting with their peers was relatively more helpful than speaking with faculty members about their concerns. In an ensuing study, Shen-Miller and colleagues (2015) interviewed a subset of the participants from the earlier study to ask about the factors that impacted their willingness to take action after detecting a peer had a problem of professional competence. Issues of perceived trainers' competence, approachability, caring, and receptivity; relationships among students and faculty; the programs' culture; fears of repercussion; and diversity considerations figured prominently in participants' motivation or reticence to take action regarding their concerns about peers with competence problems. These findings suggest that broad systemic factors are vital in the identification and addressing of trainees determined to have competence problems.

Demyan et al. (2018) asked a small group of marriage and family therapy students to envision how they would respond to trainees identified as having professional competence problems. The researchers shared seven vignettes that had previously been administered to a group of supervisors. Demyan et al. found that students typically suggested consulting with the trainee in question or with faculty members, that trainees' responses varied depending on the nature and severity of the identified problem, and that participants were most likely to recommend dismissal in vignettes related to dishonesty. Participants were more likely than the previous sample of supervisors to permit hypothetical trainees with mental health problems to continue seeing clients and more likely than supervisors to recommend dismissal for hypothetical trainees who submitted late case notes. In all, though limited by the use of case vignettes rather than actual peers, this study suggests that students have both similar and dissimilar approaches to remediating trainees with professional competence problems.

Noting that nearly all of the literature on trainees who have been identified with problems of competence had been conducted either with trainers or peers of those with identified problems, Kallaugher and Mollen (2017) conducted a study with trainees who themselves had been remediated during graduate school. Participants reported an array of experiences pursuant to their remediation, including both supportive and unhelpful experiences with trainers, contextual factors including perceptions of trainers' competence problems, failure for trainers to acknowledge their contributions to problems, and diversity variables impacting trainers' impressions and introducing biases.

Trainers' Experiences

Gizara and Forrest (2004) interviewed 12 university counseling center psychologists at three sites to gauge their impressions and experiences working with trainees identified with competence problems. Many of the psychologists reported feeling unprepared to address competence problems among the students they helped train. Some elucidated contextual issues such as the effect of supervisors' personalities, importance of supervisor–trainee relationships, similarities between supervisors and supervisees affecting the identification and remediation of problems, and impact of supervisors' relationships with one another as alternatively helpful or hindering resolution of identified problems. These findings suggest the importance of considering context, individual differences, and relationships among staff members and trainees.

Employing an ethical framework, Jacobs and colleagues (2011) provided guidance to trainers in initiating and facilitating conversations with trainees identified as having competence problems. They identified personal barriers (trainers' competence in engaging in difficult conversations; avoidance; resentment and fear, including of legal action; and empathy as it can result in overidentification with trainees), training setting and system barriers (program culture, policies, confidentiality, training model, and disagreements among trainers), and the interaction between personal and contextual factors. They offered several useful suggestions for approaching discussions with trainees regarding competence problems.

Forrest and colleagues (2013) studied a group composed mainly of training directors of APA-accredited doctoral programs and assessed faculty members in their programs as a blend of those with appreciable, tangible skills in managing trainees with competence problems, such as the ability to suspend judgment and employ perspective taking, as well as those with poor skills, such as avoidance and fearing negative outcomes. Results further indicated the identification of both effective (early problem identification, program-level decision making, willingness to participate in difficult conversations, employing multicultural perspectives) and ineffective (avoidance culture, individualistic approaches, ignoring diversity) programmatic strategies.

Reflecting the increasing and sustained interest in improving the process of identifying, addressing, and ameliorating issues that arise for trainees identified with competence problems, Vacha-Haase and colleagues (2019) developed a series of suggestions for trainers regarding remediation plans. They framed their ideas within the system of the program; that is, they urged trainers to ensure issues of remediation are carefully incorporated into programmatic policies and procedures, linked to designated competencies, and executed within a communitarian, transparent approach to training. Moreover, they suggested that trainers ground remediation expectations behaviorally, note clear expectations for successful completion of remediation, and engage in ongoing assessment.

Revisiting the Case Vignette
Applying a feminist–multicultural approach to the case of Alex illuminates how integral cultural context is to effectively address TPPC. Dr. Stanton neither acknowledged nor incorporated the cultural differences between himself and Alex into his approach to address Alex's professional competence issue. There was a lack of clarity and alignment on what professionalism means, as Dr. Stanton mentioned only physical appearance. Potentially, Dr. Stanton's criticism of Alex's nonbinary gender presentation as "more flamboyant" may represent an unexplored bias. Further, Dr. Stanton's reasoning was framed as if Alex's personal appearance was a flaw that did not adhere to traditional norms of professionalism and directly contributed to Alex's difficulties with clients. The request that Alex receive therapy further communicated that this is Alex's personal issue for Alex to fix, which also contributed to their decline.

Employing a feminist–multicultural approach, trainers would consider cultural contexts, power, and norms individually and systemically. Drs. Hill and Stanton would acknowledge the cultural differences between them and Alex and question the potential effect of their own biases on their perceptions of Alex's professionalism. For example, how might Alex's gender, biracial identity, or age contribute to their current understanding of and presentation of professionalism? How might Alex's perceptions of professionalism be different from theirs? Systemically, they would ask critical questions of the training program and training site to assess whether their existing definitions and policies regarding professionalism may be biased regarding gender identity and expression. Employing this more balanced approach does not begin with the assumption that something is wrong with Alex's professionalism but holds the training faculty and evaluation process accountable for their own biases or multicultural limitations.

Individually, Drs. Stanton and Hill would assess how their potentially biased ideals of professionalism are communicated to Alex (i.e., is it possible that they are making stereotypical assumptions about Alex's physical presentation that are communicated through microaggressions? How might that affect Alex's perceived competence?). They would contextualize Alex's response to the initial critical feedback by considering that the feedback may have contributed significantly to their ensuing difficulties and whether their response to the feedback may make cogent sense rather than rise to a remediable concern. Drs. Hill and Stanton then could use some culturally responsive interventions such as including Alex in the evaluation process by asking Alex about their current contextual understanding of professionalism to reduce power imbalance and help gain a more accurate conceptualization of the professional competency of concern. From there, Drs. Hill and Stanton could develop a more culturally responsive and unbiased remediation plan that intervenes on systemic and individual levels. They could make necessary updates to policies and procedures and collaborate with Alex to identify specific ways they can assist in fostering Alex's competence (such as normalizing Alex's experience and providing support for Alex's acculturative process at their practicum site).

RECOMMENDATIONS

Grounding their work in feminist–multicultural and social-ecological theory, scholars encourage training faculty to establish TPPC procedures that infuse a clear diversity focus (Mintz et al., 2009) and examine cultural context at multiple levels of the training system (Forrest et al., 2008; Knutson et al., 2022; McWhirter & McWhirter, 2007). Employing a systems approach prevents framing TPPC as a personal deficit and allows faculty to more accurately contextualize how systemic and cultural factors affect TPPC issues (Ng & Smith, 2009; Rappolt-Schlichtmann et al., 2018).

Training faculty can create a diversity training statement that acknowledges cultural variation in ideals of professionalism and identifies trainee and trainer diversity-related needs (Mintz et al., 2009). Trainers can identify contextual factors that contribute to TPPC concerns and examine how dominant culture, power, faculty–trainee interactions, and faculty level of cultural competence influences assessment of trainee competence (Forrest et al., 2008; Knutson, 2022). Mintz et al. (2009) recommended that training faculty be willing to engage in their own analysis of wrestling with training values, what they mean, and where they come from for trainers and trainees. For example, trainers can question program policies on professionalism that uphold traditional gender norms or exclude nonbinary people. They can ask how these policies are communicated, expressed, and enforced with trainees and whether faculty address these issues in culturally sensitive ways (Knutson et al., 2022).

Faculty can establish preventative training evaluation processes and interventions that use multiple perspectives among faculty and trainees, identify issues within both faculty and trainees, adopt an ecological perspective, and identify ways faculty can advocate for students' skill development or diversity-related needs (Forrest et al., 2008). McWhirter and McWhirter (2007) proposed a shift toward using an emancipatory communitarian model, first coined by Prilleltensky (1997), which is a social justice–focused approach that aims to liberate students and faculty from oppression and injustice through engaging in community and compassion (see Chapter 1, this volume). Training faculty could use this strengths-based approach by applying the five emancipatory communitarian values (care/compassion, self-determination, human diversity, collaboration and participation, and distributive justice) when addressing TPPC with diversity-related issues to dismantle oppressive systems in the training program.

Given the literature demonstrating the microaggressions students of color experience from White faculty, some scholars suggest that faculty trainers working with students from marginalized groups may benefit from exploring other approaches to trainee/student mentorship beyond traditional approaches. One such approach is "othermothering," a student-centered/ advocate approach most widely used among Black faculty and students with historical roots dating back to the enslavement of African people (P. H. Collins, 2000). A notable quality of othermothering is Black students' feeling heard by their faculty (Guiffrida, 2005). Trainers could lessen the power imbalance during the TPPC process and have a more accurate understanding of the problem by asking for trainees' perspectives of the professional competency of concern and incorporating them into the evaluation process. Further, faculty could implement strengths-based approaches like capacity building, an approach that considers neurodiversity with students with disabilities by approaching student difficulties as a way to assess how they can help increase students' capacity for learning rather than viewing performance difficulties as student deficits (Rappolt-Schlichtmann et al., 2018). Training faculty could use a similar approach to TPPC with diversity issues by reframing the TPPC issue within their cultural contexts as an opportunity for trainees and trainers to increase their understanding of professional competencies and identify ways to help strengthen trainees' knowledge, skills, and attitudes.

REFERENCES

American Psychological Association. (2017). *Ethical principles of psychologists and code of conduct* (2002, amended effective June 1, 2010, and January 1, 2017). https://www.apa.org/ethics/code/index.aspx

Americans With Disabilities Act of 1990, Pub. L. No. 101–336, 104 Stat. 328 (1990).

Barnett, J. E., Doll, B., Younggren, J. N., & Rubin, N. J. (2007). Clinical competence for practicing psychologists: Clearly a work in progress. *Professional Psychology: Research and Practice, 38*(5), 510–517. https://doi.org/10.1037/0735-7028.38.5.510

Collins, C., Falender, C., & Shafranske, E. (2011). Commentary on Rebecca Schwartz-Mette's 2009 article, "Challenges in addressing graduate student impairment in academic professional psychology programs." *Ethics & Behavior, 21*(5), 428–430. https://doi.org/10.1080/10508422.2011.604547

Collins, P. H. (2000). *Black feminist thought: Knowledge, consciousness, and the politics of empowerment*. Routledge.

Constantine, M. G., & Sue, D. W. (2007). Perceptions of racial microaggressions among Black supervisees in cross-racial dyads. *Journal of Counseling Psychology, 54*(2), 142–153. https://doi.org/10.1037/0022-0167.54.2.142

Crumb, L., Haskins, N., Dean, L., & Avent Harris, J. (2020). Illuminating social-class identity: The persistence of working-class African American women doctoral students. *Journal of Diversity in Higher Education, 13*(3), 215–227. https://doi.org/10.1037/dhe0000109

Demyan, A. L., Abraham, C. M., & Bui, N. H. (2018). Trainees looking through the lens of a supervisor: Remediation and gatekeeping responses to hypothetical problems of professional competency. *The American Journal of Family Therapy, 46*(1), 67–80. https://doi.org/10.1080/01926187.2018.1428128

Elman, N. S., & Forrest, L. (2007). From trainee impairment to professional competence problems: Seeking new terminology that facilitates effective action. *Professional Psychology: Research and Practice, 38*(5), 501–509. https://doi.org/10.1037/0735-7028.38.5.501

Epstein, R. M., & Hundert, E. M. (2002). Defining and assessing professional competence. *JAMA, 287*(2), 226–235. https://doi.org/10.1001/jama.287.2.226

Falender, C. A., Collins, C. J., & Shafranske, E. P. (2009). "Impairment" and performance issues in clinical supervision: After the 2008 ADA Amendments Act. *Training and Education in Professional Psychology, 3*(4), 240–249. https://doi.org/10.1037/a0017153

Forrest, L., Elman, N. S., Huprich, S. K., Veilleux, J. C., Jacobs, S. C., & Kaslow, N. J. (2013). Training directors' perceptions of faculty behaviors when dealing with trainee competence problems: A mixed method pilot study. *Training and Education in Professional Psychology, 7*(1), 23–32. https://doi.org/10.1037/a0032068

Forrest, L., Shen-Miller, D. S., & Elman, N. S. (2008). Psychology trainees with competence problems: From individual to ecological conceptualizations. *Training and Education in Professional Psychology, 2*(4), 183–192. https://doi.org/10.1037/1931-3918.2.4.183

Fouad, N. A., Grus, C. L., Hatcher, R. L., Kaslow, N. J., Hutchings, P. S., Madson, M. B., Collins, F. L., Jr., & Crossman, R. E. (2009). Competency benchmarks: A model for understanding and measuring competence in professional psychology across training levels. *Training and Education in Professional Psychology, 3*(4, Suppl. 4S), S5–S26. https://doi.org/10.1037/a0015832

Gardner, S. K. (2008). Fitting the mold of graduate school. A qualitative study of socialization in doctoral education. *Innovative Higher Education, 33*(2), 125–138. https://doi.org/10.1007/s10755-008-9068-x

Gardner, S. K. (2010). Contrasting the socialization experiences of doctoral students in high- and low-completing departments: A qualitative analysis of disciplinary contexts at one institution. *The Journal of Higher Education, 81*(1), 61–81. https://doi.org/10.1080/00221546.2010.11778970

Gizara, S. S., & Forrest, L. (2004). Supervisors' experiences of trainee impairment and incompetence at APA-accredited internship sites. *Professional Psychology: Research and Practice, 35*(2), 131–140. https://doi.org/10.1037/0735-7028.35.2.131

Goldberg, A. E., Kuvalanka, K., & Dickey, l. (2019). Transgender graduate students' experiences in higher education: A mixed-methods exploratory study. *Journal of Diversity in Higher Education, 12*(1), 38–51. https://doi.org/10.1037/dhe0000074

Guiffrida, D. (2005). Othermothering as a framework for understanding African Americans Students' definitions of student-centered faculty. *Journal of Higher Education, 76*(6), 701–723. https://doi.org/10.1353/jhe.2005.0041

Hatcher, R., Fouad, N., Grus, C., Campbell, L., McCutcheon, S., & Leahy, K. (2013). Competency benchmarks: Practical steps toward a culture of competence. *Training and Education in Professional Psychology, 7*(2), 84–91. https://doi.org/10.1037/a0029401

Jacobs, S. C., Huprich, S. K., Grus, C. L., Cage, E. A., Elman, N. S., Forrest, L., Schwartz-Mette, R., Shen-Miller, D. S., Van Sickle, K. S., & Kaslow, N. J. (2011). Trainees with professional competency problems: Preparing trainers for difficult but necessary conversations. *Training and Education in Professional Psychology, 5*(3), 175–184. https://doi.org/10.1037/a0024656

Kallaugher, J., & Mollen, D. (2017). Student experiences of remediation in their graduate psychology programs. *Training and Education in Professional Psychology, 11*(4), 276–282. https://doi.org/10.1037/tep0000175

Killian, K. D. (2001). Differences making a difference: Cross-cultural interactions in supervisor relationships. *Journal of Feminist Family Therapy, 12*(2–3), 61–103. https://doi.org/10.1300/J086v12n02_03

Kissil, K., Davey, M., & Davey, A. (2013). Foreign-born therapists in the United States: Supervisors' multicultural competence, supervision satisfaction, and counseling self-efficacy. *The Clinical Supervisor, 32*(2), 185–211. https://doi.org/10.1080/07325223.2013.846746

Knutson, D., Matsuno, E., Goldbach, C., Hashtpari, H., & Smith, N. G. (2022). Advocating for transgender and nonbinary affirmative spaces in graduate education. *Higher Education, 83*, 461–479. https://doi.org/10.1007/s10734-020-00673-5

Koch, J. M., Procopio, S. J., Knutson, D., Loche, R. W., III, Jayne, A., Jaybem, C., & Loche, L. (2018). Counseling psychology students' perceptions of faculty multicultural competence. *Scholarship of Teaching and Learning in Psychology, 4*(3), 140–150. https://doi.org/10.1037/stl0000116

Leigh, E. W., Pak, K., & Phuong, J. (2021). Defining ourselves: Exploring our leader and activist identities as Asian American women doctoral students. *Journal of Diversity in Higher Education, 14*(2), 174–188. https://doi.org/10.1037/dhe0000173

Maton, K. I., Wimms, H. E., Grant, S. K., Wittig, M. A., Rogers, M. R., & Vasquez, M. J. T. (2011). Experiences and perspectives of African American, Latina/o, Asian American, and European American psychology graduate students: A national study. *Cultural Diversity & Ethnic Minority Psychology, 17*(1), 68–78. https://doi.org/10.1037/a0021668

McWhirter, B. T., & McWhirter, E. H. (2007). Toward an emancipatory communitarian approach to the practice of psychology training. In E. Aldarondo (Ed.), *Advancing social justice through clinical practice* (pp. 391–416). Lawrence Erlbaum Associates.

Mintz, L. B., Jackson, A. P., Neville, H. A., Illfelder-Kaye, J., Winterowd, C. L., & Loewy, M. I. (2009). The need for a counseling psychology model training values statement addressing diversity. *The Counseling Psychologist, 37*(5), 644–675. https://doi.org/10.1177/0011000009331931

Moxley, R. E. (2020). Not by the job, nor the day, but by my life: Black student resilience in academia. In D. A. Kleiber & E. Delgado-Romero (Eds.), *Social psychology and counseling: Issues and applications* (pp. 269–281). Nova Science.

Ng, K., & Smith, S. D. (2009). Perceptions and experiences of international trainees in counseling and related programs. *International Journal for the Advancement of Counseling, 31*(1), 57–70. https://doi.org/10.1007/s10447-008-9068-7

Nicholson Perry, K., Donovan, M., Knight, R., & Shires, A. (2017). Addressing professional competency problems in clinical psychology trainees. *Australian Psychologist, 52*(2), 121–129. https://doi.org/10.1111/ap.12268

Prilleltensky, I. (1997). Values, assumptions, and practices: Assessing the moral implications of psychological discourse and action. *American Psychologist, 52*(5), 517–535. https://doi.org/10.1037//0003-066x.52.5.517

Rappolt-Schlichtmann, G., Boucher, A. R., & Evans, M. (2018). From deficit remediation to capacity building: Learning to enable rather than disable students with dyslexia. *Language, Speech, and Hearing Services in Schools, 49*(4), 864–874. https://doi.org/10.1044/2018_LSHSS-DYSLC-18-0031

Ridley, C. R., Mollen, D., & Kelly, S. M. (2011). Beyond microskills: Toward a model of counseling competence. *The Counseling Psychologist, 39*(6), 825–864. https://doi.org/10.1177/0011000010378440

Rodolfa, E., & Schaffer, J. (2019). Challenges to psychology education and training in the culture of competence. *American Psychologist, 74*(9), 1118–1128. https://doi.org/10.1037/amp0000513

Schwartz-Mette, R. (2011). Out with impairment, in with professional competence problems: Response to commentary by Collins, Falender, and Shafranske. *Ethics & Behavior, 21*(5), 431–434. https://doi.org/10.1080/10508422.2011.604551

Shavers, M. C., & Moore, J. L. (2019). The perpetual outsider: Voices of Black women pursuing doctoral degrees at predominantly White institutions. *Journal of Multicultural Counseling and Development, 47*(4), 210–226. https://doi.org/10.1002/jmcd.12154

Shen-Miller, D. S., Forrest, L., & Burt, M. (2012). Contextual influences on faculty diversity conceptualizations when working with trainee competence problems. *The Counseling Psychologist, 40*(8), 1181–1219. https://doi.org/10.1177/0011000011431832

Shen-Miller, D. S., Forrest, L., & Elman, N. S. (2009). Training directors' conceptualizations of the intersections of diversity and trainee competence problems: A preliminary analysis. *The Counseling Psychologist, 37*(4), 482–518. https://doi.org/10.1177/0011000008316656

Shen-Miller, D. S., Grus, C. L., Van Sickle, K., Schwartz-Mette, R., Cage, E., Elman, N. S., Jacobs, S. C., & Kaslow, N. J. (2011). Trainees' experiences with peers having competence problems: A national survey. *Training and Education in Professional Psychology, 5*(2), 112–121. https://doi.org/10.1037/a0023824

Shen-Miller, D. S., Schwartz-Mette, R., Van Sickle, K., Jacobs, S. C., Grus, C. L., Hunter, E., & Forrest, L. (2015). Professional competence problems in training: A qualitative investigation of trainee perspectives. *Training and Education in Professional Psychology, 9*(2), 161–169. https://doi.org/10.1037/tep0000072

Sue, D. W., Lin, A. I., Torino, G. C., Capodilupo, C. M., & Rivera, D. P. (2009). Racial microaggressions and difficult dialogues on race in the classroom. *Cultural Diversity & Ethnic Minority Psychology, 15*(2), 183–190. https://doi.org/10.1037/a0014191

Tram, J. M., Nwankwo, N., Khan, A. N., & Sabado, J. A. (2022). Impact of faculty mentoring on ethnic and racial minority student program satisfaction. *Scholarship *of Teaching and Learning in Psychology*. Advance online publication. https://doi.org/10.1037/stl0000231

Vacha-Haase, T., Elman, N. S., Forrest, L., Kallaugher, J., Lease, S. H., Veilleux, J. C., & Kaslow, N. J. (2019). Remediation plans for trainees with problems of professional competence. *Training and Education in Professional Psychology, 13*(4), 239–246. https://doi.org/10.1037/tep0000221

Vasquez, M. (1999). Trainee impairment: A response from a feminist/multicultural retired trainer. *The Counseling Psychologist, 27*(5), 687–692. https://doi.org/10.1177/0011000099275002

West, K., & Eaton, A. A. (2019). Prejudiced and unaware of it: Evidence for the Dunning-Kruger model in the domains of racism and sexism. *Personality and Individual Differences, 146*, 111–119. https://doi.org/10.1016/j.paid.2019.03.047

5
IDENTIFICATION AND ASSESSMENT OF PROBLEMS OF PROFESSIONAL COMPETENCE

SALINA M. RENNINGER AND CONSUELO E. CAVALIERI

At a practicum site, an African American cisgender male supervisor is concerned about a White cisgender female trainee's abilities to stay abreast of clinical documentation, as her clinical chart notes are always quite delayed. Additionally, he has noticed that when they are in supervision together, she has a hard time looking directly at him and rarely shares self-assessment of her work. In his estimation, she appears to defer completely to his perspective, although when he views clinical training recordings, he rarely sees her implementing the recommendations that they have discussed. He is becoming more frustrated, as efforts to discuss this lack of follow-through only yield more acquiescent behavior during supervision meetings. He raises this issue in a supervision team meeting.

What would you recommend that the supervisors advise? This vignette illustrates several challenging dilemmas encountered when identifying and assessing problems of professional competence (PPC). PPC are identified in many ways. A problem may be identified by a troubling one-time behavior by a trainee, or it might be a result of several behaviors that occur over time. Problems may be observed in informal situations (e.g., conversation between students in the hallway between classes) or may be found through formal

---

https://doi.org/10.1037/0000340-006
Supporting Trainees With Competence Problems: A Practical Guide for Psychology Trainers, R. A. Schwartz-Mette, E. A. Hunter, and N. J. Kaslow (Editors)
Copyright © 2023 by the American Psychological Association. All rights reserved.

means of identification, such as patterns of poor client care discovered when reviewing multiple clinical therapy recordings. *Identification of PPC* refers to the ability to label and describe the PPC. Assessment is a way to measure the baseline status of a concern or development over time after PPC identification occurs. Assessment itself can also be a way to identify PPC. In such an instance, it may be that only in using the assessment tool and/or process does the assessor begin to recognize PPC. The ways to handle PPC when they arise vary by the problem(s) identified and the program-specific processes for addressing concerns. These processes are embedded in the culture of the trainees' academic program and the culture of their practical site setting, as well as within each setting's policies (Shen-Miller, 2014). Systems-based models have sought to capture the complex dynamic of PPC. A systems approach was introduced in Chapter 3 of this volume, but in this chapter the systems perspective guides a comprehensive approach to understanding, assessing, and addressing PPC.

A SYSTEM PERSPECTIVE RELATED TO ASSESSMENT

Assessment of a trainee does not occur in isolation. Rather, assessor and trainee are embedded within multiple nested systems (Bronfenbrenner, 1979), such as the larger society, the mental health profession, the university/ institution, the training program and associated training sites, and the trainee's home life. Applying Bronfenbrenner's (1979) ecological model, Forrest et al. (2008) described how different systems relate to trainee PPC. In the model, the individual develops an increasingly more complex understanding of their environment and their ability to impact their environment across multiple systems. Ecological components interacting with the individual (i.e., the trainee with their relative assets and liabilities) move from the microsystem level (e.g., a trainee's supervisor) to the macrosystem level (e.g., cultural beliefs about becoming a psychologist). Nested between these two levels lies the mesosystem (interactions between two microsystems, e.g., discussions between a supervisor and an academic training director), and exosystem (e.g., a supervisors consultation group in which the trainee is not present, state licensing boards). These systems are bidirectional, with the levels closer together having greater influences on one another than levels that are farther apart. Additionally, levels with fewer links to power have less influence on the others than levels with more links to power (e.g., a microsystem may be less able to influence the exosystem, but the exosystem, where regulation occurs, has more power to influence the microsystem). Finally, these bidirectional influences occur over time and may be further influential toward or influenced by events in time. This system is referred to as the *chronosystem*. A few examples of time-based influences are the individual development of the trainee, moments in societal history, and changes in the training environment.

Returning to the vignette, consider that we learn the following: The supervision team has five members, and two members identify with one or more marginalized racial and/or gender groups. The members have varied responses to the supervisor's concerns. Some suggest that perhaps the supervisee's behaviors are related to a gender and power-differential issue and that the supervisor should raise these possibilities directly in the supervision. Others are concerned that her behaviors are racial microaggressions (Butler-Byrd, 2010) and may reflect a lack of cultural sensitivity or competence, reflecting White fragility. Yet others are most concerned that her behaviors do not meet the minimal standards of the field in the professionalism domain because her case notes are so far behind. In this example, an individualistic view of the trainee's PPC involves focusing primarily on the trainee's behavior. But there are also issues at multiple other levels, and from a systems view the focus includes the microsystem (between supervisor and supervisee), mesosystem (supervisory team), exosystem (accreditation expectations, program standards and field-specific standards), and macrosystem (potential impacts of racism, sexism and intersectionality). As such, the supervisor's assessment may not be as simple as it initially might have seemed (i.e., get caught up on case notes and begin implementing supervisory recommendations). Once assessors begin to consider the evaluation of professional competence from this ecosystemic perspective, it is common to become overwhelmed by the interacting systems and uncertain about how to proceed. As such, we recommend the use of a team approach when responding to PPC to help identify the issues at multiple levels and prioritize responses most likely to promote the trainee's achievement of required competencies (so that no one addresses challenging issues in isolation).

Trainee-Training Program Microsystem

The relationship between a trainee and their training program is bidirectional in that they must work collaboratively, each playing their unique role, toward the development of the trainee. The summative review of students is an example of how identification and assessment of a trainee's competence occurs within this relationship. Typically, students provide self-reflective statements claiming their progress and identifying areas for development. The training programs do the same, often integrating multiple sources of feedback (i.e., the mesosystem), including that of the student. At times, a student may be uncomfortable with or disagree with feedback provided during the summative review process. Even when there have been intentional efforts by the program to give informal and direct formative oral and/or written feedback, students may balk at summative feedback that is inconsistent with their own view of themselves. This may reflect that efforts of the training program were insufficient or that the trainee has blind spots, potentially further solidifying a trainer's concern for a PPC.

Trainers may be equally as uncomfortable with assessing a trainee's competence and may wish to avoid taking responsibility for this task, especially when it's necessary to give corrective feedback (Renninger et al., 2018). Yet they shoulder gatekeeping responsibilities (Johnson et al., 2008) that require them to determine students' capacities and provide feedback to help them attain competencies. The unease experienced by trainers may reflect concerns about the use of power associated with their role and the intersecting social identities of the trainer and trainee. In these instances, it may be helpful to assist all parties by identifying varied types of power at work and discussing how to mitigate the negative impact of unequal power through culturally/identity affirming power-sharing processes (Arczynski & Morrow, 2017; Hernández & McDowell, 2010).

Formal assessment within this microsystem can be formative or summative, but most frequently it is summative in nature. Formal assessments occur in different formats and at key times during a course of training. They can include evaluations typical within academic programs such as student review outcomes, key assignment results, comprehensive exams, or dissertation evaluations. They also may include formal evaluations completed at practicum and internship training sites regarding trainee competencies. As this feedback is typically part of a training record, the feedback should be concrete and specific so that both the trainee and others who may read the evaluation fully understand the meaning of the assessment. When formal assessment includes the identification of PPC, concerns must be well operationalized. Formal assessment is often used as a tool to mark the baseline of performance. If a trainee is given an opportunity to improve upon concerns, a formal assessment tool may be used to measure progress over time.

Formal assessment can be conducted in a number of ways. Kaslow and colleagues (2009) provided a comprehensive approach with the Competency Assessment Toolkit for Professional Psychology. The toolkit describes specific competencies and defines their essential elements. The toolkit provides the foundation for the selection of various types of assessment tools that measure progress on competency development across developmental levels. Additionally, the toolkit makes recommendations on the usefulness of various tools regarding measurement of specific competencies and relative to formative and summative assessment needs. No one tool is adequate to assess all competencies, and trainers are encouraged to consider the relative strengths and limits of various approaches when determining the most effective tool to measure specific competencies. The toolkit is discussed in greater detail later in this chapter.

When programs consider their formal assessment tools, they should make hidden aspects of the curriculum transparent. Smith (2013) identified many aspects of higher education curriculum that are "hidden" so only those with sufficient social capital understand the implicit expectations. A hidden curriculum example is knowing to ask for assistance when one is struggling in school. Many students who are first generation or from underrepresented groups have schemas that they must solve their problems themselves. Hence, they do not seek assistance, putting them at a disadvantage and risking that trainers will evaluate them as not meeting the competency expectations in the domain of professionalism. Programs can identify the ways in which their processes and evaluation tools reflect and uphold the status quo of Whiteness, and other dominant ways of being and make changes to counter these biases (Finders & Kwame-Ross, 2020). Programs should also consider the varied ways their informal assessment strategies may reflect and uphold dominant perspectives and work to mitigate the impacts of these processes.

Trainers' informal observations are a key aspect of identifying PPC. Creating mechanisms for communicating about these observations is essential to early identification of potential concerns. In many instances, there is no identified process for communicating these concerns at the mesosystem level (e.g., faculty member to faculty member). Assessors may be reluctant to share their observations out of protection of the student's privacy or a sense of fairness (Forrest et al., 2021), believing that only formalized assessment processes may be used. This concern may reflect awareness that without preidentified processes or assessment markers the potential for bias and inconsistency is high. As such, programs are encouraged to create processes and tools aimed at capturing informal assessment in a systematic manner.

Equally as important as conversations at the mesosystem level is assessors' willingness to give feedback directly and clearly to trainees regarding their informal assessments. This type of assessment and feedback can occur as part of coursework, later in training such as during case consultation, or at a professional conference. This formative feedback is essential to trainee development and has the potential to prevent problems of PPC. If an assessor fails to share concerns, a trainee cannot know where they need further development. Without the feedback, the behaviors may continue and eventually lead to PPC. The process of addressing PPC can be complex and require multiple efforts by assessors and students (Grus & Kaslow, 2014).

A trainee's willingness to accept feedback plays a role in how quickly change can occur. It is not uncommon for students to avoid or block hearing feedback, especially if the feedback suggests that they have areas of significant needed growth. A trainee may disagree with the observation or claim that it is hurtful to their success in the program. Feedback communicated in a context of communitarian values (see the Professional Community Macrosystem section of this chapter) may be more readily accepted because feedback in this context is an expected norm for all people within the community. The additional ethical imperative of upholding personal dignity coupled with the emphasis on honesty creates opportunities for feedback to be delivered with kindness, especially as ruptures are common within supervision and other feedback-oriented relationships (Watkins et al., 2016).

Trainee-Practicum Microsystem

Similar to the trainee-training program microsystem, trainees and supervisors at a training site have a bidirectional relationship. Many of the same issues already identified for the trainee-program microsystem are at play in this microsystem too. These issues play out through the processes of informal and formative assessments during supervision, the formal and summative assessment approaches typical of sites, and in the context of monthly review of trainees during supervisor meetings. In our experience, trainees commonly express discomfort with some assessment processes at training sites. A range of concerns are expressed. For instance, trainees may say it feels uncomfortable to know that clinical supervisors meet monthly to discuss their progress and feel as though they are "being talked about." In such instances, trainees recognize the potential impact that individuals who are not in their microsystem could be having. Within a practicum setting, trainees' microsystems may involve only a select set of individuals with whom the trainee has relationships, leaving uncertainty about how they are being evaluated. Trainees may also express discomfort with having a feeling of being "watched" while carrying out all aspects of their training. Some trainees describe a hyperawareness of being evaluated, whereas others seem less impacted by the process. One strategy for addressing trainee discomfort could be to provide an overview of the settings in which they are typically evaluated, how the information is shared among trainers, the benefits to the trainee, and the training program's commitment to helping trainees meet their learning goals. Other strategies for enhancing this process and working collaboratively and effectively to support trainee development mirror the approaches described in the prior section.

Program-Practicum/Internship Site Mesosystem

As academic programs rely on off-campus practicum and internship sites, assessment also occurs in settings outside of the academic program, which can contribute to complexities in the assessment process. Most practicum sites use training forms provided by the academic program. Academic programs hold responsibility for creating forms that accurately assess the necessary competencies of the field and of their program. In theory, ongoing/formative feedback from site supervisors should line up with the assessment form. It is not clear, however, how well sites and individual supervisors align formative feedback with the assessment form used in a program. Some sites train students across multiple programs adding to the challenges of this demand. Strategies for enhancing program assessment forms are discussed later in this chapter.

Similar to academic programs, practicum and internship sites vary on how they address PPC and how quickly they include the academic program when problems are identified. For instance, there are times when a training site delays notification about issues with a trainee and the academic program is caught unaware and yet retains responsibility for the oversight of the trainee. Other times, training sites may hold different standards of performance than an academic program, and this misalignment leaves the trainee confused about what is expected. Regular communication between program and site is useful for avoiding some of these pitfalls. This communication can be brought into the formal processes and be based on maintaining a strong and open relationship between the program and site. For instance, both the program and site may benefit from a semesterly check-in between training personnel. This formalized process of communication contributes to a stronger informal relationship, thus increasing the likelihood of a site contacting the program should issues arise. In regard to internship sites, the accreditation guidelines indicate that communication between the doctoral program and the internship site should be maintained and that the doctoral program should initiate this at the start of the academic year (American Psychological Association [APA], 2015).

Practicum and Internship Exosystem

Each practicum and internship has its own way of providing psychological care and a set of practices and procedures that trainees must learn. These site structures are built to uphold the standards of the field. As such, trainees must learn how a particular site constructs their systems to meet the standards of the broader regulatory bodies. For instance, it is now typical for each site to use an electronic health care record as a way of managing documentation and other necessary tasks such as scheduling and billing. Documentation skills are an essential area of development for trainees and is an area in which some trainees struggle. It is helpful when sites conduct a sufficient orientation early in the training experience, but supervisors should also keep a close eye on how a trainee progresses in their use of the tools of the system, as well as their timeliness for charting. Here we may see challenges within the microsystem of the supervisor and trainee and the practicum or internship exosystem. If a supervisor does not hold a trainee accountable for this part of the work, the trainee may fail to recognize the importance of clinical documentation and other related tasks. It may also be helpful to assist trainees in drawing connections between the ethics of the standards with their actions that uphold these standards. If trainees do not connect these dots, they may fail to act appropriately, thus resulting in PPC. This disconnect may also be a reflection of different foci of graduate programs and training sites. Supervisor awareness regarding such "gaps" may be useful in assisting trainees in areas of needed growth while assessing whether concerns rise to the level of PPC.

Professional Community Macrosystem

A related area of focus in the literature describes the need to create competent communities in health service psychology (Johnson et al., 2012). Literature focused on the communitarian approach suggests that not only do individuals within the psychological community have ethical obligations for ethical behavior but the community has similar obligations. Foundational to this approach is the idea of reciprocity in relationship (Johnson et al., 2012, 2014). When considering identification and assessment of PPC from a reciprocity perspective, the issue at hand looks a bit different from traditional conceptions of PPC in which problems are considered from an individualistic perspective wherein the individual is identified as "having" the PPC. When we look at concerns from a reciprocal perspective, issues of power may be conceptualized with attention to trainer–trainee power differentials and the responsibility each has to each other and to serving a diverse client population. Together, trainees and trainers recognize that power comes from many places and can be mutually shared. Also, as noted by Johnson et al. (2012), when people come with a communitarian perspective, all parties feel freer to act with honesty and reduced shame—free to share assessments in a manner that honor the dignity of the other and free to reveal personal skill limitations or other issues impacting academic work or clinical practice. Within the communitarian perspective lies the potential to normalize the need to address one's limitations and thus increase openness to the learning, which is necessary to transform a limitation into a competency.

Foundational to building health service psychology communities where communitarian approaches are valued is the development of a communitarian training culture within training systems. Trainees who experience the professional community as communitarian, versus overly individualistic, have greater potential to bring these perspectives into their work across their lifetime and to more effectively build competence (Johnson et al., 2014). Key to the communitarian training culture is a caring community in which to train, trainers who model strong self-care themselves and who transparently demonstrate their competencies so as to encourage trainees to develop theirs, and training relationships focused on mentorship using egalitarian and collegial approaches.

Professional Training Macrosystem

The competency movement has been afoot for quite some time (APA, 2006). Different communities within the field have taken time to identify competencies, theorize on development of competencies, and create evaluation tools to assess the acquisition of identified competencies (Kaslow, Rubin, Forrest, et al., 2007; Rubin et al., 2007). The National Council of Schools and Programs of Professional Psychology was the first to consider competencies as important to training students to become psychologists (Hatcher et al., 2013). The core competences include relationship, assessment, intervention, research and evaluation, consultation and education, management and supervision, and diversity. Ethics is embedded in each of the competencies. The triad of knowledge, skill, and attitude (KSA) was used to recognize that knowledge itself was insufficient for effective practice. It is in the synergy of KSA that effective practice (i.e., competence) can be seen. Developmental achievement levels were formulated, with three levels from begin practicum to begin internship to complete doctoral degree (Peterson et al., 2010). The intersections between developmental achievement level, KSA, and locus of assessment (e.g., supervisor, peer, self) allowed for the creation of assessment tools that clearly specified which KSA were relevant for which competency at which level of training and thus became a model for assessment of competencies (Borden & McIlvried, 2010).

In 2002, the Competencies Conference: Future Directions in Education and Credentialing (Kaslow, 2004) kick-started a profession-wide shift to a culture of competence (Kaslow et al., 2009). Soon after, the creation of the Assessment of Competency Benchmark Workgroup led to the development of a benchmark system and the Competency Assessment Toolkit (Hatcher et al., 2013). *Benchmarks* are behavioral descriptions of a competency for a given developmental level that can be used to determine how well an individual is doing in the development of that competency (Kaslow et al., 2009). The products of this workgroup includes a guidebook regarding the competency model and benchmark system and a benchmark evaluation system that includes rating forms that can be used by training programs (American Psychological Association Work Group, 2012).

Later, the benchmark system was redesigned to include three clusters in the foundational area and three clusters in the functional area, with the competencies nested within these clusters. Foundational competencies are those that undergird the profession and cut across the functional competencies, which are the applied aspects of professional psychology (Rodolfa et al., 2005). This categorization of competencies allowed for the creation of model rating forms, which can be used by training programs, academic and practical alike (Hatcher et al., 2013). Each rating form identifies the competency, describes it, and lists essential components of the competency. The scale measures how characteristic the element is of the trainee's behavior. This type of rating scale was chosen intentionally to maximize use across multiple sites by improving upon validity and reliability relative to other rating scales. Many rating scales are designed for supervisors and other evaluators to assess whether a trainee meets expectations or has performed satisfactorily. The concern about these types of ratings is that there may be poor agreement about satisfactory performance or what meets expectations. Additionally, Likert scales designed to rate a trainee from "below expectations" to "exceeds expectations" often yield inflated results, with most trainees exceeding expectations (Hatcher et al., 2013).

Since 2015, the Standards of Accreditation (APA) for programs accredited in counseling, clinical, and school psychology call for programs to ensure that trainees are adequately capable across nine competency areas: research, ethical and legal standards, individual and cultural diversity, professional values/attitudes/behaviors, communication and interpersonal skills, assessment, intervention, supervision, and consultation and interprofessional/interdisciplinary skills.

Competency Assessment Toolkit

The Competency Assessment Toolkit was developed by a workgroup to assist stakeholders (i.e., education, training, and regulatory bodies) with the assessment of competence. The workgroup examined prior efforts in the field of medicine to identify and link a range of assessment tools to the competencies and the essential elements of each competency. Fifteen tools were identified, and the degree of usefulness for each tool, relative to the competency and its essential elements, was evaluated. Recognition of challenges such as coordinating collection of data across multiple sources, designing tools that are adequate for varied sources, and needs and the high cost of some approaches (financial and workload related) relative to benefit of the approach is also part of the toolkit (Kaslow et al., 2009). As such, programs are encouraged to be pragmatic, balancing the need to use effective assessment strategies with the need to manage cost and ease of implementation.

Different programs may elect to use different tools to assess the competencies of their students, even if the competencies being measured are the same for each program. It is recommended, however, that all programs use a range of tools that capture students' performance in a variety of tasks and in different venues (Kaslow et al., 2009). Consideration should be given to how formative and summative evaluation will occur for each of these tasks and in which settings. For instance, competency evaluation rating forms are commonly used for practicum training and can provide opportunity for formative and summative evaluation of attitude and skills by supervisors. Client outcome data might be useful for formative evaluation and assist a supervisor with developing a trainee toward the competencies identified on the evaluation rating form. Written examinations are typical for assessing baseline knowledge and are considered as a summative evaluation. Annual reviews are common in academic programs and reflect an opportunity for summative review and a chance to integrate feedback across multiple sources. The examples provided here are typical of many programs. To review detailed information on the 15 types of assessment, please see the Competency Assessment Toolkit (Kaslow et al., 2009).

System Evaluation

Forrest et al. (2008) described the need to use an ecologically based evaluation system that provides opportunity for bidirectional feedback across multiple sources. This recommendation is suggested not only for trainees but also for use with faculty, supervisors, and programs. Such evaluations have the potential to uncover issues in the training community and create opportunities for change at the micro- and mesosystem levels, which in turn may impact whether and how issues of PPC arise for trainees. Relatedly, attending to disparities in outcomes achieved within a program may reveal systemic issues in the training and evaluation system of the program.

Identification and assessment occur within the culture of a training program (Shen-Miller, 2014). A primary way that a program organizes competency identification and assessment is through the nine competencies that all APA-accredited counseling, clinical, and school psychology programs must assess (APA, 2015). Programs must identify the tools used to assess each competency, and students must achieve minimal levels of achievement (MLA) toward those competencies. It would be a mistake, however, to believe that because this assessment is of each student's achievement, the assessment is solely about the student. Indeed, a review of patterns of MLA within a program can reveal issues within the program and may allow for evaluation of issues within the mesosystem (Forrest et al., 2008). Identifying that only students from specific social locations are having difficulties in a program and that certain competencies are not being sufficiently covered to result in successful achievement of the MLA are examples of patterns that require further inquiry.

Chronosystem

The chronosystem includes changes in the individual and changes in the environments as a result of interplay between the individual and the systems over time. Relative to PPC, some examples of chronosystem influences include trainee individual development and changes to local, national, or accreditation guidelines (Forrest et al., 2008). Formative and summative assessments reflect the role of time in trainees' development and PPC.

Formative Assessment
According to Kaslow, Rubin, Bebeau, et al. (2007), "*Formative assessment* is an ongoing, developmentally informed process with direct and thoughtful feedback during training and throughout professional development to ensure attainment of higher levels of competence through learning and performance improvement" (p. 444). Formative feedback (which is based on formative assessment) is found to be essential to the learning process (Brookhart, 2018). As such, formative assessment plays an important role in identifying PPC and formative feedback is part of a necessary foundation to working with PPC, as this is the early notification system to trainees who may be having difficulties in their performance.

Formative assessment can be informal or formal. Informal formative assessment frequently occurs in real time as situations unfold. Examples of when formative assessment occurs include observing exchanges between students that reflect problematic styles of communication and conversations between a trainee and a faculty member regarding a research design or the care of a complicated client. Formal formative assessment includes feedback that is not yet conclusive but occurs at a prespecified phase of training and often uses formal assessment tools that will ultimately become summative assessments. One example of a formal formative assessment is a midterm supervision assessment that does not become part of the official record but gives the student early information regarding their progress on key assessment areas. Another example is feedback provided on a research proposal draft that is not part of a final grade but is used to assist a student in shaping their thinking.

Summative Assessment
Summative assessment is the culmination of formative assessment over time. It provides a summary of a period of development in a student's experience and is based on the accumulation of formative assessments. Summative assessment is almost exclusively formal in nature and is typically considered to be an official form of feedback. This assessment is documented and kept as part of a student record or in relation to a grade. Examples include end-of-term supervision evaluations and feedback on a course paper that is linked to an earned grade. When PPC are identified, this type of assessment becomes part of the record substantiating concerns and serving as part of formal notification and due process for the student.

Self-Assessment
Identification and assessment of PPC are typically discussed in the context of those doing the assessment (i.e., supervisor or faculty member) and those being assessed (i.e., student). It is worth mentioning that self-assessment is another avenue toward the identification of PPC and is a recommended approach to ongoing assessment of developmental changes. Reflective practice (Knapp et al., 2017) is part of competency development and as such is both a competency and an identification and assessment tool. For instance, within the Standards of Accreditation (APA, 2015), self-reflection relates to the Professional Values and Attitudes competency, but it also is embedded in the Ethical and Legal Standards competency. One could argue that successful achievement across other competencies rests in part on the capacity for self-reflection and course correction on the basis of such reflection (e.g., Intervention competency). As such, self-reflection is a key tool for identifying and assessing PPC and may be essential to a student's acceptance of feedback and willingness to work with trainers in addressing issues once they have been identified.

A WORD ABOUT PROFESSIONALISM

Professionalism is an area worthy of specific attention as perhaps, more than any other area of the competencies, there is potential for trainees to be identified as having PPC because of implicit or vague expectations of a trainee's professionalism. But what, specifically, is professionalism? Professionalism, as defined by the Competency Benchmark Evaluation System, includes the competencies of Professional Values and Attitudes, Individual and Cultural Diversity, Ethical Legal Standards and Policy, and Reflective Practice/Self-Assessment/Self-Care (Kaslow et al., 2009). Here we focus on the first area, as this aspect of professionalism is a common area of concern relative to PPC (Kaslow, Grus, et al., 2018). The essential elements of Professional Values and Attitudes are integrity, deportment, accountability, concern for the welfare of others, and professional identity. Of these, deportment stands out as an area where problems are commonly identified.

In practice as well as academic settings, attire that is considered to be professional can vary widely. Listservs of training professionals commonly discuss attire and other professional behaviors of the trainees at their sites, often including disagreements about what is appropriate. Examples of these disagreements include whether flip-flops or wool socks and Birkenstocks are appropriate footwear, whether nylons should be required for women with bare legs, and whether it is appropriate for tattoos and piercings to be visible (to trainees' clients). A wide array of norms exist in professional settings and of beliefs across professionals themselves. Other concerns include norms of speech and language and orientation to time.

It is important to recognize that norms of deportment are culturally bound, and thus training programs are encouraged to define this concept for trainees. The benchmark evaluation description for deportment at the practicum level is "understands how to conduct oneself in a professional manner," at the internship level is "communication and physical conduct (including attire) is professional appropriate, across different settings," and at the practice level is "conducts self in a professional manner across settings and situations." Before concluding that their deportment is a form of PPC, sites and programs are encouraged to define up-front what is considered to be professional in their setting and give direct feedback to trainees whose deportment is of concern.

It is incumbent on trainers to critically examine their site's norms for the potential disparate impact their policies and resulting assessments may have on their trainees. Many of our norms are culturally bound to Euro American roots. This has implications for trainers in their duty to uphold training standards that equitably reflect and affirm trainee's cultures and their identities. For instance, consider the experience of a trainee who is left to navigate a new professional setting on their own and blunders into mistakes, which leads them to be evaluated poorly. In this situation, the trainee is comfortable referring to supervisors and professors by their first name but upon joining a site where formal titles are used, they violate the site norms. Unless they receive specific orientation about these norms, they continue to refer to individuals by their first name and are later seen in a negative light. In fact, this is not an uncommon situation. Academic programs and applied training sites are encouraged to educate their trainees about the variety of norms in the field, advocate for trainees, and educate sites when trainees make these errors. It is important that programs and sites stay open to hearing from their trainees about why they comport themselves in the manner they do. Cultural humility is encouraged for both the trainer and the trainee (Abbott et al., 2019; Kaslow, Grus, et al., 2018) as a mechanism for understanding each other. Sites and programs should be open to changing norms that may be unintentionally oppressive to some trainees. Self-reflection at all levels of the ecological system is recommended as a means toward enhancing one's ability to develop sophisticated and nuanced appreciation for diverse expressions of professionalism as trainers and trainees (Kaslow, Grus, et al., 2018; Knapp et al., 2017).

KEY CONSIDERATIONS IN THE IDENTIFICATION AND ASSESSMENT OF COMPETENCIES

Assessment of competencies that is ongoing throughout a student's training reflects a proactive approach to handling competence problems and may even serve as a mechanism to prevent PPC. Assessment and ongoing feedback are necessary components of a student's movement from doctoral study to professional employment (Kaslow, Bangasser, et al., 2018). Trainees should be aware of how they will be evaluated and what will happen if performance is not up to expectation. This information can be provided at admissions time, in the training or program handbook, in key coursework, and as needed as one moves throughout a program. It is important to include formative and informal assessments, along with formal and summative assessments.

Assessment should occur in the context of communitarian principles (Johnson et al., 2012). Students have specific roles and obligations, as do those serving in assessment positions (e.g., faculty, supervisors). Additionally, the various stakeholders in a student's development (e.g., academic programs, training sites) should work collaboratively to perform competent assessment. Johnson et al. (2008) referred to the "hot potato game" (p. 590) in describing the tendency of stakeholders to pass students with PPC along while blaming the other for the issue. To combat this tendency, stakeholders need to work together and with humility, each owning their place in the micro-, meso-, and exosystems. With this perspective, it becomes easy to see shared responsibility; rather than focusing on deflecting or assigning blame, all parties can play a role in helping a trainee address their PPC.

Some trainees have overall discomfort with the process of evaluation, and this can be a barrier to receiving feedback based on assessment. It also may be a form of PPC. Because learning occurs through an iterative process of ongoing assessment and feedback (either from external or self-assessment processes), difficulty with assessment can be a barrier to development. For example, years ago a colleague worked with a supervisee who cried every time they received feedback. This reaction occurred whether the feedback was affirming or corrective. Although tears in supervision are to be expected periodically, this student's response became problematic because they often failed to internalize the feedback, as efforts to manage emotion became the focus. Consequently, some on-site supervisors avoided giving feedback. The student also was not able to self-assess because of their deep avoidance of evaluation. As a result, the student did not develop many skills over the course of the practicum and eventually required a remediation plan, further feeding their discomfort with evaluation and feedback. This particular issue is one of the more challenging types of PPC, as the very processes aimed at supporting change are also part of triggering challenges.

Just as some trainees may struggle with evaluation, so can evaluators. Discomfort by trainers can make them not want to evaluate but can have poor consequences if it is avoided (Hoffman et al., 2005). Assisting students in the development of competency is an ethical imperative (Johnson et al., 2013). Jacobs and colleagues (2011) described the personal and contextual factors that impede effective communication when addressing PPC. In the personal realm, lack of competency in having difficult conversation, coping style of avoidance, resentment regarding the situation, or fears related to handling their own emotions or legal action may be at play. Contextual factors include program culture, program policies (or lack of policies), concerns about confidentiality, program type (applied vs. research focused), and trainer disagreement. One antidote to some of these concerns is the specificity of the current tools that can be used to assess competencies. When behaviors are specifically described, it may be easier for evaluators to provide the necessary feedback. Further recommendations when there are issues of PPC are that evaluators work in teams and that programs take the time to attend to contextual factors. For instance, Forrest et al. (2021) addressed common concerns about confidentiality and recommended strategies for managing such issues through improved policies at both the local level (i.e., program) and national level (i.e., ethics code and accreditation guidelines).

Clear communication throughout the identification and assessment process is key. Remediation should never come as a surprise to a student. The assessment communication should allow students to receive programmatic support and be clear on the steps necessary for competency development. A typical process would be to give verbal feedback, then written feedback if the PPC does not improve. At these two points of feedback, nothing formal such as a remediation plan is developed. The student is told what needs to change, each parties' roles in what needs to occur, and what will happen if development is not observed. There should be identified support from multiple sources and clarity about how evaluation will occur. Additionally, it can be useful to name the context in which the concerns arose (e.g., civil unrest and protest, pandemic) and an effort made to affirm existing strengths, even as PPC is identified as an area of significant concern. This process might be called "early identification" and be the precursor to more formal solutions should the need arise.

CONCLUSION

These ecological systems and communitarian perspectives are essential to best practices in the areas of identification and assessment of PPC. Some aspects of traditional assessment approaches pull for an individualistic approach to PPC. The process through which assessment occurs can interrupt this. Academic programs and clinical training sites need to identify their own processes to best serve their program goals while upholding the ideals of the communitarian perspective and understanding the interplay of systems. Programs are encouraged to take time to review their programs processes and policies through the lens of the ecological model and communitarian perspectives to determine processes that will best serve their programs.

Returning to the example presented at the beginning of the chapter, how do we now look at the issues described? Does it look different when we take into account the communitarian perspective? How might we think about reciprocity of relationship? How do we imagine resolving communication of the assessment issues? What avenues might there be to uphold the dignity of both supervisor and supervisee during the assessment process. What variables might we consider as we navigate assisting this student in growth and recognizing that the supervisor may have areas of development as well? How do the social locations of the supervisor and supervisee impact their experiences? And how do the relationships and various perspectives on the supervision team potentially impact the next steps? We encourage you to grapple with these questions, knowing there are many "right" answers.

REFERENCES

Abbott, D. M., Noelany, P., & Mercier, C. (2019). Cultural humility and the teaching of psychology. *Scholarship of Teaching and Learning in Psychology, 5*(2), 169–181. https://doi.org/10.1037/stl0000144

American Psychological Association. (2006). *APA Taskforce on the Assessment of Competence in Professional Psychology: Final report.* https://www.apa.org/ed/resources/competency-revised.pdf

American Psychological Association. (2015). *Standards of accreditation for health service psychology and accreditation operating procedures.* https://www.apa.org/ed/accreditation/about/policies/standards-of-accreditation.pdf

American Psychological Association Work Group. (2012). *A practical guide for the Competency Benchmarks.* https://www.apa.org/ed/graduate/guide-benchmarks.pdf

Arczynski, A. V., & Morrow, S. L. (2017). The complexities of power in feminist multicultural psychotherapy supervision. *Journal of Counseling Psychology, 64*(2), 192–205. https://doi.org/10.1037/cou0000179

Borden, K., & McIlvried, E. (2010). Applying the competency model to professional psychology education, training, and assessment: Mission bay and beyond. In M. Kenkel & R. Peterson (Eds.), *Competency-based education for professional psychology* (pp. 43–53). American Psychological Association. https://doi.org/10.1037/12068-002

Bronfenbrenner, U. (1979). *The ecology of human development.* Harvard University Press.

Brookhart, S. M. (2018). Summative and formative feedback. In A. A. Lipnevich & J. K. Smith (Eds.), *The Cambridge handbook of instructional feedback* (pp. 52–78). Cambridge University Press. https://doi.org/10.1017/9781316832134.005

Butler-Byrd, N. M. (2010). An African-American supervisor's reflections on multicultural supervision. *Training and Education in Professional Psychology, 4*(1), 11–15. https://doi.org/10.1037/a0018351

Finders, M. J., & Kwame-Ross, T. (2020). "You're just being oversensitive": White talk moves in higher education. *Change, 52*(5), 25–28. https://doi.org/10.1080/00091383.2020.1807879

Forrest, L., Elman, N. S., Bodner, K. E., & Kaslow, N. J. (2021). Trainee confidentiality: Confusions, complexities, consequences, and possibilities. *Training and Education in Professional Psychology.* Advance online publication. https://doi.org/10.1037/tep0000364

Forrest, L., Shen-Miller, D. S., & Elman, N. S. (2008). Psychology trainees with competence problems: From individual to ecological conceptualizations. *Training and Education in Professional Psychology, 2*(4), 183–192. https://doi.org/10.1037/1931-3918.2.4.183

Grus, C. L., & Kaslow, N. J. (2014). Professionalism: Professional values and attitudes in psychology. In W. B. Johnson & N. J. Kaslow (Eds.), *Oxford handbook of education and training in professional psychology* (pp. 491–509). Oxford University Press.

Hatcher, R., Fouad, N., Grus, C., Campbell, L., McCutcheon, S., & Leahy, K. (2013). Competency Benchmarks: Practical steps toward a culture of competence. *Training and Education in Professional Psychology, 7*(2), 84–91. https://doi.org/10.1037/a0029401

Hernández, P., & McDowell, T. (2010). Intersectionality, power, and relational safety in context: Key concepts in clinical supervision. *Training and Education in Professional Psychology, 4*(1), 29–35. https://doi.org/10.1037/a0017064

Hoffman, M., Hill, C., Holmes, S., & Freitas, G. (2005). Supervisor perspective on the process and outcome of giving easy, difficult, or no feedback to supervisees. *Journal of Counseling Psychology, 52*(1), 3–13. https://doi.org/10.1037/0022-0167.52.1.3

Jacobs, S. C., Huprich, S. K., Grus, C. L., Cage, E. A., Elman, N. S., Forrest, L., Schwartz-Mette, R., Shen-Miller, D. S., Van Sickle, K. S., & Kaslow, N. J. (2011). Trainees with professional competency problems: Preparing trainers for difficult but necessary conversations. *Training and Education in Professional Psychology, 5*(3), 175–184. https://doi.org/10.1037/a0024656

Johnson, W. B., Barnett, J. E., Elman, N. S., Forrest, L., & Kaslow, N. J. (2012). The competent community: Toward a vital reformulation of professional ethics. *American Psychologist, 67*(7), 557–569. https://doi.org/10.1037/a0027206

Johnson, W. B., Barnett, J. E., Elman, N. S., Forrest, L., & Kaslow, N. J. (2013). The competence constellation model: A communitarian approach to support professional competence. *Professional Psychology: Research and Practice, 44*(5), 343–354. https://doi.org/10.1037/a0033131

Johnson, W. B., Barnett, J. E., Elman, N. S., Forrest, L., Schwartz-Mette, R., & Kaslow, N. J. (2014). Preparing trainees for lifelong competence: Creating a communitarian training culture. *Training and Education in Professional Psychology, 8*(4), 211–220. https://doi.org/10.1037/tep0000048

Johnson, W. B., Elman, N. S., Forrest, L., Robiner, W. N., Rodolfa, E., & Schaffer, J. B. (2008). Addressing professional competence problems in trainees: Some ethical considerations. *Professional Psychology: Research and Practice, 39*(6), 589–599. https://doi.org/10.1037/a0014264

Kaslow, N. J. (2004). Competencies in professional psychology. *American Psychologist, 59*(8), 774–781. https://doi.org/10.1037/0003-066X.59.8.774

Kaslow, N. J., Bangasser, D. A., Grus, C. L., McCutcheon, S. R., & Fowler, G. A. (2018). Facilitating pipeline progress from doctoral degree to first job. *American Psychologist, 73*(1), 47–62. https://doi.org/10.1037/amp0000120

Kaslow, N. J., Grus, C. L., Allbaugh, L. J., Shen-Miller, D., Bodner, K. E., Veilleux, J., & Van Sickle, K. (2018). Trainees with competence problems in the professionalism domain. *Ethics & Behavior, 28*(6), 429–449. https://doi.org/10.1080/10508422.2018.1438897

Kaslow, N. J., Grus, C. L., Campbell, L. F., Fouad, N. A., Hatcher, R. L., & Rodolfa, E. R. (2009). Competency Assessment Toolkit for professional psychology. *Training and Education in Professional Psychology, 3*(4, Suppl.), S27–S45. https://doi.org/10.1037/a0015833

Kaslow, N. J., Rubin, N. J., Bebeau, M. J., Leigh, I. W., Lichtenberg, J. W., Nelson, P. D., Portnoy, S. M., & Smith, I. L. (2007). Guiding principles and recommendations for the assessment of competence. *Professional Psychology: Research and Practice*, *38*(5), 441–451. https://doi.org/10.1037/0735-7028.38.5.441

Kaslow, N. J., Rubin, N. J., Forrest, L., Elman, N. S., Van Horne, B. A., Jacobs, S. C., Huprich, S. K., Benton, S. A., Pantesco, V. F., Dollinger, S. J., Grus, C. L., Behnke, S. H., Miller, D. S. S., Shealy, C. N., Mintz, L. B., Schwartz-Mette, R., Van Sickle, K., & Thorn, B. E. (2007). Recognizing, assessing, and intervening with problems of professional competence. *Professional Psychology: Research and Practice*, *38*(5), 479–492. https://doi.org/10.1037/0735-7028.38.5.479

Knapp, S., Gottlieb, M. C., & Handelsman, M. M. (2017). Enhancing professionalism through self-reflection. *Professional Psychology: Research and Practice*, *48*(3), 167–174. https://doi.org/10.1037/pro0000135

Peterson, R., Peterson, D., Abrams, J., Stricker, G., & Ducheny, K. (2010). The National Council of Schools and Programs of Professional Psychology: Educational model 2009. In M. Kenkel & R. Peterson (Eds.), *Competency-based education for professional psychology* (pp. 13–42). American Psychological Association. https://doi.org/10.1037/12068-001

Renninger, S. M., Sovereign, A. E., Jennings, L., & Picard, K. (2018, August 9–12). *Gatekeeping aspirations, ambiguities, and angst: Preliminary findings on graduate program practices and policies* [Poster presentation]. 126th Annual American Psychological Association Convention, San Francisco, CA, United States.

Rodolfa, E., Bent, R., Eisman, E., Nelson, P., Rehm, L., & Ritchie, P. (2005). A cube model for competency development: Implications for psychology educators and regulators. *Professional Psychology: Research and Practice*, *36*(4), 347–354. https://doi.org/10.1037/0735-7028.36.4.347

Rubin, N. J., Bebeau, M., Leigh, I. W., Lichtenberg, J. W., Nelson, P. D., Portnoy, S., Smith, I. L., & Kaslow, N. J. (2007). The competency movement within psychology: An historical perspective. *Professional Psychology: Research and Practice*, *38*(5), 452–462. https://doi.org/10.1037/0735-7028.38.5.452

Shen-Miller, D. S. (2014). Trainee evaluation in professional psychology. In W. B. Johnson & N. J. Kaslow (Eds.), *The Oxford handbook of education and training in professional psychology* (Vol. 1, pp. 251–271). Oxford University Press.

Smith, B. (2013). *Mentoring at-risk students through the hidden curriculum of higher education*. Lexington Books.

Watkins, C. E., Jr., Hook, J. N., Ramaeker, J., & Ramos, M. J. (2016). Repairing the ruptured supervisory alliance: Humility as a foundational virtue in clinical supervision. *The Clinical Supervisor*, *35*(1), 22–41. https://doi.org/10.1080/07325223.2015.1127190

6 REMEDIATION, COUNSELING OUT, AND DISMISSAL

REBECCA A. SCHWARTZ-METTE

CONTEXTUALIZING REMEDIATION AS SUPPORTIVE INTERVENTION

Remediation can be understood, simply, as corrective action taken in response to observed competency problems. This action typically involves a series of strategies designed by trainers to assist trainees in overcoming identified barriers to competent performance and/or deficiencies in attaining professional standards (Vacha-Haase et al., 2019). Although this conceptualization is relatively straightforward, it is important to acknowledge that the term *remediation* may carry much more meaning and weight for trainees and trainers alike. Remediation can trigger intense emotions—such as shame, guilt, humiliation, and anger—for trainees who may misunderstand or overpersonalize its function (Kallaugher & Mollen, 2017). Remediation may even feel extreme, punitive, or otherwise distressing to trainers who are unprepared

---

Appreciation is extended to Drs. Linda Forrest, Evelyn Hunter, and David Shen-Miller. Together with this author, the group has prepared and taught several workshops on this topic, and much of the information in this chapter reflects the group's efforts.

https://doi.org/10.1037/0000340-007
Supporting Trainees With Competence Problems: A Practical Guide for Psychology Trainers, R. A. Schwartz-Mette, E. A. Hunter, and N. J. Kaslow (Editors)
Copyright © 2023 by the American Psychological Association. All rights reserved.

for or avoidant toward their full gatekeeping responsibilities (Jacobs et al., 2011; Robiner et al., 1993). In any case, remediation is not typically met with joy and excitement on either end. So what is it, really, and is it as bad as it seems?

Remediation is what we do *for* and *with* students when their competencies have not reached expected levels (given training and experience in the context of developmental stage) or when their competence (once attained) has diminished in some way. It is not what we do *to* or *at* trainees, as it may sometimes feel. Any given competence problem could be attributable to trainee challenge(s), trainer challenge(s), a combination of the two, or none of the above. In some ways, the core source of difficulty matters less than our commitment to being in this process with our trainees to support their growth. Moreover, remediation should not merely be a consequence that punctuates a difficult road. Rather, remediation should be a door through which we walk with our trainees to invite them into new possibilities, new growth, and a new level of functioning.

In terms of the function and utility of remediation, the goal is to provide an opportunity for trainees to develop and exhibit the requisite competencies to meet minimal professional standards (Kaslow, Rubin, Forrest, et al., 2007). The aim is not to simply shock students into never exhibiting competence problems again. The success (or failure) of remediation may depend, in large part, on the creation, implementation, and evaluation of a good remediation plan. Perhaps ironically, designing, implementing, and evaluating remediation plans for trainee competence problems is an area of trainer competence that most trainers only have an opportunity to develop when in the midst of supporting students with competency concerns. This scenario is akin to building a plane (and learning to fly said just-built plane) while the plane is in the air, in the middle of a severe storm. Not ideal! As such, the goal of this chapter is to help better prepare trainers to develop these remediation competencies ahead of time, so that their support of trainees with competence problems yields the best possible outcomes. With a step-by-step description of remediation processes, trainers will be better positioned to meet the needs of all trainees.

GETTING CLEAR ON THE PROBLEM AND COMMUNICATING TO TRAINEES

To develop supportive remediation for our trainees, we must be clear on what the problem is. Assessing competencies and identifying competence problems is an area of discussion requiring depth in its own right (e.g., Rodolfa et al.,

2005; see also Chapters 2, 3, and 5, this volume). Some programs use existing evaluation systems such as the one built around the *competency benchmarks model* (see Fouad et al., 2009; Kaslow et al., 2009), which provides a framework for summative evaluation to be conducted at regular intervals and includes behavioral anchors for each competency domain. Having behavioral indicators for professional competencies enables trainers and trainees alike to have a clear understanding of what behaviors are expected and to better identify and articulate competency problems when they are observed (Kaslow, Rubin, Bebeau, et al., 2007).

Vague, general, or otherwise nonbehavioral descriptions (e.g., "personality problems") are not only unclear and confusing, but they could also resemble trainer articulation of a trainee's core psychological issues. This inadvertently creates an ethically problematic multiple relationship for trainers (e.g., training, psychological assessment; Falender et al., 2009). Trainers should avoid psychological assessment of trainees and speculation about root causes of competence problems at all costs (Collins et al., 2011; Elman & Forrest, 2007; Schwartz-Mette, 2011). Instead, it is important to gather information about the circumstances that gave rise to the competence problem (i.e., barriers to competence). For example, if the competence problem is reflected in timely completion of an assessment report, the barrier might be lack of knowledge or poor time management. If a problem is strained relationships with trainers, the barrier might be lack of communication skills or professionalism deficits. Articulation of barriers to competence, particularly in the areas of interpersonal functioning, requires careful consideration and attention to the intersection of trainees' personal and professional functioning and raises questions about what trainers can and should not discuss. As a good rule of thumb, trainers should only address personal factors that are clearly apparent in and/or negatively impacting the trainee's professional context (see Chapter 7). For example, a trainee's substance use is a personal behavior that, outside of affecting professional functioning, would not be addressed by trainers. However, a trainer would be ethically obligated to address a trainee's substance use that was apparent in their professional context (e.g., arrives to work intoxicated) and/or negatively impacting professional functioning (e.g., misses deadlines or appointments).

Finally, the problem behavior and associated competency domain must be clearly linked to the training goals of the program and profession (Forrest et al., 1999). Again, using an established system to evaluate competencies at regular intervals (e.g., Kaslow et al., 2009) communicates these goals to trainees so that if and when competence problems arise, they are already clearly linked. The process of communicating about competence problems directly to trainees involves a series of possible steps, including proximal feedback, the program letter, the trainee response, and release(s) of information. Each is discussed in detail next. Note that any given competence problem situation may require alterations to the steps proposed.

Proximal Feedback

Once trainers are clear that there is an observable competency concern linked to program and/or professional training goals and standards, the ideal first step is to verbally communicate the concern directly to the trainee in the context in which the problem arose (Falender & Shafranske, 2004). This type of communication would be considered formative feedback to be followed by more formal documentation at the program level. For example, if a student is observed to engage in nonfunctional or overly personal self-disclosure with clients during therapy sessions and to have a hard time containing their own emotional reactions to clients in session, a supervisor may bring these observations to the student in their next supervision meeting for discussion. As another example, a student may be observed to fail to follow established protocols in running research subjects through a laboratory study. In a regular meeting with the research mentor, the mentor may communicate this observation.

To be clear, informal formative feedback regarding the competence problem does not need to (and likely should not) be as extensive and detailed as a formal, program-level communication that fully articulates the issue(s) and the subsequent remediation plan. The trainer may articulate the concern to the student and note that more detailed feedback and discussion will occur soon. The trainer would then benefit from discussing the issues with program faculty at length to gather information (e.g., about the student's performance in other contexts) and ensure that the problem observed is indeed related to training goals and requires remediation. It is important, though, to communicate to the trainee as early as possible in the process that a concern exists. The "law of no surprises" that guides our summative evaluation processes should certainly apply here, so that long periods of time do not go by following observation of the issue without acknowledging the issue to the student (Forrest & Elman, 2014). Timely communication to the student is further essential to demonstrating adequate due process. Failure to do so may invite scrutiny regarding the program's processes and open the program up to appeal by the student (see the Dismissal section of this chapter and also Chapter 9).

A brief note about thresholds for remediation is warranted here. Although representative, empirical data are sorely lacking, many remediation plans result from competency concerns that have been repeatedly communicated to students over time and become subject to formal remediation only after the trainee fails to course correct in a developmentally expected time frame (e.g., failing to document clinical sessions appropriately, mild unprofessional behavior). In other instances, a competency concern may be of a kind that, in and of itself and on its first occurrence, may be enough to formally remediate (e.g., significant unprofessional or unethical behavior, failing a required course). Finally, and fortunately rare, some competency concerns could be so significant that immediate dismissal from the program (without remediation) is the appropriate course (e.g., felonious action impacting the program, client, or public welfare; Kaslow et al., 2018; Katz et al., 2010; Veilleux et al., 2012). In the latter case, programs should be sure to consult legal counsel before moving to remove a student without remediation (Gilfoyle, 2008).

Program Letter

The next step is to formally document the competence problem and directly communicate this to the trainee, again, in a timely fashion. If a competence problem is identified in the context of formal evaluation (e.g., summative evaluation at semester, rotation, or end of year), then a program letter may follow this document and elaborate on the concerns. Oftentimes, though, competence problems may arise in between such formal assessments, and a letter could come on its own, following delivery of informal, formative feedback about the issue (e.g., within a supervision meeting or research mentor meeting) as discussed earlier. The letter should make clear that the concern comes from the training program as a whole, and not just from a single trainer. Taking a program-level stance on competency concerns prevents inadvertent communication that the competence issue is merely a disagreement between a single trainer and trainee and helps to avoid potential triangulation between trainee, trainer, and other faculty members. The program letter also should articulate the observed competence problem(s) in behavioral terms and link this with professional competency standards. Finally, the letter should articulate next steps, as known to this point in the process.

Trainee Response

It can be helpful at this stage to elicit feedback from the trainee regarding the observed competency problems. For example, in articulating next steps, the program letter may invite a response from the trainee, asking them to reflect on the problem, what competencies are involved, what might have led to the problem, and what support they may need to attain requisite competence. To be clear, the program is not obligated to embrace these explanations or suggestions for remediation. However, in the spirit of supporting students with competence problems, eliciting such a letter invites collaboration between trainees and trainers and considers trainee voice in this process. This aspect of the remediation process further promotes a communitarian training culture (as discussed throughout this volume). Having an opportunity to be heard also is an essential element of due process afforded the student.

Student reflections may also provide useful information that trainers can use in creating the remediation plan. For example, a student may offer information that helps the trainers conceptualize the problem in functional terms and illuminate obstacles to competent performance. Alternatively, a lack of insight or self-reflection at this stage in the process (e.g., student is strongly defensive, does not acknowledge competence issue, or blames others) also can be informative in what additional support may be necessary. Asking for such reflection in writing gives the student time and space to process the feedback they have received and communicate back to the program in a less-demanding and pressure-filled context. Should this feedback be elicited verbally in front of all program faculty, a trainee could likely feel particularly stressed and perhaps would be less able to articulate their thoughts and reflections. The student response letter can and should become part of their file, assisting with documentation of the remediation process.

Release(s) of Information

At this stage in the process, it also is helpful to have the trainee sign any relevant releases of information (if necessary) in order for the program to be able to communicate concerns about competencies and remediation information to relevant parties such as external practicum site supervisors, graduate programs if an intern, or any other individuals outside of the training program who interface with the students' training. Releases should be solicited in consideration of Family Educational Rights and Privacy Act of 1974 (FERPA) regulations and "who needs to know" and thus should not be overly broad to include those who are not directly involved in the trainee's educational experience (Forrest et al., 2021; see also Chapters 7 and 9, this volume).

Importantly, trainees should be informed about any entity that will receive information about remediation without their explicit authorization, such as internship sites. Programs have been encouraged to (and often do) share information about whether a trainee has participated in remediation and the outcomes of remediation activities in the training director's portion of the Association of Psychology Postdoctoral and Internship Centers (APPIC) internship applications. If this is the case, the trainee should be informed early in the process, before remediation begins.

DESIGNING AN EFFECTIVE REMEDIATION PLAN

As noted, the success (or failure) of a remediation plan largely depends on the utility of the plan itself. If a program has been clear about the observed behaviors of concern (that align directly with program and professional standards for competence), then creation of the plan itself can commence (Wu et al., 2010). In addition to the reasons discussed earlier, if the description of problem behavior is unclear or vague, then it will be very difficult for a program to later evaluate whether remediation has been successful.

Who Is Involved?

Multiple relevant stakeholders should be involved in the process of creating and reviewing the plan (Kaslow et al., 2014; Katz et al., 2010). Although each party may not be directly involved in articulating specific remediation activities per se, various stakeholders can be included in discussions about the plan, and some parties must review the plan to ensure a united front. Stakeholders certainly include the trainee and all relevant trainers, who may be both within (e.g., training program director) and outside (e.g., external supervisor) of the training program environment. In addition, if the training program is situated within a university or professional school, department administrators and graduate school leadership should be involved to ensure comprehensive communication of action plans. It also is very helpful to have legal counsel review a draft remediation plan to minimize liability and ensure that program requests are permissible under the law (Gilfoyle, 2008). Other parties that may be relevant include student affairs, Title IX coordinators, support and accessibility services, and equal opportunity consultants. Keep in mind that the content of the remediation plan (e.g., articulation of problem behavior and remediation strategies) is really up to the trainers. Other parties are involved for communication's sake and to provide additional feedback where relevant. For example, legal counsel can be helpful in giving feedback to trainers regarding any gaps in the conceptualization of observable problem behaviors or remediation strategies.

What Is Included?

As an overarching guideline, the remediation plan should be individualized and tailored to the specific competence problems and needs of the trainee. Vacha-Haase and colleagues (2019) provided a helpful checklist for the essential, specific components of effective remediation plans. As discussed, the plan should include clear articulation of the competence problem and the area of professional competency to be remediated. The problem must be tied to training program goals and professional competency standards, and specific criteria for determination of remediation success (e.g., competency benchmarks) should be included. Next, multiple mechanisms for remediation should be articulated. Specifically, the plan should list the planned activities to be implemented in order to acquire or reacquire competence. Along with each, the plan should further articulate the time frame for completion, the designated supervisor(s), the responsibilities of the trainee and supervisor(s), the assessment strategies to be used to evaluate success, and the expected level of achievement for each assessment at completion. In addition, the remediation plan should specify the specific consequences of successful remediation or failure to remediate. Finally, the plan should clarify what information in the remediation process will be shared and with whom, who was involved in the design of the remediation plan, and who will be involved in the implementation and evaluation of the remediation plan. Signatures from the trainee, director of training, and any relevant trainers (direct mentors or supervisors) also are included. A helpful remediation plan template created by the Ad Hoc Working Group on Trainees With Competence Problems can be found in Appendix C to this volume.

SELECTING AND IMPLEMENTING REMEDIATION ACTIVITIES

Transparency is key in identifying specific remediation activities for each competence issue, just as it is in linking competence problems to professional standards. The more clearly a competence problem is linked to a specific learning opportunity, the more likely the remediation strategy is to be successful. Moreover, good remediation plans articulate potential mechanisms of action that help bridge the trainee's engagement in any given remediation activity and the desired competency outcomes. For example, it may be suggested that a trainee review a video recording of a therapy session to promote self-awareness and deportment skills. The plan could then articulate that deliberate practice, an evidence-based technique incorporating repetition to develop mastery (e.g., Anders Ericsson, 2008; Rousmaniere, 2016), may be used in the context of this activity to promote competence development in these areas. Next, two competency target domains that may be of focus during remediation are described, including foundational and functional competencies. Each is followed by a nonexhaustive discussion of potential remediation strategies. We also include a section on considerations in suggesting personal psychotherapy as part of remediation.

Enhance Foundational Competencies

Foundational competencies involve basic, cross-cutting skills that inform all areas of psychologists' work such as interpersonal skills and multicultural competencies (Kaslow, Rubin, Forrest, et al., 2007). Professionalism, another foundational skill, has historically been understudied in psychology (Grus & Kaslow, 2014; Grus et al., 2017), rendering remediation in this domain quite challenging (Bennett et al., 2005; Papadakis et al., 2008). Some possible activities for remediation of foundational competencies could include the following:

- watch therapy videos (one's own and/or others) and analyze particular skills;
- utilize deliberate practice to hone attunement and emotion regulation strategies in therapy sessions;
- develop a concrete self-care plan and monitoring strategies;
- articulate professional values with which one is struggling;
- obtain, compare, and integrate self-, peer, and trainer assessments (e.g., 360-degree evaluation);
- practice reflective journaling following professional activities; and/or
- consult with others who have successfully navigated similar challenges (e.g., Kaslow et al., 2018; Vacha-Haase et al., 2019).

Enhance Functional Competencies

Functional competencies involve precise, technical skills required to carry out specific activities of psychologists such as assessment, intervention, research, and consultation (Kaslow, Rubin, Forrest, et al., 2007). To develop functional competencies in a specific area, a trainee may do the following:

- repeat a failed course,
- attend external trainings,
- obtain tutoring or additional mentorship,
- conduct a literature or systematic review,

- read and report about a book,
- teach a class or workshop session,
- administer and score additional assessments,
- take on additional clients with certain presenting problems or use certain intervention approaches,
- engage in additional supervision,
- transcribe therapy sessions and identify choice points, and/or
- respond to vignettes or other problem-based learning techniques (e.g., Vacha-Haase et al., 2019).

What About Personal Psychotherapy?

Personal psychotherapy has, historically, been a common remediation strategy for trainees exhibiting competence problems (Elman & Forrest, 2004; Forrest et al., 1999). This suggestion presumably flows from an understandable belief by trainers that a trainee's professional functioning may benefit from engagement in personal psychotherapy, particularly if the competence problems are related to professionalism and/or interpersonal functioning. However, as Forrest and colleagues (2021) discussed, requiring personal psychotherapy as part of a remediation plan invites a host of ethical challenges involving boundary and role violations, voluntariness, and confidentiality. Requiring psychotherapy as part of remediation smacks of speculation about psychological root causes for professional competence problems; as noted earlier, this places trainers in a problematic and unethical multiple relationship with the trainee, which is not appropriate. Further, in most cases, therapy should be a choice of the client involved. Mandating therapy for trainees who do not wish to engage in therapy is unlikely to be productive. In addition, there is an equity in requiring therapy that may come at significant cost for uninsured or underinsured trainees. Finally, although trainees are not afforded identical confidentiality protections by trainers as clients are by their therapists, trainees as clients are importantly protected by client confidentiality regulations. This is an important benefit for the trainee, but it becomes difficult for a training program to monitor trainee progress in personal psychotherapy when these confidentiality restrictions are in place.

Under certain conditions, personal psychotherapy may be a helpful adjunct, but should not be a central component, to remediation plans centered on educational activities. If a trainee chooses to receive psychotherapy as part of their remediation (e.g., as part of self-care action plans, in response to documented and disclosed conditions), this could be appropriate. A therapist unaffiliated with the training program should provide the treatment, the focus of treatment should be clear, and the sharing of information (or lack thereof) with the program should be clarified at the outset. For example, if a trainee elects to receive therapy and is willing to do so, they could sign a release of information for the therapist to receive information about the remediation plan and/or for the therapist to relay certain information with trainers (e.g., attendance, general progress comments). In short, trainers may recommend personal psychotherapy, but it should not be required. (For extended discussions of this issue, see Forrest & Elman, 2005, 2014; Forrest et al., 2021; and Chapter 7, this volume.)

EVALUATING REMEDIATION PLANS

Perhaps one of the more challenging aspects of remediation is evaluating whether it has been successful. However, this task can be made easier (or at the very least, more transparent) by accurate assessment of the competence problem vis-à-vis professional standards and training program goals, clear linkages of the competence problem(s) and learning opportunities (i.e., remediation activities), direct descriptions of expected performance (and deadlines for exhibiting competent behavior), and unambiguous articulation of outcomes of successful versus unsuccessful remediation. In other words, without a strong foundation early in the process of remediation, trainers may be left with difficult decisions about what to do next, not to mention the ethical and legal risks associated with the tension between providing adequate support and due process for the student versus upholding essential gatekeeping responsibilities (Cobb & Jordan, 1989; Gaubatz & Vera, 2006; Johnson et al., 2008).

The goal of evaluation is to identify whether progress has been made and if this progress is sufficient to meet minimal competency standards. Such evaluation must occur for each target behavior identified in the remediation plan itself. Recall that in your well-crafted remediation plan, you have already identified minimal standards for reaching each threshold of competence and the time frame in which this goal attainment is expected. You also have articulated who is responsible for monitoring the implementation and evaluation of each activity and how the outcomes of these activities will be assessed.

Just as it was recommended that multiple remediation activities be linked with each target behavior in order to offer the student several learning opportunities in which they can demonstrate improved competency, a multitrait, multimethod, multi-informant approach to assessing the outcomes of remediation is recommended (Kaslow et al., 2018). Self-assessments, trainer assessments, peer assessments, and observations may be used. See Exhibit 6.1 for an example of remediation activities and associated evaluation plans for a trainee who is struggling with accurate statistical analysis and reporting of research results. As demonstrated in this excerpt of a sample remediation plan, activities and evaluation involve multiple trainers, not just the trainer(s) who first identified the competency issue. This communicates that remediation (and evaluation of remediation activities) is a program-level process and not the result of a single trainer's agenda. Involving multiple trainers helps to prevent potential splitting and triangulation, particularly in remediation situations in which the student may be particularly distressed or uncooperative with the process. Moreover, the more trainers involved, the more fair the process can be for the student because bias across evaluation will likely be minimized.

EXHIBIT 6.1. Sample Excerpt From a Trainee Remediation Plan

Competence problem	Conducting accurate statistical analyses	Creating accurate reports of statistical results
Associated competency standard(s): Competency Benchmarks 6A, Scientific Mindedness; and 6B, Scientific Foundations of Psychology		
Learning Opportunity 1	Retake statistics course (PSY 650: General Linear Models I)	Read a book focused on reporting statistical results, such as *Write It Up* by Paul J. Silvia (2015)
Supervisor(s)	Dr. A. Nova (course instructor), Dr. D. C. Training (program director)	Dr. A. D. Visor (research mentor)
Expected level of competency	Obtain a passing course grade	Accurately extract strategies for writing results
Evaluation	Complete weekly homework assignments, midterm exam, and final exam; self-assessment of statistical skills	Develop an outline of strategies; meet with research mentor to discuss
Time frame	Fall semester	Spring semester
Learning Opportunity 2	Attend external statistical workshop	Prepare Results section of master's thesis
Supervisor(s)	Workshop instructor (to be determined), Dr. A. D. Visor (research mentor)	Dr. A. D. Visor (research mentor), Master's Thesis Committee
Expected level of competency	Engage with workshop; reflect learning objectives; articulate applications of learning to master's research	Write an accurate Results section with minimal errors (appropriate to stage of training)

EXHIBIT 6.1. Sample Excerpt From a Trainee Remediation Plan (*Continued*)

Competence problem	Conducting accurate statistical analyses	Creating accurate reports of statistical results
Evaluation	Present documentation of attendance; write a brief reflection paper (one to two pages) on major takeaways; meet with mentor to discuss applications to master's research project	Review of written Results section by committee; give oral presentation of results in committee meeting
Time frame	Spring semester	Summer semester
Learning Opportunity 3	Present mini-lesson in department research seminar	Prepare conference presentation proposal
Supervisor(s)	Dr. R. Brownbag (seminar instructor), Research Training Committee	Supervisor: Dr. A. D. Visor (research mentor), Research Training Committee
Expected level of competency	Understand basic applications of research methodology and data analysis; accurately communicate basic data analytic strategies (e.g., moderated regression)	Prepare a conference presentation proposal with minimal (developmentally appropriate) assistance from mentor; accurately report results in the proposal
Evaluation	Obtain a research seminar evaluation form (completed by attending faculty, peer trainees, and trainee)	Review of conference proposal by mentor and committee
Time frame	Spring semester	Summer semester

Note. Additional required elements for a remediation plan are not included. See the template in Appendix C of this volume for additional categories to include.

PROVISION OF ONGOING FEEDBACK

Feedback regarding the trainee's progress (or lack thereof) toward expected competency should be provided at ongoing in-person meetings at regular intervals throughout the remediation process. Attendees should include the trainee, trainers, and any trainee advocates, if requested by the trainee. Documentation of each meeting should be clear and included in the trainee's student file.

Feedback also should be provided in written format. To this point in the process, the trainee will have received (a) a letter identifying the competence problem and soliciting the trainee's self-assessment of the issue and (b) a letter detailing the remediation plan or the remediation plan itself. The trainee should also be provided all letters with updates on the process, their progress, and any changes made to the plan (if needed). Care should be taken at each stage to consider any ethical, legal, and training implications of any changes to the remediation plan. Of course, a final letter detailing the outcome of the overall evaluation of the remediation plan and the trainee's status following evaluation (e.g., no longer on remediation) should be provided at the conclusion of the remediation period. A program may wish to reiterate in this final letter whether and what information about remediation will be included in the training director's portion of the trainee's APPIC (n.d.) application or in communication to licensure and other regulatory boards or credentialing organizations. At all points during this process, trainers should clearly communicate whether the trainee's progress is satisfactory and continue to discuss with the trainee what will happen if competency standards are not met following remediation (e.g., further remediation, probationary status, dismissal).

MINDING THE SYSTEMIC CONTEXT OF REMEDIATION

It has been acknowledged and underscored by competency scholars that a systemic, or ecological, approach to understanding and supporting competence problems is critically important (e.g., Behnke, 2008; Elman et al., 1999; Forrest et al., 2008; Johnson et al., 2014; see also Chapter 4, this volume). We know that trainees' competence problems do not occur in isolation, in terms of both their causes and their consequences, and these problems have the potential to negatively impact all levels of a system (e.g., peer trainees, trainers; Shen-Miller et al., 2011, 2015). As such, it is important to prepare the system for successful remediation efforts.

Trainees With Competence Problems

It is essential for trainers to keep in mind that trainees are very likely to feel distressed at times during, or even throughout, this process. In the only study to specifically examine the experiences of trainees during remediation, Kallaugher and Mollen (2017) discussed that trainees may be confused if the process is unclear, they may feel angry and resentful if they perceive remediation to be malicious in nature, and they may suspect that negative perceptions (by other trainees and/or trainers) will follow them throughout their time in the program, regardless of whether they successfully complete their remediation plan. Further, trainees may have concerns about their ability to progress through the professional pipeline, beyond their time in residence in the program (e.g., internship or licensure).

Peer Trainees

Peers of trainees with competence problems also appear to be impacted, potentially negatively, by the experience. Some studies suggest that peers are often the first (and sometimes only) to know about a trainee who is struggling with competence, yet they often avoid direct confrontation or action and may instead withdraw from and/or talk with other trainees about the peer (Gaubatz & Vera, 2006; Rosenberg et al., 2005; Shen-Miller et al., 2011, 2015). In any event, peers of struggling trainees consistently report strong emotional reactions to these situations, including anger, frustration, and resentment (e.g., Mearns & Allen, 1991; Oliver et al., 2004; Shen-Miller et al., 2015; Veilleux et al., 2012).

Trainers

Like struggling trainees and their peers, trainers themselves also are deeply affected by the experience of intervening with competence problems. Jacobs and colleagues (2011) detailed myriad challenges associated with confronting trainees with competence problems, including both fear and empathy regarding the trainee. Gizara and Forrest (2004) further highlighted that the personal impact of trainees with competence problems on trainers is often among the most difficult parts of the process to manage. Supervisors in their qualitative study discussed the experience as "painful" and "gut-wrenching," particularly when the struggling trainee engaged in retaliatory behavior toward trainers.

Training Program Culture

Just as addressing competence problems can positively influence a system, it also has a high potential for "cultural fallout," given the necessary ethical and legal restrictions on sharing information across a system. Specifically, trainees' shame, misinterpretation of remediation, and level of disclosure about competence issues to peers, coupled with trainers' necessary public silence on the issues, may lead to confusion among peers and even other trainers not directly involved. In extreme cases, these issues can lead to splitting, triangulation, enmeshment, alliances, backlash, and high levels of ongoing distress (Forrest et al., 2013).

So how can we uphold our legal and ethical obligations to provide high-quality training, support students, uphold professional standards, and protect the public, all while preventing cultural damage to our programs? Proactive steps are suggested for trainers to best prepare their systems for addressing problems of professional competence. Trainers should clearly articulate expected competencies and methods of evaluating competency, including the steps involved, what information is shared and with whom, due process procedures, and FERPA restrictions. This information must be shared not just in a program handbook but also in orientations, group program meetings, ethics courses, supervision sessions, and mentor meetings. Some programs benefit from having incoming students (a) review information related to competence evaluation and remediation and (b) provide informed consent to receive this information and to follow expectations.

What's more, and beyond the logistical aspects of our programs, we must create healthy and safe environments where trainees and trainers alike have protected space to succeed, fail, and grow (e.g., "error culture"; Harteis et al., 2008; Leicher et al., 2013). Such an environment is one in which trainers can conceptualize trainees in ecological systemic context; competency attainment can be collaborative, growth oriented, and communitarian in nature; remediation can be normalized as a natural part of training; and the ethical and legal contexts can be acknowledged not just to minimize risk and liability but also to promote fairness to trainees.

NAVIGATING UNSUCCESSFUL REMEDIATION

Infrequently, the outcome of remediation may be unsuccessful. Recall that good remediation plans will articulate what happens if the required competencies are not attained following remediation efforts. These outcomes typically involve dismissal, which may or may not be voluntary in nature (sometimes referred to as "counseling out"). In any event, programs should avoid a second remediation for an identical competence issue. Although well meaning, a second remediation may be perceived as stringing a student along. It requires additional and unnecessary financial commitment by the student, if eventually dismissed, and undermines a clear message about professional competency standards. Moreover, it may create future legal jeopardy, opening up the program's future decisions to second-guessing.

Counseling Out

Sometimes, following unsuccessful remediation, the trainee, in collaboration with feedback from trainers, may decide to voluntarily discontinue their training (Knoff & Prout, 1985). In this case, the program can provide support and assistance in determining the trainee's future options. It is important to involve the trainee in conversations during this process so they understand what to expect. Keep in mind that the trainee requires additional support during this time because they are, in effect, in the midst of a career crisis. A program may help a trainee brainstorm other career possibilities and support "face-saving" strategies with peers or other trainees (where accurate and appropriate). It may be possible for the trainee to enter another degree program within the department or university. This helps create a joint sense of collaboration and potential positive future and may reduce the program's liability to an appeals process or future court challenges. It is important to consider our ethical obligations in facilitating transfer, however, if a student hopes to enter another program that will require similar competencies. For example, if a student leaves a doctoral program as a result of insufficient clinical skills, then simply transferring to a master's level program in which clinical work is central may not be indicated. The ethical responsibilities of gatekeeping remain in the context of the counseling out process.

Dismissal

In the case of unsuccessful remediation and if the trainee does not voluntarily leave the program, a program may decide to dismiss the trainee. Dismissal may be academic or disciplinary (see Forrest et al., 1999). *Academic dismissals* are based on academic standards articulated by the training program and/or profession. These academic standards include both functional and foundational competencies, such as interpersonal and/or relational functioning necessary for professional competence. *Disciplinary dismissals* pertain to misconduct, illegal activity, or other violations of rules that typically are separate from the training program and may be handled by other parts of the training institution, such as student affairs. Due process standards in disciplinary dismissals can be more stringent, as they may require more of a moral (as opposed to academic) judgment regarding trainee behavior (Meyer, 1980).

Trainees have multiple avenues for challenging program decisions regarding dismissal. Internally, they can follow the training program or organization's appeals policies and/or file discrimination claims on the basis of identity. Trainers should keep in mind that, at some institutions, trainees are considered employees and thus are protected by and subject to human resources policies and protections. External to the training environment, trainees may pursue legal action by hiring a lawyer and filing a legal complaint; historically, these types of complaints have focused primarily on due process issues. They may also elect to file a discrimination complaint with the U.S. Equal Employment Opportunity Commission. Interns may file a complaint with APPIC. Other avenues for complaints include the American Psychological Association (APA) Commission on Accreditation, the APA Ethics Committee, or state licensing boards.

Court decisions have typically reflected a respect for faculty and/or program rights to determine educational standards and deference to program decisions (see Forrest et al., 1999; and Chapter 9, this volume). This is because courts tend to view trainers as the most knowledgeable to make decisions about professional standards and as the gatekeepers to the profession. As such, challenges to program decisions about trainees with competence problems are typically unsuccessful, provided the program has followed its policies. Common legal risks for trainers in these situations include deprivation of due process (substantive or procedural), promissory estoppel, and defamation. Each is briefly discussed next; more detailed discussions are provided in the literature (Forrest & Campbell, 2012; Gilfoyle, 2008) and in Chapter 9 of this volume.

Deprivation of due process refers to a program's negligence in providing adequate and fair action in response to competence issues (Gilfoyle, 2008). Training programs must afford trainees both substantive and procedural due process (Kerl et al., 2002; McAdams & Foster, 2007). With regard to trainees with competence problems, *substantive due process* focuses on the substance of a program's decision and whether trainers have behaved in an arbitrary or capricious manner toward the trainee. Managing substantive due process risk involves applying policies consistently and fairly; linking evaluations, warnings, and remediation and/or dismissal decisions to established training goals and professional standards or patient care concerns; and treating trainees in similar situations consistently. *Procedural due process* pertains to the process of decision making and whether the trainee has been given proper notice regarding academic and professional standards, evaluations, notice of deficient performance, and an opportunity to be heard. Managing procedural due process risk involves clearly articulating training standards and policies, providing timely and written notice of any problems, allowing the trainee to be heard and to respond to notices of deficient performance, and keeping detailed and accurate documentation of actions taken.

Promissory estoppel refers to a situation in which a program representative (e.g., trainer) misrepresents established training requirements (e.g., evaluation criteria, graduation requirements; Gilfoyle, 2008). Trainees raising promissory estoppel claims must demonstrate that they relied on this misrepresentation to their detriment. In response, a court may choose to enforce the misrepresented statement (which "estops" the program from enforcing its actual rules). To manage this type of risk, programs should periodically review their policies to ensure that all trainers are aware of and enforcing program procedures. Trainers should be regularly reminded that policies, procedures, rules, and actions must be in line with one another and must be applied fairly and consistently across all trainees. Any trainer who does not comply should be met with immediate corrective feedback.

Defamation refers to uttering (slander) or publishing (libel) false facts or implied facts that are damaging to a trainee's reputation (Gilfoyle, 2008). This risk exists for trainers but also for training administrators, and those who publish or otherwise repeat statements may also be liable. Managing defamation risk involves relegating any oral and written statements pertaining to trainees' deficient performance only to the arena of evaluating trainee competence. Any negative opinions of trainee performance should be shared with trainers who have evaluative responsibility to the trainee. If evaluation meetings involve large groups of trainers, this should be specified in program policies (e.g., a handbook), as this provides a basis for trainees' informed consent for information about competency and performance to be shared among group members.

Nonlegal Advice

As a nonlegal scholar, I offer nonlegal guidance for navigating the complexities of dismissal decisions. Any decisions regarding trainee dismissal require specific legal advice from institutional legal representatives, as each competence problem situation will vary depending on organizational policy, state law, and the circumstances of each case. As is hopefully clear, transparency is key, and the law of no surprises should guide each step of the process. All trainers must follow all policies for all students all of the time, and major decisions about remediation and dismissal should reflect a program (as opposed to individual trainer) stance. Policies and procedures are contractual, forming the basis of trainee informed consent, and thus should be readily available to trainees and trainers throughout. All evaluations, warnings, decisions, and actions should be directly tied to program training goals, professional standards, and/or patient care. Document in detail each and every step along the way. Finally, consult, consult, consult. As is apparent in this volume, we encourage a communitarian approach to competence. No single trainer is the penultimate exemplar of competence in any given competence problem situation. Consulting the competency and training literature, as well as individual colleagues with expertise in this area, undoubtedly enhances trainers' ability to successfully support trainees with competence problems and the complexities of remediation and its aftermath.

TAKING STOCK AFTER THE DUST SETTLES

Although it may be tempting to quickly move on from trainee competence problem situations, particularly those that are complex and contentious, it is highly recommended to review what happened in (yes) another meeting. Most of what trainers know about responding to problems of professional competence is learned from experience; remember, this is a trainer competency that must develop. Programs often are not steeped in the professional competence problems literature and thus, however unintentionally, take a reactive approach. As such, a follow-up debriefing session with stakeholders (including the trainee when possible) is essential for learning and moving forward with increased competence. In this meeting, trainers can reflect on what was learned, what could be improved for next time, and whether any policies and procedures should be revised accordingly. The scholarly literature on competence issues also should be consulted to determine whether any new guidance or information is available. This meeting also may be helpful for processing and repairing, if necessary, any ruptures in trainer relationships or trainee–trainer relationships that may have occurred during the process.

CARING FOR OURSELVES IN THIS PROCESS

Situations involving trainees with professional competence problems present a curious dialectic in which we must (a) take action to uphold our training and gatekeeping responsibilities and (b) navigate the range of negative emotions that result from effects on the trainee and peer trainees, disagreements among trainers, and cultural changes in our programs. As psychologists, we can do hard things; ironically, we are often trained to do the very hard things required in competence problem situations (e.g., have difficult conversations). Yet these skills are difficult to apply to ourselves, our trainees, and our colleagues. We do not often readily escape our own humanity, as we—like trainees with competence problems themselves—can feel an understandable avoidance of these situations because they can so deeply impact us both personally and professionally. As one participant in the Gizara and Forrest (2004) study so aptly recalled,

> I think the emotional elements of this experience don't get validated because there's not enough out there on the topic. So knowing people's affective reactions to working on these situations. To get validation. I think I'd like that for myself personally. . . . I would find that helpful. (p. 137)

To maintain good balance in order to navigate this challenging dialectic, we must attend to ourselves and our needs in this process. There surely is no one-size-fits-all approach for any given trainer or any given trainee competence problem situation. However, we can use what we know as psychology trainers and humbly apply it to ourselves. First, we must get over ourselves, in a sense. We are human, we are imperfectible, and we cannot, no matter how hard we try, ensure that we will never make a mistake, always avoid emotional reactions, or be able to prevent or remedy every trainee competence issue. Acceptance of this can go a long way in helping us to set down any defensiveness that is understandably triggered in these situations. Second, we must acknowledge the need for self-care and support. As easily surmised from the literature or from talking to just about any trainer who has been in these situations, we have emotional reactions (e.g., stress, sadness, frustration) that deserve (and I would argue, require) attention. We regularly teach others how to care for themselves and ask for support. It's high time we followed suit. Finally, let's look out for one another. As is self-care, colleague care is an ethical imperative (see Standards 1.04, Informal Resolution of Ethical Violations, and 2.06, Personal Problems and Conflicts, in APA, 2017). Reach out to your colleagues navigating these challenges. Ask them what they need. Talk about your own experiences. Be a visible part of their competent community.

REFERENCES

American Psychological Association. (2017). *Ethical principles of psychologists and code of conduct* (2002, amended effective June 1, 2010, and January 1, 2017). https://www.apa.org/ethics/code/index

Anders Ericsson, K. (2008). Deliberate practice and acquisition of expert performance: A general overview. *Academic Emergency Medicine, 15*(11), 988–994. https://doi.org/10.1111/j.1553-2712.2008.00227.x

Association of Psychology Postdoctoral Internship Centers. (n.d.). *Sample APPI.* https://www.appic.org/Portals/0/downloads/Example_AAPI_Online_Application_Basic_2017.pdf

Behnke, S. H. (2008). Discussion: Toward elaborating and implementing a conceptualization of healthy, safe training environments. *Training and Education in Professional Psychology, 2*(4), 215–218. https://doi.org/10.1037/a0014008

Bennett, A. J., Roman, B., Arnold, L. M., Kay, J., & Goldenhar, L. M. (2005). Professionalism deficits among medical students: Models of identification and intervention. *Academic Psychiatry, 29*(5), 426–432. https://doi.org/10.1176/appi.ap.29.5.426

Cobb, N. H., & Jordan, C. (1989). Students with questionable values or threatening behavior: Precedent and policy from discipline to dismissal. *Journal of Social Work Education, 25*(2), 87–97. https://doi.org/10.1080/10437797.1989.10672117

Collins, C., Falender, C., & Shafranske, E. (2011). Commentary on Rebecca Schwartz-Mette's 2009 article, "Challenges in addressing graduate student impairment in academic professional psychology programs." *Ethics & Behavior, 21*(5), 428–430. https://doi.org/10.1080/10508422.2011.604547

Elman, N., Forrest, L., Vacha-Haase, T., & Gizara, S. (1999). A systems perspective on trainee impairment: Continuing the dialogue. *The Counseling Psychologist, 27*(5), 712–721. https://doi.org/10.1177/0011000099275005

Elman, N. S., & Forrest, L. (2004). Psychotherapy in the remediation of psychology trainees: Exploratory interviews with training directors. *Professional Psychology: Research and Practice, 35*(2), 123–130. https://doi.org/10.1037/0735-7028.35.2.123

Elman, N. S., & Forrest, L. (2007). From *trainee impairment* to *professional competence problems*: Seeking new terminology that facilitates effective action. *Professional Psychology: Research and Practice, 38*(5), 501–509. https://doi.org/10.1037/0735-7028.38.5.501

Falender, C. A., Collins, C. J., & Shafranske, E. P. (2009). "Impairment" and performance issues in clinical supervision: After the 2008 ADA Amendments Act. *Training and Education in Professional Psychology, 3*(4), 240–249. https://doi.org/10.1037/a0017153

Falender, C. A., & Shafranske, E. P. (2004). *Clinical supervision: A competency-based approach*. American Psychological Association. https://doi.org/10.1037/10806-000

Family Educational Rights and Privacy Act. 20 U.S.C. § 1232g; 34 CFR Part 99 (1974).

Forrest, L., & Campbell, L. F. (2012). Emerging trends in counseling psychology education and training. In N. Fouad, J. Carter, & L. Subich (Eds.), *APA handbook of counseling psychology: Vol. 1. Theories, research, and methods* (pp. 119–154). American Psychological Association. https://doi.org/10.1037/13754-005

Forrest, L., Elman, N., Gizara, S., & Vacha-Haase, T. (1999). Trainee impairment: A review of identification, remediation, dismissal, and legal issues. *The Counseling Psychologist, 27*(5), 627–686. https://doi.org/10.1177/0011000099275001

Forrest, L., & Elman, N. S. (2005). Psychotherapy for poorly performing trainees: Are there limits to confidentiality? *Psychotherapy Bulletin, 40*(4), 29–37.

Forrest, L., & Elman, N. S. (2014). Trainees with problems of professional competence. In W. B. Johnson & N. J. Kaslow (Eds.), *The Oxford handbook of education and training in professional psychology* (pp. 314–335). Oxford University Press.

Forrest, L., Elman, N. S., Bodner, K. E., & Kaslow, N. J. (2021). Trainee confidentiality: Confusions, complexities, consequences, and possibilities. *Training and Education in Professional Psychology*. Advance online publication. https://doi.org/10.1037/tep0000364

Forrest, L., Elman, N. S., Huprich, S. K., Veilleux, J. C., Jacobs, S. C., & Kaslow, N. J. (2013). Training directors' perceptions of faculty behaviors when dealing with trainee competence problems: A mixed method pilot study. *Training and Education in Professional Psychology, 7*(1), 23–32. https://doi.org/10.1037/a0032068

Forrest, L., Shen-Miller, D. S., & Elman, N. S. (2008). Psychology trainees with competence problems: From individual to ecological conceptualizations. *Training and Education in Professional Psychology, 2*(4), 183–192. https://doi.org/10.1037/1931-3918.2.4.183

Fouad, N. A., Grus, C. L., Hatcher, R. L., Kaslow, N. J., Hutchings, P. S., Madson, M. B., Collins, F. L., Jr., & Crossman, R. E. (2009). Competency benchmarks: A model for understanding and measuring competence in professional psychology across training levels. *Training and Education in Professional Psychology, 3*(4, Suppl.), S5–S26. https://doi.org/10.1037/a0015832

Gaubatz, M. D., & Vera, E. M. (2006). Trainee competence in master's level counseling programs: A comparison of counselor educators' and students' views. *Counselor Education and Supervision, 46*(1), 32–43. https://doi.org/10.1002/j.1556-6978.2006.tb00010.x

Gilfoyle, N. (2008). The legal exosystem: Risk management in addressing student competence problems in professional psychology training. *Training and Education in Professional Psychology, 2*(4), 202–209. https://doi.org/10.1037/1931-3918.2.4.202

Gizara, S. S., & Forrest, L. (2004). Supervisors' experiences of trainee impairment and incompetence at APA-accredited internship sites. *Professional Psychology: Research and Practice, 35*(2), 131–140. https://doi.org/10.1037/0735-7028.35.2.131

Grus, C. L., & Kaslow, N. J. (2014). Professionalism: Professional values and attitudes in psychology. In W. B. Johnson & N. J. Kaslow (Eds.), *Oxford handbook of education and training in professional psychology* (pp. 491–509). Oxford University Press.

Grus, C. L., Shen-Miller, D. S., Lease, S. H., Jacobs, S. C., Bodner, K. E., Van Sickle, K. S., Veilleux, J., & Kaslow, N. J. (2017). Professionalism: A competency cluster whose time has come. *Ethics & Behavior, 28*(6), 450–464. https://doi.org/10.1080/10508422.2017.1419133

Harteis, C., Bauer, J., & Gruber, H. (2008). The culture of learning from mistakes: How employees handle mistakes in everyday work. *International Journal of Educational Research, 47*(4), 223–231. https://doi.org/10.1016/j.ijer.2008.07.003

Jacobs, S. C., Huprich, S. K., Grus, C. L., Cage, E. A., Elman, N. S., Forrest, L., Schwartz-Mette, R., Shen-Miller, D. S., Van Sickle, K. S., & Kaslow, N. J. (2011). Trainees with professional competency problems: Preparing trainers for difficult but necessary conversations. *Training and Education in Professional Psychology, 5*(3), 175–184. https://doi.org/10.1037/a0024656

Johnson, W. B., Barnett, J. E., Elman, N. S., Forrest, L., Schwartz-Mette, R., & Kaslow, N. J. (2014). Preparing trainees for lifelong competence: Creating a communitarian training culture. *Training and Education in Professional Psychology, 8*(4), 211–220. https://doi.org/10.1037/tep0000048

Johnson, W. B., Elman, N. S., Forrest, L., Robiner, W. N., Rodolfa, E., & Schaffer, J. B. (2008). Addressing professional competence problems in trainees: Some ethical considerations. *Professional Psychology: Research and Practice, 39*(6), 589–599. https://doi.org/10.1037/a0014264

Kallaugher, J., & Mollen, D. (2017). Student experiences of remediation in their graduate psychology programs. *Training and Education in Professional Psychology, 11*(4), 276–282. https://doi.org/10.1037/tep0000175

Kaslow, N. J., Grus, C. L., Allbaugh, L. J., Shen-Miller, D., Bodner, K. E., Veilleux, J., & Van Sickle, K. (2018). Trainees with competence problems in the professionalism domain. *Ethics & Behavior, 28*(6), 429–449. https://doi.org/10.1080/10508422.2018.1438897

Kaslow, N. J., Grus, C. L., Campbell, L. F., Fouad, N. A., Hatcher, R. L., & Rodolfa, E. R. (2009). Competency Assessment Toolkit for professional psychology. *Training and Education in Professional Psychology, 3*(4, Suppl.), S27–S45. https://doi.org/10.1037/a0015833

Kaslow, N. J., Johnson, W. B., & Schwartz, A. C. (2014). When training goes awry. In W. B. Johnson & N. J. Kaslow (Eds.), *The Oxford handbook of education and training in professional psychology* (pp. 377–393). Oxford University Press.

Kaslow, N. J., Rubin, N. J., Bebeau, M. J., Leigh, I. W., Lichtenberg, J. W., Nelson, P. D., Portnoy, S. M., & Smith, I. L. (2007). Guiding principles and recommendations for the assessment of competence. *Professional Psychology: Research and Practice, 38*(5), 441–451. https://doi.org/10.1037/0735-7028.38.5.441

Kaslow, N. J., Rubin, N. J., Forrest, L., Elman, N. S., Van Horne, B. A., Jacobs, S. C., Huprich, S. K., Benton, S. A., Pantesco, V. F., Dollinger, S. J., Grus, C. L., Behnke, S. H., Miller, D. S. S., Shealy, C. N., Mintz, L. B., Schwartz-Mette, R., Van Sickle, K., & Thorn, B. E. (2007). Recognizing, assessing, and intervening with problems of professional competence. *Professional Psychology: Research and Practice, 38*(5), 479–492. https://doi.org/10.1037/0735-7028.38.5.479

Katz, E. D., Dahms, R., Sadosty, A. T., Stahmer, S. A., Goyal, D., & the CORD-EM Remediation Task Force. (2010). Guiding principles for resident remediation: Recommendations of the CORD Remediation Task Force. *Academic Emergency Medicine, 17*(Suppl. 2), S95–S103. https://doi.org/10.1111/j.1553-2712.2010.00881.x

Kerl, S. B., Garcia, J. L., McCullough, S., & Maxwell, M. E. (2002). Systematic evaluation of professional performance: Legally supported procedure and process. *Counselor Education and Supervision, 41*(4), 321–332. https://doi.org/10.1002/j.1556-6978.2002.tb01294.x

Knoff, H. M., & Prout, H. T. (1985). Terminating students from professional psychology programs: Criteria, procedures, and legal issues. *Professional Psychology: Research and Practice, 16*(6), 789–797. https://doi.org/10.1037/0735-7028.16.6.789

Leicher, V., Mulder, R. H., & Bauer, J. (2013). Learning from errors at work: A replication study in elder care nursing. *Vocations and Learning, 6*(2), 207–220. https://doi.org/10.1007/s12186-012-9090-0

McAdams, C. R., III, & Foster, V. A. (2007). A guide to just and fair remediation of counseling students with professional performance deficiencies. *Counselor Education and Supervision, 47*(1), 2–13. https://doi.org/10.1002/j.1556-6978.2007.tb00034.x

Mearns, J., & Allen, G. J. (1991). Graduate students' experiences in dealing with impaired peers compared with faculty predictions: An exploratory study. *Ethics & Behavior, 1*(3), 191–202. https://doi.org/10.1207/s15327019eb0103_3

Meyer, R. G. (1980). Legal and procedural issues in the evaluation of clinical graduate students. *The Clinical Psychologist, 33*(4), 15–17.

Oliver, M. N. I., Bernstein, J. H., Anderson, K. G., Blashfield, R. K., & Roberts, M. C. (2004). An exploratory examination of student attitudes toward "impaired" peers in clinical psychology training programs. *Professional Psychology: Research and Practice, 35*(2), 141–147. https://doi.org/10.1037/0735-7028.35.2.141

Papadakis, M. A., Arnold, G. K., Blank, L. L., Holmboe, E. S., & Lipner, R. S. (2008). Performance during internal medicine residency training and subsequent disciplinary action by state licensing boards. *Annals of Internal Medicine, 148*(11), 869–876. https://doi.org/10.7326/0003-4819-148-11-200806030-00009

Robiner, W. N., Fuhrman, M., & Ristvedt, S. L. (1993). Evaluation difficulties in supervising psychology interns. *The Clinical Psychologist, 46*, 3–13.

Rodolfa, E., Bent, R., Eisman, E., Nelson, P., Rehm, L., & Ritchie, P. (2005). A cube model for competency development: Implications for psychology educators and regulators. *Professional Psychology: Research and Practice, 36*(4), 347–354. https://doi.org/10.1037/0735-7028.36.4.347

Rosenberg, J. I., Getzelman, M. A., Arcinue, F., & Oren, C. Z. (2005). An exploratory look at students' experiences of problematic peers in academic professional psychology programs. *Professional Psychology: Research and Practice, 36*(6), 665–673. https://doi.org/10.1037/0735-7028.36.6.665

Rousmaniere, T. (2016). *Deliberate practice for psychologists: A guide to improving clinical effectiveness*. Taylor & Francis. https://doi.org/10.4324/9781315472256

Schwartz-Mette, R. (2011). Out with *impairment*, in with *professional competence problems*: Response to commentary by Collins, Falender, and Shafranske. *Ethics & Behavior, 21*(5), 431–434. https://doi.org/10.1080/10508422.2011.604551

Shen-Miller, D. S., Grus, C. L., Van Sickle, K., Schwartz-Mette, R., Cage, E., Elman, N. S., Jacobs, S. C., & Kaslow, N. J. (2011). Trainees' experiences with peers having competence problems: A national survey. *Training and Education in Professional Psychology, 5*(2), 112–121. https://doi.org/10.1037/a0023824

Shen-Miller, D. S., Schwartz-Mette, R., Van Sickle, K., Jacobs, S. C., Grus, C. L., Hunter, E., & Forrest, L. (2015). Professional competence problems in training: A qualitative investigation of trainee perspectives. *Training and Education in Professional Psychology, 9*(2), 161–169. https://doi.org/10.1037/tep0000072

Silvia, P. J. (2015). *Write it up: Practical strategies for writing and publishing journal articles*. American Psychological Association. https://doi.org/10.1037/14470-000

Vacha-Haase, T., Elman, N. S., Forrest, L., Kallaugher, J., Lease, S. H., Veilleux, J. C., & Kaslow, N. J. (2019). Remediation plans for trainees with problems of professional competence. *Training and Education in Professional Psychology, 13*(4), 239–246. https://doi.org/10.1037/tep0000221

Veilleux, J. C., January, A. M., VanderVeen, J. W., Reddy, L. F., & Klonoff, E. A. (2012). Differentiating amongst characteristics associated with problems of professional competence: Perceptions of graduate student peers. *Training and Education in Professional Psychology, 6*(2), 113–121. https://doi.org/10.1037/a0028337

Wu, J. S., Siewert, B., & Boiselle, P. M. (2010). Resident evaluation and remediation: A comprehensive approach. *Journal of Graduate Medical Education, 2*(2), 242–245. https://doi.org/10.4300/JGME-D-10-00031.1

7
TRAINEE CONFIDENTIALITY
The Hidden Challenge of Competence Problems

LINDA M. FORREST AND NANCY S. ELMAN

A thorough coverage of the topic of trainees[1] with problems of professional competence (TPPC) requires attention to trainee confidentiality (TC). Yet scholarship focused on TC in psychology training is limited to one article focused on TC (Forrest et al., 2022), a few articles that comment on TC issues (Behnke, 2014; Elman & Forrest, 2004; Forrest & Elman, 2005, 2014; Gilfoyle, 2008; Kaslow et al., 2007), and coverage of TC in the supervision literature (American Psychological Association [APA], 2014; Ellis, 2017; Thomas, 2010). We surmise that TC has received little attention by training programs, except perhaps when TC concerns surface when responding to TPPC. The effects of TC are likely out of trainers' awareness, function covertly, and create unintentional sub rosa program dynamics. In this chapter, we synthesize the existing knowledge on TC while focusing on complexities and consequences created by current TC practices that reverberate across the training system. We present systemic frameworks (communitarian, secrets

---

[1] We have chosen to use the terms *trainer* and *trainee* because each of these terms is inclusive and captures multiple categories of individuals. The term *trainer* includes faculty, supervisors, and others involved in overseeing and evaluating trainees. The term *trainee* includes students, interns, and postdoctoral trainees.

https://doi.org/10.1037/0000340-008
Supporting Trainees With Competence Problems: A Practical Guide for Psychology Trainers, R. A. Schwartz-Mette, E. A. Hunter, and N. J. Kaslow (Editors)
Copyright © 2023 by the American Psychological Association. All rights reserved.

in systems, and just culture) to expand awareness of TC effects beyond the individual trainee to interactions and/or dynamics among training components. We propose that TC exists along a continuum from substantial to more limited, and we explore the benefits of expanding the boundaries of TC to include greater transparency and openness across the training program. We close with recommendations to assist training programs, trainers, and trainees in dealing effectively with TC.

To meet trainer gatekeeper responsibilities and provide transparency to the profession and public (Bodner, 2012), TC may need to be limited. Yet we know little about when, where, and why trainers place limits on TC or whether programs provide trainees with adequate informed consent about limits to their confidentiality. Without clear TC policies, trainers may not have addressed disagreements among themselves about limits to TC and may be uncertain about what they can share with other trainers or peer trainees. Trainees may think they have confidentiality only to discover at the worst possible moment that they do not. Such surprises may cause trainees to lose trust and confidence in their trainers, making remediation efforts unnecessarily challenging (Kallaugher & Mollen, 2017; Vacha-Haase et al., 2019). Peers of the TPPC may be confused and uncertain about their responsibilities (e.g., address the TPPC directly, share concerns with faculty, or question whether it is even their business). In addition, trainers may believe that confidentiality protects a TPPC from any further psychological harm and stigma, while they also struggle with what to share with other trainers and trainees who come to them with concerns about a TPPC. Most troublesome is when peers request confidentiality prior to sharing their concerns about a fellow trainee. Our consultations over the last 2 decades with training directors, faculty, and supervisors have anecdotally identified and confirmed many of the above-listed concerns.

Some of the uncertainty associated with TC may be the result of an unexamined application of psychology's high standard of client confidentiality to trainees. Yet trainees are not clients; they are engaged in training to become professional psychologists (Forrest et al., 2022). Joining a profession requires an individual to agree to be evaluated and regulated by training programs and licensing boards (Vacha-Haase et al., 2019). The *right to privacy* provides freedom from exposure or intrusion into one's personal matters (Moskop et al., 2005). Psychology trainees are afforded this privacy for personal information as long as it is not relevant to professional competence. In contrast, *confidentiality* refers to the duty of professionals to disclose information only with consent except when allowed or required by ethical or legal standards. Responsibility for decisions about the limits of confidentiality rests with trainers, not trainees. Because personal backgrounds can affect professional performance and may result in client safety issues, trainers hold the responsibility for determining and communicating the limits of TC and under what circumstances it will be breached (Behnke, 2014; Bodner, 2012; Forrest et al., 2022).

Although little has been published on TC, we believe how programs manage TC greatly influences relationships among trainees, between trainers and trainees, and among trainers as well as program outcomes (e.g., remediations, dismissals). Our goal in this chapter is to help prepare trainers and trainees to successfully address TC within programs and throughout their professional careers.

IMPACT OF TRAINEE CONFIDENTIALITY ON TRAINING ENVIRONMENT

Confusion, misinformation, and disagreements exist among trainers about how to manage TC. In this section, we review unintended consequences of TC on relationships and communications (a) among trainees, (b) between trainers and trainees, and (c) among trainers. See Forrest et al. (2022) for a full description of tensions created by TC.

Tensions Among Peer Trainees

There is a growing empirical literature on peer trainees' perceptions and reactions to the presence of a TPPC. We identified 13 studies of peer trainees: Ten used survey data (Brown-Rice & Furr, 2013, 2019; Furr & Brown-Rice, 2018; Gaubatz & Vera, 2006; Magsam, 2021; Mearns & Allen, 1991; Oliver et al., 2004; Rosenberg et al., 2005; Shen-Miller et al., 2011; Veilleux et al., 2012) and three used interview data (Foster et al., 2014; Parker et al., 2014; Shen-Miller et al., 2015). Across these studies, peers reported knowing someone in their program with problems of professional competence (PPC); the percentages varied from 44% (Shen-Miller et al., 2011) to 95% (Mearns & Allen, 1991). Peers reported having deep concerns about TPPC, losing trust in their trainers, and experiencing isolation, helplessness, and conflict for the TPPC and themselves. Together these studies described an uncertain, stressful, and disrupted training environment (DeCino et al., 2020).

Peers endorsed observing myriad TPPC responses, including a tendency to withdraw from the peer group, express or hide with shame and embarrassment, exhibit defensiveness, criticize trainers, assert unfair treatment or biased evaluations, and pressure peers to take sides. When asked about their own emotional and behavioral responses to the presence of a TPPC, peers reported gossiping, withdrawing, experiencing negative feelings (e.g., frustration, anger, and resentment), worrying about the impact of the TPPC on their clients and program, having frustrating conversations with trainers, and believing trainers' responses were inadequate (Rosenberg et al., 2005; Shen-Miller et al., 2011, 2015). These attitudes and behaviors (e.g., gossip, avoidance) are not the skills future psychologists or the profession need (e.g., giving feedback to colleagues about competence concerns) to maintain a competent and strong psychology workforce. Trainers may be unaware of peer group struggles or known struggles may go unaddressed because communications are silenced by concerns about TC. When trainer involvement is lacking, trainees may be bereft of professional guidance, leaving unhealthy peer group responses to the TPPC and TC unaddressed and creating opportunities for trainees to develop unprofessional habits that make both them and the profession more vulnerable.

Trainees tend to believe that they have a fuller picture of the degree and depth of their peers' competence problems than faculty do (Foster & McAdams, 2009; Gaubatz & Vera, 2006; Mearns & Allen, 1991; Shen-Miller et al., 2015). Trainees are together more often and in more varied situations (e.g., between classes, informal gatherings), in which more is revealed and less attention is given to professional impression management. Not surprisingly, peers tend to believe that they are under more distress than trainers (Brown-Rice & Furr, 2013; Gaubatz & Vera, 2006). Reasons include loyalty to peer friendships, support and affirmation sought by or provided to the TPPC in ways that are exhausting and disrupt learning environments, greater focus on the TPPC by both trainers and trainees than on their own growth and development, and lack of faculty involvement to mitigate damaging group and program dynamics.

Further complicating peer group dynamics is the lack of attention in training programs to how diverse backgrounds (e.g., cultural differences associated with privacy, confidentiality, and sharing) intersect with judgments about competence problems (Goodrich & Shin, 2013; Letourneau, 2016; Shen-Miller et al., 2009, 2015; also see Chapters 1 and 4, this volume). Shen-Miller et al. (2012) found that faculty differed in how they conceptualized the intersection between diversity and competence: some trainers described a color-blind approach, whereas others reported using a culturally attentive approach that integrates attention to race, gender, and other identity variables. These approaches, if also present in trainee groups, may further exacerbate already contentious peer relationships. The presence of institutional racism, sexism, and other isms in training settings creates an uneven playing field for trainees, especially for those who pay the biggest individual price for these institutional practices. Acknowledgment or denial of these institutional effects adds tension to peer group dynamics.

Tensions Between Trainees and Trainers

In the peer studies cited earlier, participants varied in their knowledge of PPC program policies and what responsibilities or actions they, as peers, should take. Although many participants reported that they were aware of their program's PPC policies, they stated that there was no clear policy or guidance about what they should do if they observed or were concerned about a fellow trainee's professional competence or well-being. Although trainees often had little doubt about a peer's competence problems, most were uncertain about their responsibilities and did not know what to do. Some trainees reported that they sought advice from the training director (or another trainer), yet they were often dissatisfied with the response. Trainees noted that they felt left in the dark, had little idea what the faculty did with the information they provided, and judged the program policies describing trainee responsibilities as inadequate (Parker et al., 2014). Trainees also indicated that based on their experience, they would be unlikely to talk with faculty in a similar situation (Shen-Miller et al., 2015) and were concerned about whether faculty were doing enough to address the TPPC. Trainees reported accepting that trainers were not able to share their responses and actions to address the TPPC due to TC (Oliver et al., 2004), but they worried as they watched their peer progress through the program without any direct knowledge of trainers' actions. Deeper concerns were expressed about trainers with PPC whose behaviors intersected with and protected the TPPC (Shen-Miller et al., 2015) or resulted in reduced trainee commitment to the profession and decreased self-efficacy for addressing PPC (Magsam, 2021). Overall, these studies suggest that trainees have a poor sense of their responsibilities; worry about whether their input is welcome, respected, or valued; and do not believe that program policies adequately clarify their responsibilities as peers. According to Rose and Persutte-Manning (2020), trainers would benefit from knowing more about trainees' emotional reactions, confusion, and uncertainty related to TPPC. Peers' concerns and lack of trainer clarification about peer responsibilities may be rooted in assumptions about TC.

We found only one study of trainees on remediation. Trainees disclosed that their remediation experiences had more complicated and negative effects on the trainee–trainer relationship (Kallaugher & Mollen, 2017). Themes identified from the trainee interviews included the following: (a) wanting more clarity, support, and empathy from trainers; (b) under- or overfocusing by trainers on cultural background, resulting in cultural mistrust; (c) believing remediators did not have a full context for their struggles (e.g., health challenges); (d) experiencing the remediation as punishing; and (e) perceiving remediators as having hostile intent.

Differences in personal culture, professional culture, and multicultural competence may contribute to greater conflict and misunderstanding between trainers and trainees (Letourneau, 2016), further complicating the already complicated dynamics created by the presence of a TPPC and TC. Trainers and trainees from dominant cultural backgrounds may feel more at ease in making judgments about other trainees' professional competence (Goodrich & Shin, 2013) because these standards may be more aligned with the dominant cultural values and behaviors (Council of Chairs of Training Councils [CCTC], 2020). Individuals from marginalized backgrounds who have lived experiences of racism, sexism, and/or other isms, including being under greater surveillance, may be more apprehensive about speaking up about peer competence problems (Shen-Miller et al., 2015). We suspect that power and cultural differences as well as institutional racism and sexism intersect with TPPC and TC to further exacerbate conflicts between trainers and trainees.

Tensions Among Trainers

Trainers are not always on the same page about how to proceed when they identify a TPPC (Behnke, 2014; Gizara & Forrest, 2004), especially when trainers are acting without clear TC policies in place (Forrest et al., 2022). Trainers often focus on confidentiality protections for the individual trainee and act to limit communications among trainers or with other trainees to avoid further stigmatization for the trainee. On the other hand, TPPC scholars have argued that addressing PPC is a professional competency that requires faculty to be knowledgeable about PPC scholarship, develop skills for addressing TPPC (Forrest et al., 2013; Jacobs et al., 2011; Kerl & Eichler, 2005), and establish TC policies (Forrest et al., 2022) to support professional communications about competence standards. Others believe that programs should include the topic of PPC in the curriculum, and trainees should intentionally develop PPC competencies (Foster & McAdams, 2009; Freeman et al., 2020), including knowledge about TC consequences.

TC is central to conflicts that arise among trainers, especially communications between academic training and internship programs. Internships ask specific questions about competence problems on the application to facilitate communication between programs and internships (Behnke, 2014). Yet trainers remain hesitant to convey information about trainee struggles, especially when remediations have been successful. Even though communication standards have been well established between academic and internship training programs (APA, 2017b; Association of Psychology Postdoctoral and Internship Centers, n.d.), internship trainers continue to be wary about whether academic programs have been fully forthcoming about PPC, and academic training directors struggle with exactly how much information to reveal about a trainee's past or current PPC on their application and in letters of recommendation. Uncertainties and disagreements about the boundaries of TC may make trainer–trainer relationships across the training system more contentious and less trustworthy.

In summary, TC decisions create dysfunctions across training systems (e.g., silence, incorrect assumptions, misunderstandings, spread of misinformation). Strict TC means that trainers are limited in how they communicate with others. The presence of a TPPC and TC creates a training environment that is fraught with communication constraints, putting professional relationships under stress and impeding ethical and successful gatekeeping. Most notable are trainees' uncertainty about their professional responsibilities, the troublesome and disruptive peer group dynamics, and the failure of trainers to respond in a manner that makes trainees confident that trainers are taking seriously their responsibility as gatekeepers to the profession.

SYSTEMIC PERSPECTIVES ON TRAINEE CONFIDENTIALITY

A broadly systemic, communitarian, and multicultural perspective on TPPC forms the overall perspective of this edited volume. Chapter 1 ("Creating a Communitarian, Multiculturally Sensitive, and Socially Just Training Culture") and Chapter 4 ("Systemic Perspectives on Trainees With Problems of Professional Competence") enlarge and inform our systemic view of TC. Along with the ecological view of TC tensions described earlier, we propose three systemic perspectives (communitarian systems, secrets in systems, and just culture organizations) as frameworks to further delineate the role and nature of TC.

Communitarian Systems

A communitarian perspective on determining the extent of TC stems from basic assumptions about the moral and/or ethical responsibility for the care of self and others as well as evidence-based knowledge about how a cooperative community (a "village") enhances and supports improvements for professional development and competence. A communitarian training culture (Johnson et al., 2014) refocuses the mandate from managing one's own competence (highly valued in an individualistic culture) to a professional and ethical obligation to engage with others with PPC (highly valued in collectivist cultures focused on family and group responsibility). Evidence for the importance of limiting TC based on a communitarian cultural perspective includes research on errors of self-assessment (e.g., overestimating one's own competence, being unaware of one's incompetence, or inaccurately appraising oneself, especially of multicultural competence; Johnson et al., 2012; Schwartz-Mette, 2009). A communitarian-oriented training program provides an opportunity to model and teach transformative trainer–trainee relationships that are more reciprocal, more egalitarian, and less hierarchical (Johnson et al., 2014)—qualities that are also desirable in training environments attuned to multicultural and social justice aims (Scheel et al., 2018). To accomplish these transformative goals, CCTC (2020) published the Social Responsiveness in Health Service Psychology Education and Training Toolkit, a resource for creating a communitarian training culture.

Impact of Secrets in Systems

Secrets and secrecy provide a conceptual perspective to further understand the effects of TC on an individual TPPC and the entire training system. Confidentiality—by definition—implies secrecy, as some individuals are on the inside and have knowledge, whereas others are on the outside and denied knowledge. There is no way to avoid secrecy when TC is present. Although secrecy may be easily confused with privacy, a secret has been defined as "a piece of information deliberately kept from others" (John et al., 2020, p. 99), making secrecy and thus confidentiality, at its most basic, both interpersonal and systemic. There is a rich literature on secrets in family systems theory and practice (Afifi & Steuber, 2010; Imber-Black, 1998; Orgad, 2015), including disclosure of secrets on well-being and cognitive functioning (Critcher & Ferguson, 2014), and organizational behavior and function (Birchall, 2011). This scholarship on secrets elaborates and expands our systemic perspective on TC. Next, we describe the effects of secrets on the individual with a secret, a person holding another's secret, those outside the secret, and interactional dynamics in the system.

Factors that likely motivate an individual to keep a secret include the control of information, management of the perceived effects on oneself and others, and the quality of the community or system within which the secret exists. Secrecy is often related to a negative view of the self as somehow inadequate, along with fear of and efforts to avoid shame and stigma (Goffman, 1963; Slepian et al., 2020) and an experience of inauthenticity (Slepian et al., 2017). We believe that these factors underlie the lack of voluntary disclosure and secret-keeping efforts by TPPC and sometimes their trainers. Evidence suggests that keeping secrets is associated with the following:

- increased isolation, fatigue, rumination, hypervigilance when with others, mind-wandering to the secret, and monitoring for leakage (Slepian et al., 2017);
- increased defensiveness, lowered trust, and poorer relationships (Afifi & Olson, 2005; Afifi & Steuber, 2010);
- cognitive depletion, including deficits in intellectual acuity, interpersonal restraint, physical stamina, and executive functioning (Critcher & Ferguson, 2014); and
- anticipation of negative outcomes from a perceived forbidding environment (Slepian et al., 2016).

Across several studies, positive outcomes of confiding a secret to another included reduced mind-wandering (Barasch, 2020), increased social support (Slepian & Kirby, 2018), enhanced coping efficacy, and enhanced coping efficacy and reappraisal (Slepian & Moulton-Tetlock, 2019). When individuals disclose secrets, they "can receive social support, feel more capable in coping with the secret, and cope more effectively" (Slepian & Moulton-Tetlock, 2019, p. 482). These research findings suggest that overreliance on TC may (a) exacerbate the stigma and shame attached to developmental challenges of competency attainment; (b) increase trainee defensiveness (resulting in poorer relationships with both trainers and peers); (c) increase mind-wandering, cognitive depletion, and distraction when a focus on skill enhancement and competence is most needed; and (d) fail to model and normalize the importance of seeking support for competence challenges.

The effects of keeping another's secret are also complex and multiply determined. Although holding another's secret may initially foster increased feelings of closeness and being valued, over time it may feel like a burden, reduce the quality of interactions, and ultimately harm the relationship (Slepian & Greenaway, 2018). Consequences for the secret keeper include mind-wandering to the secret (like the person who originated the secret), divided loyalties, risk of triangulation with others, loss of trust in one's judgment, and misunderstandings based on cultural expectations about secrets

(Cowan, 2020). Trainees who know about a peer's PPC hidden by TC may experience these same negative consequences for holding secrets, whether at the request of the TPPC or their peers; consequences of holding secrets may help explain findings from the peer studies cited earlier.

When trainers keep trainees' secrets, they may initially experience closeness to the TPPC (e.g., a desire to nurture and mentor). Yet over time, trainers realize that the secrecy impinges on relationships with peer trainees and faculty colleagues. Trainers may also behave self-protectively, fear being stigmatized about their own lack of competence, and anticipate disagreements among trainers (Gizara & Forrest, 2004), especially if the trainer is less powerful in the system (e.g., nontenured trainers fearful of their own competence evaluation, members of underrepresented racial and ethnic groups). Faculty or supervisors outside those holding the secret lack needed information, cannot collaborate in problem solving, and may feel angry or betrayed if or when problems erupt into program-level decision making, public challenges, or legal actions.

The effect of sharing a secret seems to be determined in part by the response of the other person according to the perceived or real cost–benefit appraisal (Barasch, 2020). When the other person is aggressive or critical, the likelihood of further sharing or disclosing is reduced and may result in a cycle of concealment (Afifi & Steuber, 2010). These findings suggest that trainers' response to TPPC disclosures (supportive of openness or assistance with next steps vs. criticism, avoidance, or silence) will influence how much the TPPC shares or conceals over time.

Although the literature is silent about secrets in psychology training systems, a number of factors might contribute to the failure to disclose relevant trainee issues. Some examples include preexisting mental health problems (e.g., depression, anxiety, or trauma history; Grice et al., 2018), sensitive health issues (e.g., HIV or another concealable stigmatized identity or disability; Camacho et al., 2020), illness or other life challenges that arise during training (Sosoo & Wise, 2022), or response to stresses and challenges of doctoral training (Levecque et al., 2017; Schwartz-Mette, 2009). In addition, disclosure of gender or sexual preference, multicultural differences, and challenges to social justice and equity issues within the program may all be silenced in programs that prioritize TC over a communitarian openness to supporting competence. In a study of British mental health trainees, Grice et al. (2018) found that the likelihood of disclosing a personal mental health problem was negatively associated with maladaptive perfectionism and anticipated stigma. The authors concluded that "training institutions, clinical supervisors, and trainees should jointly champion a training environment that encourages openness and transparency relating to mental health. This may also promote wider social acceptance of MHPs [mental health problems]" (p. 722).

Organizational Behavior and Culture

Confidentiality and the balance of secrecy and disclosure bidirectionally impact an organization and its cultural norms. Research on family systems and organizational behavior has shown that secrecy negatively affects how well the system meets the needs of its members and accomplishes its objectives. Secrets in families often create triangles that may destabilize and shift power in hierarchies and responsibilities. This destabilization may result from excluding others from the closeness and secrecy between two members (e.g., a mother and child keep secrets from a father or other siblings) or by scapegoating them, thus impeding the family's ability to collaborate and problem solve as well as limiting closeness and comfort. Although some secrets may serve individuation and developmental processes (e.g., adolescent privacy), toxic secrets withhold information that others need or have a right to know (Imber-Black, 1998), creating guilt, suspicion about truthfulness, and doubt about one's own perceptions about others. Affirming or disconfirming family environments impact voluntary disclosure (Afifi & Steuber, 2010), partly determined by the power of dependence and punishment. Negative responses, especially by a trainer upon whom one is dependent or who may mete out punishment, lead to increased secrecy over time, resulting in cycles of concealment or chilling effects (e.g., protecting oneself, protecting others, or reducing the sense of communication efficacy; Afifi & Olson, 2005). Training programs are characterized by some qualities of family systems. For example, negative or punitive responses by those upon whom a trainee is dependent may promote similar cycles of concealment, whereas supportive, problem-solving responses may yield further openness and transparency.

According to Birchall (2011), organizational secrecy acts in tension with transparency. Research on organizational behavior and leadership has increasingly shown that better functioning organizations are characterized by (a) increasing openness and intentional transparency; (b) making disclosures that are clear, accurate, and timely; (c) creating, maintaining, and repairing trust; and (d) conveying leadership aims to be perceived as trustworthy (Schnackenberg & Tomlinson, 2016). An organizational model that we believe has promise for aiding training programs to locate themselves along the TC continuum is the just culture approach. The concept of a *just culture* developed in professions in which mistakes can result in great harm, such as medicine, nursing, and aviation (Boysen, 2013; Global Aviation Information Network, 2004), and is characterized by an atmosphere of trust in which people are encouraged to share essential safety-related information (Reason, 1997). Rather than a blame culture, emphasis in a just culture is placed on (a) sharing; (b) revealing errors, problems, and mistakes to foster learning; (c) improving accountability and competence; and (d) reducing future risk. Rather than isolating a TPPC via TC to stop trainee information from leaking, programs could introduce a just culture approach that emphasizes transparency and trust and thus reduces blame about misjudgments or mistakes, with a goal of improved functioning and alleviating risk not just for the TPPC but for everyone associated with the training program. A just culture has much in common with a communitarian framework, with its emphasis on shared responsibility for supporting and enhancing competence.

Creating a just culture requires organizational change—a paradigm shift—that modifies what people think and do in their daily work and interaction. It takes time and the efforts of many people to be successful. One example of a just culture initiative in health care emphasized the following steps:

- get buy-in, starting with visible and active senior leadership support;
- adopt common language and processes that support a just culture;
- engage and train leaders, managers, and health care workers;
- build awareness and share information about just culture with patients and the public; and
- measure progress (Health Quality Council of Alberta, n.d.).

These organizational and cultural perspectives offer new insights to trainers and the training system and support intentional TC management. As with other cultural changes, creating a just culture must be intentional on the part of those responsible (faculty, supervisors, and administrators), and it must be taught and modeled for trainees. Conceptualizing TC within system frameworks (communitarian, secrets, and just culture) introduces the possibility of viewing TC along a continuum from promising complete confidentiality, like that accorded to clients, to upholding privacy but not promising confidentiality. In between the extremes of the continuum are gradations of confidentiality appropriate for trainee professional development, which may shift for a specific trainee as issues of PPC arise and require more communication to maintain healthy training environments. See Figure 7.1 for a visual representation of the TC continuum. We believe that training programs should be intentional in determining the extent of TC afforded trainees and should clarify their position along the TC continuum in their program policies and practices.

FIGURE 7.1. Trainee Confidentiality Continuum

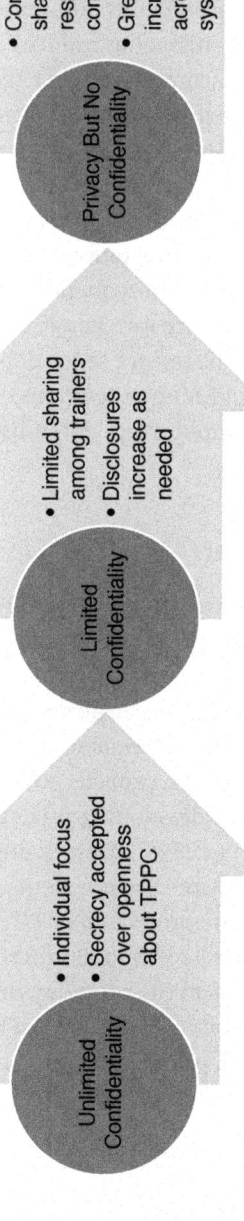

Note. TPPC = trainees with problems of professional competence.

RECOMMENDATIONS

Thus far, we have focused on the challenges and tensions resulting from an overreliance on TC and described systemic perspectives as background to argue for shifting the status quo along the TC continuum toward more openness and transparency. Our recommendations are aimed at helping programs and trainers prepare for more planful and reasoned limits to TC for TPPC, improving TC policies, and enhancing trainees' competence to address PPC throughout their careers. Such changes first require assessing a program's current functioning (e.g., degree of faculty conflict or collegiality, healthiness of current training culture, faculty multicultural competence) and its readiness and capacity for change (e.g., faculty openness to moving toward a communitarian approach, faculty capacity to give and receive feedback about their own and others' competence, faculty ability to recognize their potential misuse of power and consequent harm to trainees). Determining current functioning and capacity for change must also include holding discussions with various administrators (e.g., department chairs or representatives from legal affairs and human relations) who will be involved in and responsible for enacting, supporting, defending, and evaluating program policy changes.

Preparing Programs and Trainers

Trainer competence in effectively managing PPC and TC is an ethical mandate (see Standards 2.06, Personal Problems and Conflicts; 7.04, Student Disclosure of Personal Information; and 7.06, Assessing Student and Supervisee Performance; APA, 2017a) as well as an accreditation requirement (see Accreditation Standard III, Students, 3. Feedback and Remediation; APA, 2017b). Program leadership that has the capacity to foster trainer preparation and development is essential for developing proactive policies and practices to address TC in relationship to TPPC. Trainer preparation involves providing opportunities to surface and air disagreements about the limits of TC along the continuum from complete protection of TC to privacy only or no promise of TC. The following should be included in trainer preparation: a thorough review of past TC challenges in the program, analysis of current TC policies and practices, and discussions of the potential benefits and costs of making changes to TC policies and practices (e.g., faculty skill deficits that must be addressed to enact new TC policies). Trainers might also consider the following in program policies:

- Highlight that developing and maintaining professional competencies cannot be a private matter. Describe under what circumstances TC will be limited and when and where trainees will learn about these limits (e.g., admission, orientation, handbook, professional seminars). Notification in advance provides trainees with due process.

- Highlight that (a) decisions to limit TC rest with trainers, (b) voluntary disclosure by trainees about competence problems is preferred yet is not always possible, and (c) trainers will break confidence without trainee consent when the risk to client safety or others is sufficient to warrant intervention.

- Articulate the distinction between personal/private functioning and personal functioning that affects professional competence and thus requires communication and decision making by trainers (e.g., evaluation, remediation, and dismissal). Here are some examples of possible wording for policy statements: "personal privacy is honored as long as personal issues do not affect professional performance" (see Standard 7.04, Student Disclosure of Personal Information in APA, 2017a, p. 9); "unprofessional behavior requires feedback and open communication about requirements to meet professional standards"; or "a decision to become a professional involves recognizing that you have no confidentiality related to your professional competence, performance, or behaviors."

- Clarify (a) that all psychologists, including trainees, have a professional and ethical responsibility to engage peers and colleagues who are struggling to maintain professional standards (Standard 1.04, Informal Resolution of Ethical Violations in APA, 2017a); (b) trainees' responsibilities to disclose to trainers their concerns about peers whose problems interfere with professional competence, including what must be shared and with whom; (c) the benefits of voluntary disclosure by the TPPC to peers; and (d) peer involvement when competence problems occur.

- Identify (a) who is included in the training faculty; (b) who is involved in trainee evaluation decisions about advancement, remediation, and dismissal; and (c) with whom trainee evaluations will be shared. Emphasize that these actions are taken by the program, not individual faculty.

- Clarify the limits of confidentiality in personal psychotherapy when it is recommended as part of remediation; and clarify in advance with the trainee and treating therapist what needs to be shared with the program (Forrest & Elman, 2005).

- Clarify that trainees have a responsibility to become competent in giving and receiving feedback focused on professional competencies, especially when professional standards are in jeopardy. Trainers assist the TPPC with what requires disclosure, to whom, and by whom (e.g., other trainers or the TPPC).
- Provide trainees with an opportunity to understand these policies and acknowledge having read and consented to them, preferably in writing.

At a systemic level, program policies created or changed based on these recommendations require review, clarification, and approval by institutional leadership and legal review. Program preparation also involves attending to the training culture, including the communitarian ethic of care for oneself and others; just culture concepts to create safe, transparent, and successful outcomes; and organizational strategies that reduce silence and secrecy and promote transparency and trust. Adapting the organizational culture to respond to TC and TPPC challenges should include mechanisms for evaluating the outcomes associated with TC policy changes and practice.

Besides TC policy and training culture improvements, trainers need opportunities to develop their PPC professional competencies (knowledge, skills, and attitudes). Knowledge requires being up to date on PPC and TC scholarship. The scholarship on secrets in systems, just culture, organizational transparency, and trust provides additional foundational knowledge. Skills for good PPC and TC management may best be accomplished by using case vignettes and enacting role-plays. Examples include engaging in difficult conversations, having discussions to distinguish between privacy and secrecy or when personal issues affect professional functioning, teaching principles for giving and receiving feedback in a productive and professional manner, and exploring cultural values and power in organizational behavior that impact openness and transparency. Trainer preparation should also include an intentional plan to address well-documented negative trainee, trainer, and program dynamics that are known to surface because of TC and may undermine trustworthiness in relationships and the program. Finally, trainers must determine how to evaluate the effects of their TC policies on all aspects of the training system.

Preparing Trainees

Systematic education of trainees about TC challenges and complexities is imperative. Ethical, legal, and accreditation standards require programs to disclose policies in advance (e.g., recruitment, program handbook, and course syllabi) about competence standards and trainee evaluation, remediation, and dismissal (see Chapters 6, 8, and 9). When TPPC situations arise, well-documented evidence suggests that trainees are either unaware of their program's policies or uncertain about what they can or should do and what faculty can or will do. As a result, trainees may respond in ways that exacerbate problems within the training program, and they may observe their trainers failing to model professional behavior in intervening with a TPPC, often because the trainee's behavior is treated as confidential and dealt with "behind the curtain" (Freeman et al., 2020, p. 570).

Educating trainees toward competency in addressing TC when dealing with PPC—theirs or others—requires curricular material to be introduced at developmentally appropriate competence levels (e.g., Freeman et al., 2020), just like other competencies. Educating trainees about TC as part of PPC can be threaded into the program's existing training that addresses the professionalism competency and added to existing courses (e.g., professional issues, ethics, and supervision courses). Trainees preparing to become supervisors and trainers themselves, as well as those preparing for full-time practice, will need knowledge, skills, and attitudes about PPC and TC in their future work environments (APA, 2014).

Curricula suggestions for knowledge development are as follows:

1. Provide in-depth explanations of program policies on TC and informed consent.

2. Make clear distinctions between confidentiality for trainees versus clients.

3. Expose trainees to secrecy theory and research, understanding TC benefits and costs.

4. Expose trainees to the organizational literature on openness and transparency.

5. Include coverage of the communitarian ethic of care (e.g., limited accuracy of self-assessment that results in the need for others' involvement in maintaining professional competence).

6. Discuss gatekeeping requirements (e.g., admission decisions, evaluation of professional competencies, remediation, dismissal, or court challenges).

7. Include coverage of social justice, equity, diversity, inclusion, power dynamics in groups and training systems, and their influences on professional competence evaluations.

8. Discuss the characteristics of a communitarian training culture that promote a just culture and transparency, trust, and safety.

Curricula suggestions for skill and attitude development are as follows:

1. Role-play scenarios focused on competence concerns about the self, peer, or trainer as well as dialogues with a peer and/or faculty, benefits and costs of limiting TC, and increasing capacity to share.
2. In supervision courses and practica, discuss possible limits to TC, draft TC statements for inclusion in supervision contracts, practice giving and receiving feedback, and provide supervision (e.g., for a first-year trainee) that focuses on PPC and TC skill development.
3. In case studies of limited TC, perform assessments to determine the need for remediation and shared engagement process (e.g., faculty and peers), creation of remediation and assessment of outcome, and communication challenges (e.g., peers, field sites, internship, or postdoctoral fellowship).
4. Prepare trainees for challenges that produce PPC, including mental health issues that trainees bring to the program (Grice et al., 2018) or develop in response to program stressors (Levecque et al., 2017).
5. Provide opportunities to examine attitudes toward shared responsibilities for competence (self and others) and mitigating effects of TC on TPPC and peers.

CLOSING THE CIRCLE: NATIONAL TRAINING SYSTEM CHANGES

This chapter focused on how trainers and training programs can better address TC. Training programs are situated in a professional ecosystem, nested in institutional (master's, doctoral, internship, postdoctoral), professional (licensure, accreditation), ethical, legal, and cultural systems. As programs develop TC policies and practices, these eco- and macrosystems will also need to address the negative consequences of confidentiality and secrets and the benefits of increased transparency. We have recommended specific eco- and macrosystem changes elsewhere (see Forrest et al., 2022). CCTC and professional psychology training councils are well suited to create these changes, because they capture the diversity of training models and contribute to establishing national professional standards and best practices. Contributions include (a) developing or offering continuing education focused on PPC and TC, (b) proposing model TC policies that address greater transparency, (c) collecting data throughout the training sequence and across programs (e.g., impact of limiting TC on the success of training program-to-internship transition), and (d) developing long-needed prospective research to determine the effects of differing TC limits on program success and career-long professionalism of its graduates.

REFERENCES

Afifi, T. D., & Olson, L. (2005). The chilling effect in families and the pressure to conceal secrets. *Communication Monographs, 72*(2), 192–216. https://doi.org/10.1080/03637750500111906

Afifi, T. D., & Steuber, K. (2010). The cycle of concealment. *Journal of Social and Personal Relationships, 27*(8), 1019–1034. https://doi.org/10.1177/0265407510378301

American Psychological Association. (2014). *Guidelines for clinical supervision in health service psychology.* https://www.apa.org/about/policy/guidelines-supervision.pdf

American Psychological Association. (2017a). *Ethical principles of psychologists and code of conduct* (2002, amended effective June 1, 2010, and January 1, 2017). https://www.apa.org/ethics/code/index

American Psychological Association. (2017b). *Multicultural guidelines: An ecological approach to context, identity, and intersectionality, 2017.* https://www.apa.org/about/policy/multicultural-guidelines.pdf

Association of Psychology Postdoctoral Internship Centers. (n.d.). *Sample APPI.* https://www.appic.org/Portals/0/downloads/Example_AAPI_Online_Application_Basic_2017.pdf

Barasch, A. (2020). The consequences of sharing. *Current Opinion in Psychology, 31,* 61–66. https://doi.org/10.1016/j.copsyc.2019.06.027

Behnke, S. (2014). Remedial and disciplinary interventions in graduate psychology training programs: Twenty-five essential questions for faculty and supervisors. In W. B. Johnson & N. J. Kaslow (Eds.), *Oxford handbook of education and training in professional psychology* (pp. 356–376). Oxford University Press.

Birchall, C. (2011). Introduction to 'secrecy and transparency': The politics of opacity and openness. *Theory, Culture & Society, 28*(7–8), 7–25. https://doi.org/10.1177/0263276411427744

Bodner, K. (2012). Ethical principles and standards that inform educational gatekeeping practices in psychology. *Ethics & Behavior, 22*(1), 60–74. https://doi.org/10.1080/10508422.2012.638827

Boysen, P. (2013). Just culture: A foundation for balanced accountability and patient safety. *The Ochsner Journal, 13*(3), 400–406. https://pubmed.ncbi.nlm.nih.gov/24052772/

Brown-Rice, K., & Furr, S. (2019). Am I my peers' keeper? Problems of professional competence. *Teaching and Supervision in Counseling, 1*(1), 33–46. https://doi.org/10.7290/tsc010104

Brown-Rice, K. A., & Furr, S. (2013). Preservice counselors' knowledge of classmates' problems of professional competence. *Journal of Counseling and Development, 91*(2), 224–233. https://doi.org/10.1002/j.1556-6676.2013.00089.x

Camacho, G., Reinka, M. A., & Quinn, D. M. (2020). Disclosure and concealment of stigmatized identities. *Current Opinion in Psychology, 31,* 28–32. https://doi.org/10.1016/j.copsyc.2019.07.031

Council of Chairs of Training Councils. (2020). *CCTC 2020: Social responsiveness in health service psychology education and training toolkit.* https://www.appic.org/Portals/0/downloads/TrainingDocs/CCTC_Socially-Responsive-HSP-Ed-Training.pdf

Cowan, S. K. (2020). Secrets and social networks. *Current Opinion in Psychology, 31,* 99–104. https://doi.org/10.1016/j.copsyc.2019.07.038

Critcher, C. R., & Ferguson, M. J. (2014). The cost of keeping it hidden: Decomposing concealment reveals what makes it depleting. *Journal of Experimental Psychology: General, 143*(2), 721–735. https://doi.org/10.1037/a0033468

DeCino, D. A., Waalkes, P. L., & Dalbey, A. (2020). "They stay with you": Counselor educators' emotionally intense gatekeeping experiences. *The Professional Counselor, 10*(4), 548–561. https://doi.org/10.15241/dad.10.4.548

Ellis, M. V. (2017). Clinical supervision contract & consent statement and supervisee rights and responsibilities. *The Clinical Supervisor, 36*(1), 145–159. https://doi.org/10.1080/07325223.2017.1321885

Elman, N. S., & Forrest, L. (2004). Psychotherapy in the remediation of psychology trainees: Exploratory interviews with training directors. *Professional Psychology: Research and Practice, 35*(2), 123–130. https://doi.org/10.1037/0735-7028.35.2.123

Forrest, L., & Elman, N. S. (2005). Psychotherapy for poorly performing trainees: Are there limits to confidentiality? *Psychotherapy Bulletin, 40*(4), 29–37.

Forrest, L., & Elman, N. S. (2014). Trainees with problems of professional competence. In W. B. Johnson & N. J. Kaslow (Eds.), *The Oxford handbook of education and training in professional psychology* (pp. 314–335). Oxford University Press.

Forrest, L., Elman, N. S., Bodner, K. E., & Kaslow, N. J. (2022). Trainee confidentiality: Confusions, complexities, consequences, and possibilities. *Training and Education in Professional Psychology, 16*(3), 306–314. https://doi.org/10.1037/tep0000364

Forrest, L., Elman, N. S., Huprich, S. K., Veilleux, J. C., Jacobs, S. C., & Kaslow, N. J. (2013). Training directors' perceptions of faculty behaviors when dealing with trainee competence problems: A mixed method pilot study. *Training and Education in Professional Psychology, 7*(1), 23–32. https://doi.org/10.1037/a0032068

Foster, J. M., Leppma, M., & Hutchinson, T. S. (2014). Students' perspectives on gatekeeping in counselor education: A case study. *Counselor Education and Supervision, 55*(3), 190–203. https://doi.org/10.1002/j.1556-6978.2014.00057.x

Foster, V., & McAdams, C., III. (2009). A framework for creating a climate of transparency for professional performance assessment: Fostering student investment in gatekeeping. *Counselor Education and Supervision, 48*(4), 271–284. https://doi.org/10.1002/j.1556-6978.2009.tb00080.x

Freeman, B., Woodliff, T., & Martinez, M. (2020). Teaching gatekeeping to doctoral students: A qualitative study of a developmental experiential approach. *The Professional Counselor, 10*(4), 562–580. https://doi.org/10.15241/bf.10.4.562

Furr, S., & Brown-Rice, K. (2018). Psychology doctoral students' perceptions of peers' problems of professional competency. *Training and Education in Professional Psychology, 12*(2), 118–124. https://doi.org/10.1037/tep0000184

Gaubatz, M. D., & Vera, E. M. (2006). Trainee competence in master's level counseling programs: A comparison of counselor educators' and students' views. *Counselor Education and Supervision, 46*(1), 32–43. https://doi.org/10.1002/j.1556-6978.2006.tb00010.x

Gilfoyle, N. (2008). The legal exosystem: Risk management in addressing student competence problems in professional psychology training. *Training and Education in Professional Psychology, 2*(4), 202–209. https://doi.org/10.1037/1931-3918.2.4.202

Gizara, S. S., & Forrest, L. (2004). Supervisors' experiences of trainee impairment and incompetence at APA-accredited internship sites. *Professional Psychology: Research and Practice, 35*(2), 131–140. https://doi.org/10.1037/0735-7028.35.2.131

Global Aviation Information Network. (2004). *A roadmap to a just culture: Enhancing the safety environment.* https://flightsafety.org/files/just_culture.pdf

Goffman, E. (1963). *Stigma: Notes on the management of spoiled identity.* Simon & Schuster.

Goodrich, K. M., & Shin, R. Q. (2013). A culturally responsive intervention for addressing problematic behaviors in counseling students. *Counselor Education and Supervision, 52*(1), 43–55. https://doi.org/10.1002/j.1556-6978.2013.00027.x

Grice, T., Alcock, K., & Scior, K. (2018). Mental health disclosure amongst clinical psychologists in training: Perfectionism and pragmatism. *Clinical Psychology & Psychotherapy, 25*(5), 721–729. https://doi.org/10.1002/cpp.2192

Health Quality Council of Alberta. (n.d.) *Just culture: Culture change resource.* https://justculture.hqca.ca

Imber-Black, E. (1998). *The secret life of families: Truth-telling, privacy, and reconciliation in a tell-all society.* Bantam Books.

Jacobs, S. C., Huprich, S. K., Grus, C. L., Cage, E. A., Elman, N. S., Forrest, L., Schwartz-Mette, R., Shen-Miller, D. S., Van Sickle, K. S., & Kaslow, N. J. (2011). Trainees with professional competency problems: Preparing trainers for difficult but necessary conversations. *Training and Education in Professional Psychology, 5*(3), 175–184. https://doi.org/10.1037/a0024656

John, L. K., Slepian, M. L., & Tamir, D. (2020). Editorial overview: Tales of two motives: Disclosure and concealment. *Current Opinion in Psychology, 31*, iv–vii. https://doi.org/10.1016/j.copsyc.2019.11.002

Johnson, W. B., Barnett, J. E., Elman, N. S., Forrest, L., & Kaslow, N. J. (2012). The competent community: Toward a vital reformulation of professional ethics. *American Psychologist, 67*(7), 557–569. https://doi.org/10.1037/a0027206

Johnson, W. B., Barnett, J. E., Elman, N. S., Forrest, L., Schwartz-Mette, R., & Kaslow, N. J. (2014). Preparing trainees for lifelong competence: Creating a communitarian training culture. *Training and Education in Professional Psychology, 8*(4), 211–220. https://doi.org/10.1037/tep0000048

Kallaugher, J., & Mollen, D. (2017). Student experiences of remediation in their graduate psychology programs. *Training and Education in Professional Psychology, 11*(4), 276–282. https://doi.org/10.1037/tep0000175

Kaslow, N. J., Rubin, N. J., Bebeau, M. J., Leigh, I. W., Lichtenberg, J. W., Nelson, P. D., Portnoy, S. M., & Smith, I. L. (2007). Guiding principles and recommendations for the assessment of competence. *Professional Psychology: Research and Practice, 38*(5), 441–451. https://doi.org/10.1037/0735-7028.38.5.441

Kerl, S., & Eichler, M. (2005). The loss of innocence: Emotional costs to serving as gatekeepers to the counseling profession. *Journal of Creativity in Mental Health, 1*(3–4), 71–88. https://doi.org/10.1300/J456v01n03_05

Letourneau, J. L. H. (2016). A decision-making model for addressing problematic behaviors in counseling students. *Counseling and Values, 61*(2), 206–222. https://doi.org/10.1002/cvj.12038

Levecque, K., Anseel, F., DeBeuckelaer, A., Van der Heyden, J., & Gisle, L. (2017). Work organization and mental health problems in PhD students. *Research Policy, 46*(4), 868–879. https://doi.org/10.1016/j.respol.2017.02.008

Magsam, E. L. (2021). *Trainers with problems of professional competence: Relationships with trainee professional commitment and self-efficacy for addressing competency issues* (Publication No. 28646385) [Dissertation, University of Memphis]. ProQuest Dissertations and Theses Global.

Mearns, J., & Allen, G. J. (1991). Graduate students' experiences in dealing with impaired peers compared with faculty predictions: An exploratory study. *Ethics & Behavior, 1*(3), 191–202. https://doi.org/10.1207/s15327019eb0103_3

Moskop, J. C., Marco, C. A., Larkin, G. L., Geiderman, J. M., & Derse, A. R. (2005). From Hippocrates to HIPAA: Privacy and confidentiality in emergency medicine—Part I: Conceptual, moral, and legal foundations. *Annals of Emergency Medicine, 45*(1), 53–59. https://doi.org/10.1016/j.annemergmed.2004.08.008

Oliver, M. N. I., Bernstein, J. H., Anderson, K. G., Blashfield, R. K., & Roberts, M. C. (2004). An exploratory examination of student attitudes toward "impaired" peers in clinical psychology training programs. *Professional Psychology: Research and Practice, 35*(2), 141–147. https://doi.org/10.1037/0735-7028.35.2.141

Orgad, Y. (2015). The culture of family secrets. *Culture and Psychology, 21*(1), 59–80. https://doi.org/10.1177/1354067X15568979

Parker, L. K., Chang, C., Corthell, K. K., Walsh, M. E., Brack, G., & Grubbs, N. K. (2014). A grounded theory of counseling students who report problematic peers. *Counselor Education and Supervision, 53*(2), 111–125. https://doi.org/10.1002/j.1556-6978.2014.00052.x

Reason, J. (1997). *Managing the risks of organizational accidents*. Ashgate Publishing.

Rose, J. S., & Persutte-Manning, S. (2020). Students with problems of professional competency and their impact on proficient students in counseling programs. *Journal of Counselor Preparation and Supervision, 13*(4). https://digitalcommons.sacredheart.edu/jcps/vol13/iss4/4

Rosenberg, J. I., Getzelman, M. A., Arcinue, F., & Oren, C. Z. (2005). An exploratory look at students' experiences of problematic peers in academic professional psychology programs. *Professional Psychology: Research and Practice, 36*(6), 665–673. https://doi.org/10.1037/0735-7028.36.6.665

Scheel, M. J., Stabb, S. D., Cohn, T. J., Duan, C., & Sauer, E. M. (2018). Counseling psychology model training program. *The Counseling Psychologist, 46*(1), 6–49. https://doi.org/10.1177/0011000018755512

Schnackenberg, A. K., & Tomlinson, E. C. (2016). Organizational transparency: A new perspective on managing trust in organization-stakeholder relationships. *Journal of Management, 42*(7), 1784–1810. https://doi.org/10.1177/0149206314525202

Schwartz-Mette, R. A. (2009). Challenges in addressing graduate student impairment in academic professional psychology programs. *Ethics & Behavior, 19*(2), 91–102. https://doi.org/10.1080/10508420902768973

Shen-Miller, D. S., Forrest, L., & Burt, M. (2012). Contextual influences on faculty diversity conceptualizations when working with trainee competence problems. *The Counseling Psychologist, 40*(8), 1181–1219. https://doi.org/10.1177/0011000011431832

Shen-Miller, D. S., Forrest, L., & Elman, N. S. (2009). Training directors' conceptualizations of intersection of diversity and trainee competence problems: A preliminary analysis. *The Counseling Psychologist, 37*(4), 482–518. https://doi.org/10.1177/0011000008316656

Shen-Miller, D. S., Grus, C. L., Van Sickle, K., Schwartz-Mette, R., Cage, E., Elman, N. S., Jacobs, S. C., & Kaslow, N. J. (2011). Trainees' experiences with peers having competence problems: A national survey. *Training and Education in Professional Psychology, 5*(2), 112–121. https://doi.org/10.1037/a0023824

Shen-Miller, D. S., Schwartz-Mette, R., Van Sickle, K., Jacobs, S. C., Grus, C. L., Hunter, E., & Forrest, L. (2015). Professional competence problems in training: A qualitative investigation of trainee perspectives. *Training and Education in Professional Psychology, 9*(2), 161–169. https://doi.org/10.1037/tep0000072

Slepian, M., & Moulton-Tetlock, E. (2019). Confiding secrets and well-being. *Social Psychological & Personality Science, 10*(4), 472–484. https://doi.org/10.1177/1948550618765069

Slepian, M. L., Chun, J. S., & Mason, M. F. (2017). The experience of secrecy. *Journal of Personality and Social Psychology, 113*(1), 1–33. https://doi.org/10.1037/pspa0000085

Slepian, M. L., & Greenaway, K. H. (2018). The benefits and burdens of keeping others' secrets. *Journal of Experimental Social Psychology, 78*, 220–232. https://doi.org/10.1016/j.jesp.2018.02.005

Slepian, M. L., & Kirby, J. N. (2018). To whom do we confide our secrets? *Personality and Social Psychology Bulletin, 44*(7), 1008–1023. https://doi.org/10.1177/0146167218756032

Slepian, M. L., Kirby, J. N., & Kalokerinos, E. K. (2020). Shame, guilt, and secrets on the mind. *Emotion, 20*(2), 323–328. https://doi.org/10.1037/emo0000542

Slepian, M. L., Masicampo, E. J., & Galinsky, A. D. (2016). The hidden effects of recalling secrets: Assimilation, contrast, and the burdens of secrecy. *Journal of Experimental Psychology: General, 145*(8), e27–e48. https://doi.org/10.1037/xge0000194

Sosoo, E. E., & Wise, E. H. (2022). When the expected happens: Facing a major life event in graduate school. *Training and Education in Professional Psychology, 16*(4), 325–332. https://doi.org/10.1037/tep0000381

Thomas, J. T. (2010). *The ethics of supervision and consultation: Practical guidance for mental health professionals*. American Psychological Association. https://doi.org/10.1037/12078-000

Vacha-Haase, T., Elman, N. S., Forrest, L., Kallaugher, J., Lease, S. H., Veilleux, J. C., & Kaslow, N. J. (2019). Remediation plans for trainees with problems of professional competence. *Training and Education in Professional Psychology, 13*(4), 239–246. https://doi.org/10.1037/tep0000221

Veilleux, J. C., January, A. M., VanderVeen, J. W., Reddy, L. F., & Klonoff, E. A. (2012). Differentiating amongst characteristics associated with problems of professional competence: Perceptions of graduate student peers. *Training and Education in Professional Psychology, 6*(2), 113–121. https://doi.org/10.1037/a0028337

8

ETHICAL ISSUES IN WORKING WITH TRAINEES WITH PROBLEMS OF PROFESSIONAL COMPETENCE

JEFFREY E. BARNETT AND W. BRAD JOHNSON

Training programs in psychology, including graduate programs and clinical training sites such as practicum sites, internship programs, and postdoctoral residencies (hereafter jointly termed "training programs"), have an ethical obligation to ensure that each trainee meets or exceeds minimal standards of performance and conduct. This obligation necessitates that these programs provide a comprehensive education and training process in line with accreditation standards that include evaluation of, and feedback provided to, trainees on an ongoing basis (American Psychological Association [APA], 2015). The ultimate goals of this process include establishing each trainee's competence in all of their professional roles and responsibilities, to include the development of their professional identity and integration of the values of the profession into that identity, all to achieve the ultimate objective of helping to create competent professionals who promote the best interests and well-being of the recipients of their professional services, both at present and in the future.

Despite each training program's best efforts at screening applicants, individuals with preexisting limitations or difficulties that may impact their

https://doi.org/10.1037/0000340-009
Supporting Trainees With Competence Problems: A Practical Guide for Psychology Trainers, R. A. Schwartz-Mette, E. A. Hunter, and N. J. Kaslow (Editors)
Copyright © 2023 by the American Psychological Association. All rights reserved.

professional functioning and conduct will be accepted into their programs. Those who enter the mental health professions have at least the same likelihood as the general public to experience mental health, substance abuse, and relationship difficulties during the course of their training and their careers (Barnett, 2008).

Like all individuals, psychology trainees are susceptible to the many stressors, demands, and challenges in their lives, both professionally and personally, guaranteeing that some trainees will experience difficulties and even deficits in their functioning and effectiveness. It is also important to note that competence in one area of professional functioning or at one point in time does not guarantee competence in other areas of functioning or at other times. Some trainees may struggle with developing and maintaining competence in certain aspects of their training and may even experience a loss of competence in some aspects of their professional functioning, possibly due to ongoing stressors or mental and/or physical health difficulties in their lives, inadequate self-care and a lack of adequate engagement with others for support and assistance, use of maladaptive coping practices, or failure to keep their knowledge and skills up-to-date over the course of their training (Wise & Reuman, 2019). In addition, not all trainees will be able to master and consistently apply the many complex competencies associated with their professional training. Thus, over time, it is likely that all training programs will have trainees with problems of professional competence (TPPC; Veilleux et al., 2012) and will need to address these issues in an ethical manner. Finally, keep in mind that the "seasons" of a trainee's development (graduate student, intern, or postdoctoral fellow) often bring different challenges to competence. For instance, while a fledgling student may be emotionally overwhelmed by the demands of starting graduate school, a postdoctoral resident may struggle to accurately articulate their boundaries of competence.

TRAINEES WITH PROBLEMS OF PROFESSIONAL COMPETENCE AND ETHICS

Trainers (to include faculty, supervisors, and administrators) have wide-ranging ethical obligations in their varied professional roles and interactions, as articulated in the APA *Ethical Principles of Psychologists and Code of Conduct* (referred to hereinafter as the APA Ethics Code; APA, 2017). The APA Ethics Code's aspirational General Principles provide trainers with direction and guidance that should influence all decisions made and actions taken. These

General Principles form the foundation of the enforceable Ethical Standards that follow in the APA Ethics Code, and they also offer guidance when ethical dilemmas pertaining to supporting TPPC arise. These General Principles, introduced in Chapter 2 of this volume, are as follows:

- *Principle A: Beneficence and Nonmaleficence.* Promote the well-being and best interests of those we serve and minimize the risks of exploitation and harm to include misuse of one's influence. Mitigate factors that may adversely impact our competence and effective functioning (e.g., trainers deliver difficult feedback to trainees and colleagues in a spirit of *carefrontation*, always communicating genuine concern for and commitment to the recipient).

- *Principle B: Fidelity and Responsibility.* Establish relationships built on trust, fulfill our obligations to others, take responsibility for our actions, and work to ensure ethical conduct by others (e.g., trainers are available, reliable, consistent, and accountable in the way they show up in and prioritize relationships with trainees and colleagues).

- *Principle C: Integrity.* Be honest and truthful at all times, do not misrepresent information, avoid unwise commitments, and work to fulfill all commitments made (e.g., trainers provide consistent, honest, and transparent formative assessments of trainee competence such that trainees never feel blindsided by summative assessments).

- *Principle D: Justice.* Promote fairness and ensure equal access to services provided and equal quality of services to all individuals. Be cognizant of biases and limitations to our competence and expertise, and work to ensure they do not negatively affect others (e.g., trainers hold themselves accountable for ensuring that a diverse array of trainees have access to them as mentors and sponsors).

- *Principle E: Respect for People's Rights and Dignity.* Demonstrate a commitment to respecting and valuing all forms of diversity and individual differences, promoting the rights of all individuals, and working to modify how we interact and communicate with diverse individuals to ensure thoughtful respect of individual differences and needs to promote their best interests in a fair and equitable manner (e.g., trainers self-educate and seek ongoing consultation related to elements of cultural difference and cultural bias that may interfere with fair and equitable assessment of trainee competence).

These General Principles offer guidance to trainers on all aspects of their professional roles, including their interactions with each other, their interactions with trainees, and their obligations to the recipients of services provided by trainees. They also provide guidance that should influence how to structure the training program, how to implement it, how to complete the trainee evaluation and feedback process, and how to respond to TPPC, to include remediation opportunities and efforts as well as decision making when these problems of professional competence persist despite the training program and trainee's best efforts. One pervasive theme emanating from psychology's ethical principles is the obligation for trainers to tirelessly pursue self-awareness, education, and competence in recognizing how cultural differences can easily lead to biased assessments of competence. For instance, female trainees more than male trainees are likely to suffer biased assessments of competence when their parenting status is public (Dias et al., 2020). Failure on the part of trainers to appreciate and mitigate the "motherhood penalty" may lead to biased assessments of female trainees.

Detailed standards of ethical conduct that address specific aspects of many of these obligations are included in the enforceable Ethical Standards of the APA Ethics Code. While these ethical standards delineate minimal expectations for ethical conduct that one must not fall below, merely meeting or barely exceeding minimal expectations misses the intent of the underlying values of our profession as articulated in the General Principles. Trainers should embrace what Handelsman et al. (2001) describe as positive or aspirational ethics. This approach to ethical decision making and conduct focuses on striving to live out the General Principles as fully as possible and doing the best we can for those we interact with and serve in our professional roles, never seeking to merely meet minimal requirements or expectations. Of course, the aspirational General Principles and the enforceable Ethical Standards of the APA Ethics Code apply equally to trainees as well. It is important that training programs infuse a focus on ethics in all aspects of training as part of inculcating trainees with the values of the profession and hold trainees accountable to these standards.

CREATING A COMMUNITARIAN CULTURE WITHIN THE TRAINING ENVIRONMENT: A FOCUS ON PREVENTION

Although training programs need to address all trainee problems with professional competence as they arise, much can be done to help prevent many such difficulties from arising and to address those that occur more thoughtfully and effectively, in compliance with ethical obligations. A focus on positive or aspirational ethics will result in training programs being structured and run based on the principles of a communitarian training culture as described by

Johnson, Barnett, et al. (2014). Rather than create a training program that promotes competitiveness among trainees, critical evaluations of trainee functioning with penalties for deviations from narrowly defined norms, and a sole focus on individual responsibility and accountability, a communitarian training culture promotes care for each other, acceptance of individual differences and needs, collegiality, mutual support and respect, and responsibility for each other's ongoing wellness and effective functioning. As described by Johnson, Barnett, et al. (2014), "an effective CTC [communitarian training culture] will promote cultural norms of interdependence, honesty, compassion, and collegial engagement likely to facilitate everyone's improved competence" (p. 215; see also Chapter 1, this volume).

The absence of a communitarian training culture may increase the likelihood of the development of trainee problems with professional competence by fueling secrecy and nondisclosure on the part of trainees who experience serious distress or diminished competence. A competitive and individualistic training culture also inhibits cooperation, engagement, and expressions of care from others in the community. Each of these factors heightens the potential for negative outcomes that will result in less competent trainees and increased risks of harm to those they serve. Because there is good evidence that trainees may be more likely than trainers to witness competence problems among other trainees (Shen-Miller et al., 2011), reducing competition among trainees and strengthening an ethical attitude of interdependence and collegial care is essential. For all of these reasons, the development of a communitarian training culture should be seen as an ethical imperative consistent with the APA Ethics Code's General Principles as well as specific ethical standards to include Standard 3.04, Avoiding Harm (APA, 2017).

Trainers play key roles in establishing and maintaining the communitarian training culture through modeling humility, authenticity, and vulnerability; through offering mutual support to colleagues; and through providing collaborative and caring responses when TPPC arise. It is also important to note that trainees are not the only ones who benefit from the presence of a communitarian training culture. Trainers benefit greatly from the support and assistance received from colleagues as they experience life's many challenges, thus promoting their own competence and modeling for trainees their commitment to the ethical ideals of the profession.

Creating a Communitarian Training Culture

To ensure the development and maintenance of a communitarian training culture, trainers must accept responsibility for the structure and demands of the training program. Consistent with the General Principles of the APA Ethics Code, trainers should focus on developing a culture within the training program that emphasizes caring, mutual support, and communal efforts, and they should eschew competitiveness, exclusively individual responsibility for wellness and competence, and a fear-based system of accountability. Sufficient supports should be in place to help promote every trainee's ongoing effective functioning.

To create a communitarian culture, trainers may need to undergo training to educate themselves on how to create such an environment and to better understand the role they may play in promoting or unintentionally undermining effective functioning of trainees (Kaslow et al., 2014). This is consistent with Standard 2.01, Boundaries of Competence (APA, 2017), which requires that psychologists have the necessary competence to ensure they carry out their professional responsibilities effectively. Further, this ethical standard requires each psychologist's competence to include sufficient attention to diversity factors and individual differences to ensure that each individual's relevant needs and best interests are met. Senior administrators must (a) take responsibility for ensuring that the needed education and training of trainers is provided and (b) provide the needed leadership and resources. Although gatekeeper functions are essential for ensuring that training programs only graduate competent professionals, a focus on effective role modeling and mentoring, the integration of self-care into all aspects of the training program, timely evaluation and helpful feedback on an ongoing basis, and opportunities for remediation when needed that include necessary support and assistance are essential for minimizing TPPC and promoting the development of competent professionals (Johnson & Kaslow, 2014).

The focus on communitarianism must be lived by all faculty and trainees, understanding that trainees are in the midst of developing their professional identity and are often readily influenced by trainers' behaviors. Thus, trainers must accept responsibility for effective modeling of self-care and transparency while ensuring that the training program's structure and expectations do not undermine these efforts (Forrest et al., 2008). Trainers also must possess the requisite competence needed to thoughtfully and effectively attend to and address TPPC consistent with the training program's focus on a communitarian training culture.

All of this is consistent with the expectations set in Standard 7.01, Design of Education and Training Programs (APA, 2017). This standard requires that training programs are "designed to provide the appropriate knowledge and proper experiences, and to meet the requirements for licensure, certification, and other goals for which claims are made by the program." Training programs will best be served by infusing a communitarian culture within all aspects of the training experience—something that can significantly reduce the probability of TPPC and ensure the best chance possible of achieving a positive resolution when problems with professional competence do arise (Forrest et al., 2013).

Support for this focus on a communitarian training culture is found in accreditation standards as well. Section III.C, Plans to Maximize Student Success of APA's (2015) *Standards of Accreditation for Health Service Psychology and Accreditation Operating Procedures* requires that trainers engage in all needed actions to maximize student success and to minimize "preventable causes of attrition" to include "unsupportive learning environments" (p. 12). This accreditation standard also requires that training programs focus on trainees' individual differences and needs by engaging in "tailored retention/completion efforts as appropriate (e.g., accommodation of student needs and special circumstances)" (p. 15). Thus, accredited training programs must take necessary steps to create and ensure a supportive learning environment for all trainees, doing so with sensitivity to diversity and individual differences and needs.

Effective Communication and Active Information Sharing

It is hoped that training programs will make clear in all program descriptions their commitment to a communitarian training culture. This includes websites, promotional materials sent to prospective applicants, presentations to interviewees, student handbooks, and policy documents. Thus, communications with prospective trainees, members of the public, and current trainees should consistently promote this focus consistent with the ethical ideals articulated in the APA Ethics Code's General Principles (APA, 2017). It is equally important to ensure that the training program's policies and procedures are consistent with the communitarian training culture. With regard to the General Principles' ethical values, training programs must be open and transparent about their policies and procedures, expectations of trainees, program requirements and standards that must be met, evaluation criteria and methods, feedback practices, remediation and retention criteria, safeguards in place to protect trainee rights, and how these policies and procedures are implemented to promote fairness and equitable treatment of all. As is stated in Standard 7.02, Descriptions of Education and Training Programs, such program descriptions should be current and accurate. This is consistent with Standard 5.01, Avoidance of False or Deceptive Statements, which requires accuracy in all public statements regardless of the medium used (e.g., written, verbal, and online). Further, Standard 7.02 requires that "this information must be made readily available to all interested parties."

As highlighted by Vacha-Haase et al. (2004), accreditation standards require that training programs "make available written policies informing students of performance evaluation, feedback, advisement, retention and termination decisions, and due process and grievance procedures" (p. 116). These authors further stressed the importance of due process and fairness to students that takes into consideration the imbalance of power in professional relationships between training programs and trainers and their trainees. This guidance is consistent with Standards 3.04, Avoiding Harm, and 3.08, Exploitative Relationships (APA, 2017).

One important venue for transparently disseminating this required information to trainees and promoting trainees' professional identities and values is the orientation process for new trainees. A thoughtfully planned orientation will allow trainers to share information openly with trainees in an effort to ensure that trainees have a realistic understanding of the requirements and demands of the training program, the stresses of graduate training and life challenges and how they interact, and the mechanisms in place to support trainees in general and when they experience difficulties. Beyond the orientation of new trainees, it is recommended that a focus on such issues be integrated into the training experience on an ongoing basis. The orientation experience may be overwhelming, information shared may lack the context that will be present over the course of training, and issues discussed may be forgotten over time. Relevant information should be shared, discussed, and reinforced over time to support the trainee's ongoing professional growth and development. Examples of communitarian safeguards and support structures that should prove helpful in this regard include advising, mentoring, holding regularly scheduled check-in sessions with trainees, having regular meetings of trainers and administrators with training cohorts, and conducting ongoing presentations and workshops that promote the communitarian training culture and address relevant issues such as challenges to competence, work–life balance, stress management and coping skills, self-care and the promotion of wellness, time management skills, and ethical obligations.

In addition to these efforts, it is important to proactively help allied professionals and key training stakeholders to appreciate psychology ethics and the unique obligations of trainers. For example, one should not assume that stakeholder partners (e.g., organizational administration, lawyers, student advocates, or clinical faculty from allied health professions) will necessarily understand psychology's ethical principles, communitarian training commitments, or the psychologist's dual ethical obligations to both the individual trainee and the larger society. Doing so should be helpful in obtaining greater support for the communitarian training culture and a greater understanding of the focus on the promotion of professional competence and the reasons behind remediation efforts and gatekeeper functions implemented by trainers.

The Training Contract

To further ensure that trainees are aware of all information necessary for them to be successful in the training program and understand performance expectations, criteria for success, evaluation procedures, remediation opportunities, and dismissal procedures, it is recommended that an informed consent process be used to ensure that trainees possess the necessary information and that they understand the information being shared with them. This is consistent with the recommendation that all clinical supervisors use an informed consent process, typically referred to as a supervision contract, that is reviewed, discussed, and agreed to at the outset of the professional relationship (Falender & Shafranske, 2004; Thomas, 2010) and added to as needed to reflect changes in expectations and responsibilities that may occur over the course of the training experience. This is supported by General Principle B, Fidelity and Responsibility, of the APA Ethics Code, which guides psychologists to "establish relationships of trust with those with whom they work" and Standard 3.10, Informed Consent (APA, 2017).

It is recommended that the training contract be a written document that is discussed, that the trainer ensures the trainee's understanding and acceptance of the information included in the contract, and that both the trainer and trainee can refer back to as may be relevant over time. In addition, because trainees may be inundated with information about the new training experience, having a written document to refer back to and review over time can help ensure their deepening awareness of training standards, expectations, and resources.

Although Standard 7.03, Accuracy in Teaching (APA, 2017), requires that course syllabi are accurate with regard to "bases for evaluating progress, and the nature of course experiences," merely relying on course syllabi and published program descriptions is considered insufficient for ensuring trainees' understanding of the training program's expectations. The open sharing of information necessary to ensure that trainees understand their roles, responsibilities, obligations, and rights, along with program requirements and policies, is an important preventative step for initiating training relationships built on mutual trust and understanding. Trainers should use this process to initiate ongoing discussions relevant to professional competence, the myriad ways it may be threatened over time, and resources in place for proactively and thoughtfully addressing difficulties. Specific criteria for successfully competing each phase of the training experience and overall, along with specific minimal standards and expectations that must be met, should be clearly articulated.

In keeping with a communitarian training ethos, the training contract should also elaborate trainers' expectations that all trainees will assume a measure of caring responsibility for the well-functioning and competence of peers. The principle of beneficence means that trainees own an obligation to promote the best interests of colleagues while simultaneously protecting the public. A notable touchstone with the APA Ethics Code is Standard 1.04, Informal Resolution of Ethical Violations (APA, 2017). This standard enjoins psychologists to address unethical behavior on the part of other psychologists. Whenever possible, a trainee should attempt to bring concerns about competence or professionalism to the attention of a fellow trainee, with the intention of educating and seeking an informal resolution. Program documents and training faculty should reiterate this expectation, perhaps offering case illustrations of caring conversations regarding problems of professional competence and ethical behavior. Helping trainees overcome their natural reluctance to address concerns about fellow trainees' competence and professionalism is essential, as doing so may feel like betraying a colleague (Shen-Miller et al., 2011). Yet remaining silent when such concerns are present violates one's ethical obligations and may put the well-being and safety of those the trainee serves at risk. In the same vein, this solemn ethical obligation to hold colleagues accountable applies among trainers. Thus, a caring conversation with a fellow trainer who either ignores competence problems among trainees or is too quick to label trainees as incompetent is an unavoidable communitarian responsibility.

GATEKEEPER FUNCTIONS AND OBLIGATIONS

Consistent with accreditation requirements to regularly evaluate student functioning and to provide trainees with ongoing feedback and opportunities for remediation (APA, 2015), trainers have an ethical obligation to monitor trainees' ongoing functioning and professional development. Although each trainee should be afforded all reasonably available opportunities to be successful and to overcome obstacles to professional competence, training programs are ethically bound to ensure that each trainee's professional competence meets minimal standards before allowing them to advance. As

Kitchener (1992) articulated, "There is a specific ethical obligation not to graduate those who because of their incompetence or lack of ethical sensitivity would inflict harm on the consumers whom they have agreed to help" (p. 190). There is a similar obligation not to allow trainees to move on to the next level of training when they have not consistently demonstrated mastery of the competencies required for successful completion of the present training experience.

Providing trainees with corrective feedback and addressing problems with professional competence, especially when remediation efforts do not yield positive results, may be especially challenging for trainers. Trainers may fear lawsuits by or complaints from former trainees who are displeased with being dismissed from their training program, or they may be influenced by awareness of the likely impact of dismissal from a training program on trainees who are close to completion of the program. In addition, trainers may be sensitive to accreditation issues, knowing they will need to report graduation and attrition rates to accrediting bodies. Trainers may also feel an obligation to the trainee based on compassion and caring that may tempt trainers to allow a struggling trainee to move on to the next level of training. Hoping that the passage of time will resolve ongoing difficulties or assuming that subsequent trainers will address professional competence problems that remain results in what Johnson et al. (2008) described as similar to "passing a hot potato." This fails to fulfill the trainer's ethical obligations (specifically, Standard 7.06, Assessing Student and Supervisee Performance; APA, 2017) and places those the trainee provides professional services—both now and in the future—at risk.

Failure to effectively implement the gatekeeper role risks violating Standard 2.05, Delegation of Work to Others, along with Standard 3.04, Avoiding Harm (APA, 2017). Trainers should not put trainees in situations where they do not possess the necessary competence to provide needed services, keeping in mind the amount and type of supervision to be provided and the expectations of trainees based on their level of training. Trainers will want to ensure that trainees are making progress toward training goals and expectations, making good use of feedback provided to them, and demonstrating the professionalism and ethical conduct expected of a budding mental health professional. Finally, trainers must keep in mind that when trainees graduate from their program, they will likely be working independently and no longer have the oversight, evaluation, feedback, and opportunities for remediation found during the training experience. Bernard and Goodyear (2014) made this point very clearly in stating that each trainer has the responsibility to ensure that only those trainees who demonstrate the competencies and disposition needed for independent practice be allowed to graduate from the training program.

Assessment, Evaluation, and Feedback

Trainers must ethically evaluate each trainee's progress toward training goals and objective standards of competence that must be met at each level of training (see Chapter 5, this volume). In fact, being able to effectively evaluate trainees and doing so ethically and consistently based on established standards is an essential aspect of each trainer's professional competence. Evaluation procedures and standards trainees must meet should be included in relevant program materials and explained to trainees when discussing the training contract. Trainers should be transparent about the nature and frequency of evaluations of trainee functioning and the specific measures and criteria for success to be used. Further, it is recommended that trainers use assessment methods that are reliable and valid for their stated purposes and for the individuals being assessed, that reliance on a single method of evaluation be avoided, and that assessment methods comprehensively address all relevant aspects of competence necessary to achieve stated training objectives (Vacha-Haase et al., 2019). It is also recommended that direct methods of assessment that measure stated performance objectives be used (e.g., observing the trainee implement a specific skill or technique, viewing video recordings of trainees carrying out professional duties, or reviewing the trainee's documentation and comparing it with established standards and evaluation rubrics provided to the trainee) over indirect methods such as course grades and overly general verbal reports of a trainee's global performance or functioning. Consistent with Standard 3.10, Informed Consent, and Section 4, Privacy and Confidentiality (APA, 2017), it is essential that trainees clearly understand how the results of these assessments may be utilized (e.g., to determine whether one may continue in the training program) and with whom they will be shared (e.g., the program's training director).

Standard 7.06, Assessing Student and Supervisee Performance (APA, 2017), requires that "psychologists establish a timely and specific process for providing feedback to students and supervisees" and that the details of the assessment and feedback process are provided to trainees at the outset of each training experience (e.g., orientation sessions and the training contract). This ethical standard also requires that trainees are evaluated "on the basis of their actual performance on relevant and established program requirements." Thus, the APA Ethics Code requires that assessment methods are relevant to established criteria for success in the training program. Standards 3.05,

Multiple Relationships, and 3.06, Conflict of Interest, require that all evaluations of trainees be objective and impartial. Trainers must be cautious about factors that may affect their objectivity and judgment such as preexisting relationships, developing friendships, and feelings of attraction. Trainers should (a) be mindful of the imbalance of power in trainer–trainee relationships as well as the issues of dependency and trust that are relevant to these relationships and (b) work diligently not to take advantage of or exploit them.

Multiple Relationships and the Gatekeeping-Advocacy Tension

As trainees progress through their professional training, there often is a shift toward a more collegial relationship. This shift is important in that trainers are modeling professional conduct for trainees and validating their progress toward becoming autonomous professionals. Although all of this may be not only appropriate but also important for the trainee's professional growth and development, consistent with Standard 3.05, Multiple Relationships, maintaining appropriate boundaries between trainer and trainee remains of great importance (Smith & Fitzpatrick, 1995).

The APA Ethics Code enjoins psychologists to exercise considerable caution when engaging clients, students, and others in more than one relationship form. Standard 3.05, Multiple Relationships, specifically warns against adding a new relationship with a trainee if it might reasonably be expected to impair the psychologist's objectivity and effectiveness in performing their duties as a training psychologist. For example, trainers should not supervise a family member or close friend, engage in romantic or sexual relationships with current trainees, or negotiate a business partnership with a trainee that may appear exploitive now or in the future. Standard 3.05 reminds us that ensuring our objectivity and unimpaired judgment is important. In theory, all secondary relationships that hold significant potential to adversely impact the trainer's objectivity and judgment or to place the trainee at risk of exploitation or harm should be avoided (Thomas, 2010). Yet over the course of a trainee's development from neophyte to graduate, trainers may simultaneously occupy roles as instructor, evaluator, research or clinical supervisor, program advisor, and, in the best training relationships, mentor.

Excellent training relationships often evolve from transactional advising or supervision to more transformational mentoring. As this transition occurs, the dyad is likely to become more emotionally connected and the relationship exchanges defined by greater mutuality and reciprocity (Johnson, Skinner, & Kaslow, 2014). As a mentoring psychologist and a trainee begin to enjoy a more collegial connection, the mentor may develop a palpable sense of advocacy for the trainee, including an impulse to protect or shelter a trainee who is struggling with competence concerns. As Lichtenberg et al. (2007) observed, these mentoring and evaluative roles with trainees reflect "the affirming and validating functions on the one hand, and the gatekeeping functions on the other" (p. 477). From the perspective of professional ethics, this advocacy–evaluation tension is exacerbated by sometimes competing ethical obligations. For instance, the ethical principles of beneficence and nonmaleficence compel trainers to benefit those with whom they work. Yet in promoting the apparent welfare of a trainee with problems with professional competence, the mentoring trainer may inadvertently undermine the best interests of the public at large. Training psychologists must achieve a reasoned balance among communitarian care, personal support, and mentorship while safeguarding the public from incompetent professionals and rendering objective and honest formative and summative assessments of trainees. Finally, trainers must refrain from abusing the imbalance of power in the training relationship while maintaining clear and consistent boundaries, even when functioning as a mentor, so that trainee evaluations and feedback are relevant, helpful, and valid.

Feedback and Remediation

Trainers should review the results of all assessments of a trainee's functioning and performance with the trainee, providing comprehensive and accurate feedback in a supportive manner. In addition, when areas of concern or difficulty are noted, their implications should be clearly explained to the trainee. Any need for remediation, disciplinary action, or risks to the trainee's status in the training program should be discussed. Trainees may at times be reluctant to speak openly about difficulties they are experiencing. The need for open discussion is addressed in Standard 7.04, Student Disclosure of Personal Information. This standard requires trainees to discuss personal issues, conflicts, and difficulties openly with trainers (in a nonpublic setting) when "the information is necessary to evaluate or obtain assistance for students whose personal problems could reasonably be judged to be preventing them from performing their training- or professionally related activities in a competent manner" (APA, 2017). In a genuinely communitarian training culture, training leaders remain focused on and fulfill their gatekeeper role while facilitating a sense that these necessary disclosures will be met with empathy, care, and collaboration on the part of trainers. Creating a training environment perceived as a safe space for transparency and trust requires consistent openness and honesty on the part of trainers. This ethical standard also makes it clear that training programs should inform trainees of this requirement in training policy documents, to include the training contract.

Consistent with Standard 6.01, Documentation of Professional and Scientific Work and Maintenance of Records (APA, 2017), all feedback provided to trainees should be documented and stored in the trainee's official record within the training program. This is especially important in that trainers may leave the program and new trainers may not be aware of past assessments, discussions, and agreements—including formal remediation plans—related to competence problems. It is recommended that all assessment findings, recommendations made or requirements that must be met for the trainee to remain in the training program and to progress to the next level of training, and all follow-up assessments and discussions should be documented and signed by both the trainer and trainee to ensure accuracy and acceptance of decisions made by the training program about the trainee.

A mechanism also should be in place for trainers within each training program to openly share with each other concerns about trainees' competence and functioning so that what may appear to be small or isolated issues to individual trainers—but that actually represent persistent and problematic patterns—will not be overlooked. By the same token, trainee behavior that raises alarm in one trainer may be given context by another such that it may be correctly interpreted as situational versus characterological.

Feedback to trainees should be specific and attached to observable behaviors, relevant training goals, and required competencies, as is required by Standard 7.06, Assessing Student and Supervisee Performance (APA, 2017). It is hoped that prevention strategies will help to minimize trainee problems with professional competence, but for those that do arise, it is desirable that they are caught and addressed as early in the training sequence as is possible (Forrest et al., 2008). When remediation is necessary before the trainee is authorized to progress to the next level of training, trainers should determine the nature of the remediation experiences necessary. Intervention strategies should be tailored to each trainee's individual needs and trainers should keep in mind that there may be more than one way to reach desired outcomes. As described by Vacha-Haase et al. (2019), "Effective remediation plans delineate objective and achievable goals; determine an adequate time frame within which to reasonably expect trainees to gain or alter their relevant knowledge, skills, and attitudes; and explicate the consequences of success and failure" (p. 241). They further explained that effective remediation plans may seek to "(1) increase knowledge, (2) enhance skills, and (3) deepen self-awareness" (p. 241). Drafting the remediation plan in this manner helps to fulfill the requirements of Standard 3.10, Informed Consent (APA, 2017), and ensures that trainees are fully informed of expectations of them and standards to which they will be held.

Remediation actions may include repeating coursework and training experiences, with specific criteria set for successful completion of these experiences; receiving additional supervision; participating in other training experiences such as ethics or Health Insurance Portability and Accountability Act training; completing individualized tutorials to address knowledge or skill deficits; and engaging in personal psychotherapy or other treatment to address mental health difficulties that are found to be impacting the trainee's competence and functioning. At times, difficulties are significant enough that continued interactions with clients would be inappropriate and a leave of absence may be required during the remediation period (Standard 2.06, Personal Problems and Conflicts). As always, the overarching goals are to ensure that trainees possess the competence sufficient to provide appropriate professional services (Standard 2, Competence) and to ensure that the recipients of those professional services are not harmed (Standard 3.04, Avoiding Harm; APA, 2017).

With regard to mandatory individual psychotherapy, Standard 7.05, Mandatory Individual or Group Therapy, necessitates that such a requirement be included in relevant programmatic descriptions and policy documents, including the training contract. This ethical standard also states that trainees must be allowed "the option of selecting such therapy from practitioners unaffiliated with the program" (APA, 2017) and that trainers likely to be in an evaluative role with trainees never serve as the trainee's psychotherapist. For obvious reasons, Standards, 3.04, Avoiding Harm; 3.05, Multiple Relationships; and 3.06, Conflict of Interest are relevant to this requirement. Further, issues of confidentiality are especially sensitive when a trainee participates in individual psychotherapy. When personal psychotherapy is required, expectations for feedback from the psychotherapist should be clarified so that participation in the psychotherapy and the achievement of certain broadly defined goals can be shared with the training program, without requiring disclosure about the details of the content of the psychotherapy process. Standards 4.02, Discussing the Limits of Confidentiality, and 4.05, Disclosures, are relevant for ensuring that only the minimal information necessary is shared with the training program. Yet some feedback from the psychotherapist will be required so that the training program will have some assurance that the stated goals of the psychotherapy treatment have been achieved and that it will be appropriate for the trainee to return to their training setting. All such agreements should be documented and the consequences of failure to achieve the stated goals should be clearly specified.

Regardless of the type of remediation required, a written remediation plan should be used that details all required remediation, a proposed timeline that includes any agreed-upon deadlines, specific issues to be addressed, each party's responsibilities, confidentiality and its limits, financial responsibility if any fees are involved, clearly articulated goals of the remediation process and detailed criteria for success, possible consequences if success is not achieved, and due process protections for the trainee. This written remediation plan should be signed by all concerned parties and included in the trainee's official record at the training program. Doing so is consistent with the requirements of Standards 6.01, Documentation of Professional and Scientific Work and Maintenance of Records, and 3.10, Informed Consent (APA, 2017), and the guidance provided earlier in the supervision contract (see also Chapter 6, this volume).

Confidentiality

Standard 4.01, Maintaining Confidentiality, is relevant to creating a communitarian training culture, establishing trust with trainees (particularly when they might experience problems of competence), and protecting information gleaned from trainees about their personal lives and professional struggles. The ethical standard bearing on confidentiality is tied directly to the foundational principles of trust and respect. Confidentiality is recognized by most psychologists as a cornerstone of any helping relationship and is a salient element of any fiduciary relationship, including our training relationships with students and supervisees.

Yet Behnke (2014) cautioned against wholesale transfer of clinical conceptions of confidentiality to training contexts. For instance, a clinical perspective on trainee confidentiality may inhibit constructive communication among psychologists occupying different roles in the training landscape (e.g., graduate program, practicum site, internship program) such that TPPC may not be effectively identified or remediated before credentialing (Johnson et al., 2008; Vacha-Haase et al., 2019). According to Behnke, training psychologists must strike a balance between a trainee's right to privacy and the training program's accountability to the profession and the public. Unlike in psychotherapy or counseling relationships, most communications between a psychologist and a trainee are not governed by a stringent ethical requirement for confidentiality. Instead, Standard 4.04, Minimizing Intrusions on Privacy (APA, 2017), is likely to be more relevant.

Training psychologists may needlessly create tension, conflict, and distress about disclosing trainee information to the appropriate entities—such as when a trainee requires remediation or when problems with professional competence necessitate restrictions on scope of practice—simply because they fail to solicit the trainee's consent (Behnke, 2014). When a training culture is defined by collaboration, colleague care, and transparency (i.e., a communitarian culture), trainees are often quite willing to consent to disclosures of confidential information. Also see Chapter 7 in this volume for an extended discussion of trainee confidentiality.

CONCLUSIONS AND RECOMMENDATIONS

This chapter explored the ethical issues, challenges, and requirements relevant to addressing TPPCs. All trainers and training programs should be prepared to address TPPC and to do so in a manner consistent with the ethical ideals of the profession of psychology as articulated in the aspirational General Principles along with the enforceable Ethical Standards of the APA Ethics Code (APA, 2017) and accreditation requirements for training programs (APA, 2015).

The importance of a focus on prevention that includes the development of a communitarian training culture has been emphasized over a reactive approach to TPPC after they arise. This can be done by creating a training culture in which trainees are supported and where interdependence, caring, mutual support, mentoring, and effective role modeling are present. Further, it is essential to attend to and value individual differences among trainees and personalize the training program's approach to assisting each trainee to flourish.

Key ethics issues addressed in this chapter include attention to the design of training programs, development and communication of clear and relevant policies, informed consent, confidentiality, professional competence, documentation, ongoing evaluation and provision of helpful and meaningful feedback, and the gatekeeping function of trainers. For each, specific ethical guidance is provided to assist trainers and training programs to best meet the needs of their trainees, to ensure that all graduates of their training program possess the requisite competence and professionalism to practice independently, and to protect the welfare of trainees' current and future clients.

Here are several best practices for all trainers and training programs to embrace as they frame and operate within a genuinely communitarian, caring, and fundamentally ethical training milieu for TPPC:

- Engage in prevention, create a communitarian training culture, and provide all trainers with the necessary training so they may effectively implement this culture.

- Model openness, sharing, and mutual support of colleagues, never relying on oneself alone for responding to life's challenges and demands.
- Consult freely with colleagues when deciding how best to respond to concerns about a trainee's competence to help ensure the most ethical and appropriate response possible.
- Actively seek and be open to trainee input and feedback to continually enhance and improve the communitarian training culture.
- Clearly articulate training program requirements and expectations in all program materials.
- Develop and disseminate policies and procedures that address trainee performance standards, possible consequences of not meeting these standards, and trainee rights.
- Follow all written policies and ensure that due process protections are in place.
- Use a written training contract with each trainee and actively ensure their understanding of all responsibilities, expectations, standards, evaluation procedures, and possible consequences for not meeting expectations.
- Share all evaluation criteria from the outset of the training experience, ensure that criteria are behaviorally anchored and relevant to required competencies, utilize multiple valid methods of evaluation, and provide helpful ongoing feedback to trainees.
- When TPPC are present, offer meaningful remediation and additional training opportunities to trainees that are relevant and meaningful to their individual needs and differences.
- Take seriously the gatekeeping role of trainers while balancing this with mentoring in a caring and supportive training environment.

REFERENCES

American Psychological Association. (2015). *Standards of accreditation for health service psychology and accreditation operating procedures* (revisions approved August 2017, June 2018, and November 2019). https://www.apa.org/ed/accreditation/about/policies/standards-of-accreditation.pdf

American Psychological Association. (2017). *Ethical principles of psychologists and code of conduct* (2002, amended effective June 1, 2010, and January 1, 2017). https://www.apa.org/ethics/code/index

Barnett, J. E. (2008). Impaired professionals: Distress, professional impairment, self-care, and psychological wellness. In M. Herson & A. M. Gross (Eds.), *Handbook of clinical psychology: Vol. 1. Adults* (pp. 857–884). John Wiley & Sons.

Behnke, S. (2014). Remedial and disciplinary interventions in graduate psychology training programs: Twenty-five essential questions for faculty and supervisors. In W. B. Johnson & N. J. Kaslow (Eds.), *Oxford handbook of education and training in professional psychology* (pp. 356–376). Oxford University Press.

Bernard, J. M., & Goodyear, R. K. (2014). *Fundamentals of clinical supervision* (5th ed.). Pearson Education.

Dias, F. A., Chance, J., & Buchanan, A. (2020). The motherhood penalty and the fatherhood premium in employment during COVID-19: Evidence from the United States. *Research in Social Stratification and Mobility*, *69*, 100542. https://doi.org/10.1016/j.rssm.2020.100542

Falender, C. A., & Shafranske, E. P. (2004). *Clinical supervision: A competency-based approach*. American Psychological Association. https://doi.org/10.1037/10806-000

Forrest, L., Elman, N. S., Huprich, S. K., Veilleux, J. C., Jacobs, S. C., & Kaslow, N. J. (2013). Training directors' perceptions of faculty behaviors when dealing with trainee competence problems: A mixed method pilot study. *Training and Education in Professional Psychology*, *7*(1), 23–32. https://doi.org/10.1037/a0032068

Forrest, L., Shen-Miller, D. S., & Elman, N. S. (2008). Psychology trainees with competence problems: From individual to ecological conceptualizations. *Training and Education in Professional Psychology*, *2*(4), 183–192. https://doi.org/10.1037/1931-3918.2.4.183

Handelsman, M. M., Knapp, S., & Gottlieb, M. C. (2001). Positive ethics. In C. R. Snyder & S. Lopez (Eds.), *Handbook of positive psychology* (pp. 731–744). Oxford University Press.

Johnson, W. B., Barnett, J. E., Elman, N. S., Forrest, L., Schwartz-Mette, R., & Kaslow, N. J. (2014). Preparing trainees for lifelong competence: Creating a communitarian training culture. *Training and Education in Professional Psychology*, *8*(4), 211–220. https://doi.org/10.1037/tep0000048

Johnson, W. B., Elman, N. S., Forrest, L., Robiner, W. N., Rodolfa, E., & Schaffer, J. B. (2008). Addressing professional competence problems in trainees: Some ethical considerations. *Professional Psychology: Research and Practice*, *39*(6), 589–599. https://doi.org/10.1037/a0014264

Johnson, W. B., & Kaslow, N. J. (2014). On developing professional psychologists: The state of the art and a look ahead. In W. B. Johnson & N. J. Kaslow (Eds.), *Oxford handbook of education and training in professional psychology* (pp. 1–13). Oxford University Press.

Johnson, W. B., Skinner, C. J., & Kaslow, N. J. (2014). Relational mentoring in clinical supervision: The transformational supervisor. *Journal of Clinical Psychology*, *70*(11), 1073–1081. https://doi.org/10.1002/jclp.22128

Kaslow, N. J., Johnson, W. B., & Schwartz, A. C. (2014). When training goes awry. In W. B. Johnson & N. J. Kaslow (Eds.), *The Oxford handbook of education and training in professional psychology* (pp. 377–393). Oxford University Press.

Kitchener, K. S. (1992). Psychologist as teacher and mentor: Affirming ethical values throughout the curriculum. *Professional Psychology: Research and Practice*, *23*(3), 190–195. https://doi.org/10.1037/0735-7028.23.3.190

Lichtenberg, J. W., Portnoy, S. M., Bebeau, M. J., Leigh, I. W., Nelson, P. D., Rubin, N. J., Smith, I. L., & Kaslow, N. J. (2007). Challenges to the assessment of competence and competencies. *Professional Psychology: Research and Practice*, *38*(5), 474–478. https://doi.org/10.1037/0735-7028.38.5.474

Shen-Miller, D. S., Grus, C. L., Van Sickle, K., Schwartz-Mette, R., Cage, E., Elman, N. S., Jacobs, S. C., & Kaslow, N. J. (2011). Trainees experiences with peers having competence problems: A national survey. *Training and Education in Professional Psychology*, *5*(2), 112–121. https://doi.org/10.1037/a0023824

Smith, D., & Fitzpatrick, M. (1995). Patient-therapist boundary issues: An integrative review of theory and research. *Professional Psychology: Research and Practice*, *26*(5), 499–506. https://doi.org/10.1037/0735-7028.26.5.499

Thomas, J. T. (2010). *The ethics of supervision and consultation: Practical guidance for mental health professionals*. American Psychological Association. https://doi.org/10.1037/12078-000

Vacha-Haase, T., Davenport, D. S., & Kerewsky, S. D. (2004). Problematic students: Gatekeeping practices of academic professional psychology programs. *Professional Psychology: Research and Practice*, *35*(2), 115–122. https://doi.org/10.1037/0735-7028.35.2.115

Vacha-Haase, T., Elman, N. S., Forrest, L., Kallaugher, J., Lease, S. H., Veilleux, J. C., & Kaslow, N. J. (2019). Remediation plans for trainees with problems of professional competence. *Training and Education in Professional Psychology*, *13*(4), 239–246. https://doi.org/10.1037/tep0000221

Veilleux, J. C., January, A. M., VanderVeen, J. W., Reddy, L. F., & Klonoff, E. A. (2012). Differentiating amongst characteristics associated with problems of professional competence: Perceptions of graduate student peers. *Training and Education in Professional Psychology*, *6*(2), 113–121. https://doi.org/10.1037/a0028337

Wise, E. H., & Reuman, L. (2019). Promoting competent and life-long practice for psychologists: A communitarian perspective. *Professional Psychology: Research and Practice*, *50*(2), 129–135. https://doi.org/10.1037/pro0000226

9 LEGAL ISSUES IN WORKING WITH TRAINEES WITH PROBLEMS OF PROFESSIONAL COMPETENCE

SANJAY SHAH AND SARAH R. FISHEL

Supporting trainees with problems of professional competence (TPPC) would ideally be a straightforward process. Imagine that the student, supervisors, supporting faculty, and school administration can clearly identify a competency issue, work together to develop a plan to remediate the issue, effectively implement the plan, and see that the trainee is back on track to successfully complete the program. However, planning for such a smooth process can be folly. Educational institutions, students, and ultimately the public are better served by training programs that anticipate disagreement and challenges and thereby are able to formulate adequate policies and procedures to address these issues. As this chapter illustrates, an assortment of legal theories and issues can apply during the process of working with TPPC.

Often, there can be high-stakes consequences for programs with TPPC, as each party has short- and long-term interests. For trainees, these interests include completing a program and being able to embark on their chosen career path. For training programs, working with TPPC can test existing protocols and serve as precedents for working with trainees with similar problems in the future. Ultimately, the public is best served when competent trainees successfully finish their respective programs and when those with

https://doi.org/10.1037/0000340-010
Supporting Trainees With Competence Problems: A Practical Guide for Psychology Trainers, R. A. Schwartz-Mette, E. A. Hunter, and N. J. Kaslow (Editors)
Copyright © 2023 by the American Psychological Association. All rights reserved.

issues that cannot be remediated or accommodated do not. Many of the legal issues discussed in this chapter could warrant a separate chapter on their own. Therefore, we attempt to provide an overview of the critical considerations that could arise within each legal domain with greater attention given to the potential intersection between the Americans With Disabilities Act (ADA) and TPPC, due process issues, and First Amendment issues. This chapter also discusses issues related to tort, contract, and property law. We further include a review of statutory guidance regarding educational records. When possible, we reference case law, primarily to illustrate how the courts have historically viewed such issues. Though many cases referenced in this chapter largely deal with medical students, the experiential nature of graduate education in the medical and psychology fields allows for direct application of the general principles (Forrest et al., 1999; Hollander, 1996).

Although this chapter is meant to help the reader understand various legal issues and potentially differing perspectives on those issues, it is not meant to provide a precise step-by-step guide on what educational institutions should legally do when working with TPPC. The information here can help programs to inform best practices, design better policies, or simply ask better questions to legal representatives. Additionally, legal precedents vary by jurisdiction. Therefore, the cases discussed in this chapter are examples of how courts have dealt with various issues in the past and may not apply in your specific jurisdiction. Ultimately, when drafting policies or dealing with complex issues with a trainee, legal counsel should be sought.

APPLICABLE STATUTES

This section provides an overview of the intersection of applicable statutory law and TPPC. Specific attention is given to the ADA, Section 504 of the Rehabilitation Act, the Health Insurance Portability and Accountability Act (HIPAA), and the Family Educational Rights and Privacy Act (FERPA).

The ADA and Section 504 of the Rehabilitation Act

The ADA of 1990, including changes made by the ADA Amendments Act of 2008, is an important topic to cover early in this chapter. Not all cases involving TPPC will intersect with ADA (i.e., disability is not tantamount to competence problems); however, being clear on the ADA and how it could intersect with TPPC is essential for trainers. The purpose of the ADA in part is to address and eliminate discrimination against individuals with disabilities so they can fully participate in all aspects of society. A trainee with a documented disability and without the proper accommodations should, at least initially, be viewed distinctly from those with problems of professional competence. However, with sufficient accommodations such as those offered in some of the case examples referenced below, continuing competency issues could signal the need for remediation and eventual dismissal. TPPC will not always qualify as having a disability under the ADA.

The following discussion is meant to highlight certain critical issues pertaining to cases involving the ADA. A key preliminary issue, of course, is determining whether TPPC have a disability that falls under the ADA. The ADA in Section 12102 defines a *disability* in part as a "physical or mental impairment that substantially limits one or more major life activities of such individual." The ADA Amendments Act of 2008 broadened the scope of disabilities under the ADA by, for instance, expanding the term "major life activities" and including impairments that are episodic or in remission. Major life activities relevant to TPPC could include learning, reading, thinking, communicating, and working. Claimants (i.e., the person making a claim in a lawsuit) often assert ADA violations in tandem with a violation of Section 504 of the Rehabilitation Act, which states that

> no otherwise qualified individual with a disability in the United States . . . shall, solely by reason of her or his disability, be excluded from the participation in, be denied the benefits of, or be subjected to discrimination under any program or activity receiving Federal financial assistance.

The ADA applies to institutions receiving federal funding. In deciding these cases, courts are often asked to evaluate whether a disability substantially limits a major life activity, whether a plaintiff is otherwise qualified regardless of accommodations, whether requested accommodations would fundamentally alter a school's program, and whether deference should be given to an academic institution.

Whether a trainee is otherwise qualified regardless of accommodations is often an important and relevant consideration for the courts when it comes to TPPC who have a disability. The ADA uses the term *impairment*, although those involved in training should note the field's movement away from this term.[1] As Forrest and Elman (2014) explained, "Using [the term] PPC rather than impairment language reaffirms that trainees with disabilities may receive accommodations, but will still be held accountable to meet professional standards that constitute the essential functions of becoming a psychologist"

---

[1] For further, important discussions about using the term *impairment* when supporting trainees with competence problems, see Elman and Forrest (2007), Falender et al. (2009), and Schwartz-Mette (2011).

(p. 317). Trainees with disabilities who receive reasonable accommodations would still be required to meet these standards. A trainee may not be qualified for a program if more than reasonable accommodations are deemed necessary to help them meet professional standards.

As an example, a medical student brought a claim against the University of California that he had been discriminated against in violation of the ADA and Section 504 of the Rehabilitation Act (*Wong v. Regents of the University of California*, 1999). Wong was placed on academic probation after having significant difficulties in various clerkships. Wong later reported, and it was confirmed through testing, that he had a learning disability affecting his verbal abilities. He was subsequently referred to a psychologist and was provided several accommodations, including extra time to complete his clerkships and assignment to a student learning disability advisor. The 11th Circuit Court of Appeals in *Wong* laid out the evidence that Wong needed to provide in order to establish a preliminary case of discrimination, including, but not limited to, whether he was a qualified student for the School of Medicine with or without reasonable accommodations. The University of California argued that even with reasonable accommodations, Wong could not meet academic standards. Though the lower court ruled in favor of the university, the court of appeals reversed that decision because it determined that questions remained as to the reasonableness of the accommodations and the plaintiff's qualifications.

In *Pahlavan v. Drexel University College of Medicine* (2020), the trainee, Pahlavan, was receiving accommodations for attention-deficit/hyperactivity disorder and was ultimately dismissed from the medical school program after repeated unsatisfactory performance in his clinical rotations. The Clinical Promotions Committee, a group that oversees students' academic progress, concluded that there was serious doubt regarding Pahlavan's ability to finish medical school as he was given several opportunities to improve his performance. The underlying issue was whether Pahlavan was qualified regardless of receiving reasonable accommodations, which the court found he was not. Circumstances involved in the *Wong* and *Pahlavan* cases suggest that training programs could benefit from documenting the reasoning for providing certain accommodations and excluding others that could reasonably be considered. In addition, ongoing assessment of whether a trainee is benefiting from reasonable accommodations could help identify whether there is an underlying competency issue unrelated to the disability.

When it comes to determining what is a "reasonable" accommodation, institutions might argue that offering certain accommodations would lower their academic standards. Courts have noted that accommodations that fundamentally alter a curriculum are not reasonable (see *Wong v. Regents of the*

University of California, 1999; *Wynne v. Tufts University School of Medicine*, 1991; *Zukle v. Regents of the University of California*, 1999). This was the case in *Doe v. Samuel Merritt University* (2013). Doe asked that there not be a cap on the number of times she could take the American Podiatric Medical Licensing Examination, as the exam itself exacerbated her anxiety disorder. Samuel Merritt University (SMU) claimed that providing this particular accommodation would lower its academic standards and ability to produce competent professionals. Doe asserted that her eventual dismissal violated the ADA and Section 504 of the Rehabilitation Act. The court found that SMU did not clearly indicate whether additional test-taking opportunities would "substantially or fundamentally alter SMU's standards for the worse" (p. 969). As such, proactively defining how certain accommodations or the way accommodations are applied (e.g., an unlimited number of test-taking attempts) might substantially alter academic standards could be beneficial.

The issue of deference was central in cases such as *Doe* and warrants a more thorough discussion for the purposes of this chapter as a whole. In *Doe*, SMU asked that the court defer to its professional judgment. The court in *Doe* concluded that there were serious questions regarding whether denial of the specific accommodation (i.e., no limit on the number of times Doe could take the test) was entitled to deference. The court in *Wong* wrote, "We typically defer to the judgment of academics because courts generally are ill-equipped, as compared with experienced educators, to determine whether a student meets a university's reasonable standards for academic and professional achievement"; however, the deference is "not absolute," as an institution still has a duty to be aware of a student's disability, explore alternatives for accommodations, and "exercise professional judgment in deciding whether the modifications under consideration would give the student the opportunity to complete the program without fundamentally or substantially modifying the school's standards" (pp. 817–818). In *Wong*, the court found that the school's administration did not adequately assess the effectiveness of accommodations with professionals who would be knowledgeable about the student's disability. Similarly, the court in *Pahlavan* did not defer to Drexel's decision, as it found that some faculty reviewers of the student's performance did not consider his disability. The court went on to review the case de novo to determine whether Pahlavan was otherwise qualified. The court on its own (without deferring to Drexel University) ultimately concluded that Pahlavan could not meet standards as outlined in the Medical Student Handbook, despite being provided with many accommodations such as extended time on exams, a leave of absence, and one-on-one mentorship. The court also concluded that there was a lack of evidence that additional accommodations would have helped him meet academic standards.

Family Educational Rights and Privacy Act and Health Insurance Portability and Accountability Act

FERPA came into effect in 1974. It protects the privacy of students and applies to schools that receive funding under applicable Department of Education programs. This includes private postsecondary schools, such as colleges and universities that receive such federal funding. Under FERPA, schools are required to receive written permission from a parent/guardian or an eligible student (i.e., students who are at least 18 years old or attending a postsecondary institution at any age) before disclosing any records. Along with other exceptions, schools can disclose records when there is a legitimate educational interest in doing so, which can potentially apply broadly. However, schools should still consider obtaining consent from the eligible student prior to any disclosure. FERPA would essentially apply to psychology training programs if they are receiving federal funding as described above. Prior to disclosing records, it would be prudent to define and document the legitimate educational interest and obtain the consent of the trainee, if possible.

The education records covered by FERPA include "those records, files, documents, and other materials which contain information directly related to a student; and are maintained by an educational agency or institution or by a person acting or such agency or institution." Physician, psychiatrist, or psychologist treatment records are specifically excluded from this definition because those records are more appropriately covered by HIPAA. Although counseling centers, student health centers, and academic medical centers are covered under HIPAA, academic institutions are not. Education records, rather than health records, are most pertinent to TPPC and remedial and disciplinary proceedings. However, relevant to TPPC, remedial education records could possibly contain information related to a trainee's mental and behavioral health (not directly pertaining to treatment). Such records would likely be covered by FERPA (Legislative History of Major FERPA Provisions, 2002).

Perhaps the most relevant consideration regarding FERPA issues related to TPPC is whether there is a legitimate educational interest for particular personnel to have access to a student's records. FERPA is clear in stating that "school officials with legitimate educational interests" can have access to records that include personally identifiable information. Officials who have such a legitimate educational interest in the trainee's intuition include those who need to review the records to fulfill their professional responsibilities. Therefore, an institution's policies should define and guide who has a legitimate educational interest. Such a policy could inform who generally has access to records related to TPPC, such as those in administration, supervisory, or student support services. In other words, individuals working in these capacities would likely have an interest in accessing such records when formulating remedial actions.

Questions may arise regarding academic records and TPPC when they move on to another institution, such as if they transfer or pursue internship opportunities. The 1994 amendments to FERPA also suggest that an institution can disclose information about disciplinary action to other schools who would also have a legitimate educational interest in that information (Legislative History of Major FERPA Provisions, 2002). Section 99.31(a)(2) of FERPA states that the disclosure of personally identifiable information to officials of another school where the student seeks to enroll or transfer can be done without consent if the disclosing party adheres to the conditions in Section 99.34, such as making a reasonable attempt to notify the trainee, giving the trainee a copy of the records disclosed if requested, and giving the trainee an opportunity for a hearing if requested.

The Issue of Due Process

Due process is essential to the discussion of legal and ethical issues that may arise when working with TPPC. Any remediation or termination plan (if remediation is not successful) must recognize the due process rights afforded to trainees (McAdams & Foster, 2007). Due process rights, in this context, can be divided into two categories. The first, procedural due process, stands for the notion that the individual (in this case, the trainee) being deprived of the interest (such as continuing their training at a particular practicum site or institution) must receive notice of the actions taken against them and be given the opportunity to be heard, though not necessarily through a formal hearing (Kerl et al., 2002). Substantive due process, on the other hand, requires that an action taken against an individual (i.e., trainee) is neither "arbitrary" nor "capricious" (Kerl et al., 2002, p. 326).

Therefore, a challenge against the procedures by which TPPC are dismissed would be reviewed under procedural due process considerations, while the dismissal itself and the reasons for that dismissal would be reviewed as an issue of substantive due process (Gilfoyle, 2008). Though a complete discussion regarding due process in the university context is beyond the scope of this chapter, a review of salient cases follows.

Procedural Due Process and TPPC

The majority of procedural due process considerations regarding students were litigated in the 1960s through the 1980s (Mott, 2017). During this period, the United States Supreme Court set a baseline for protecting the fundamental fairness of actions against students that has largely been untouched by the court since that time, though lesser courts have provided additional, sometimes contradictory, standards in the intervening decades (Medd, 2019).

In *Ingraham v. Wright* (1977), the Supreme Court applied three factors to the question of whether due process was required in *disciplinary* cases: "(1) the nature of the interest protected; (2) the danger of error and the benefit of additional or other procedures; and (3) the burden on the government such protections would present" (Dutile, 2001, p. 265). Generally, disciplinary cases are more egregious and deal with issues of student conduct, for example, if a student were to commit what may equate to malpractice or an ethical violation. Depending on the egregiousness of the action against the student, lower courts have found that due process necessitated notice (*Gaspar v. Bruton*, 1975); an opportunity for both sides to be heard (*Dixon v. Alabama*, 1961); an opportunity to cross-examine witnesses (*Donohue v. Baker*, 1997); an opportunity to bring counsel to the hearing, though only the student could ask questions of the witnesses (*Esteban v. Central Missouri State College*, 1967); no formal hearing at all (*Martin v. Helstad*, 1983); and many other, often contradictory, standards (Dutile, 2001; Ford & Strope, 1996).

The court in *Board of Curators of the University of Missouri v. Horowitz* (1978) held that *academic* dismissals do not require the same due process standards, such as an official hearing, as those for disciplinary cases. Academic dismissals arise when the issue at hand is the student's scholastic performance, including clinical performance, rather than their conduct, for example, if a student is consistently underperforming in their coursework or clinical practice. Important to the application of the principles of due process to psychology trainees, Horowitz's case stemmed from issues in her work with clients (e.g., personal conduct, hygiene, and professionalism). Due to the experiential nature of her medical program, these concerns fell under "academic" dismissal. For academic dismissals to satisfy due process, the student must (a) know what is expected of them; (b) have the same opportunity to be heard; and (c) have been evaluated based on the procedural guidelines as set by the university, as long as they are neither arbitrary nor capricious. The court deferred to the university to determine whether the student's performance was impaired (i.e., what we would now label as a problem with professional competence) and what remediation steps were necessary to support the student and protect any clients who may be harmed by the student's impairments. These standards, along with general deference to the school's decision, were again reflected in *Regents of University of Michigan v. Ewing* (1985).

Some scholars have argued against what they see as an arbitrary distinction between the requirements attached to disciplinary and academic dismissals given that both have the same potential outcome: dismissal (Medd, 2019). Furthermore, some jurisdictions have created separate standards for whether public university students have a protected interest in their education regardless of whether they faced either disciplinary or academic dismissals (Medd, 2019; Mott, 2017), whereas the same question does not arise in private universities, where more discretion is given to the administration. Similar to *Horowitz*, virtually all dismissals from counseling and psychology programs are academic in nature, even if the problem of professional competence is an issue with the trainee's behavior (Forrest et al., 1999; Kerl et al., 2002). Vacha-Haase and colleagues (2004) noted that "inadequate clinical skills," falling under the academic prong of the due process question, was the most-cited reason psychological trainees were dismissed from their programs.

Substantive Due Process and TPPC

The majority of litigation regarding due process focuses on the procedural aspect of the protections. However, the landmark *Horowitz* and *Ewing* cases each nod to the principles underlying substantive due process. Any decision made by the administration regarding the dismissal of a student must be "careful and deliberate" (*Board of Curators of the University of Missouri v. Horowitz*, 1978, p. 87; *Schuler v. University of Minnesota*, 1986, p. 514). Deference is paid to the university "unless [its action constitutes] such a substantial departure from accepted academic norms as to demonstrate that the person or committee responsible did not actually exercise professional judgment"—for example, if a student were to be dismissed after receiving their first B grade in their coursework (*Regents of University of Michigan v. Ewing*, 1985, p. 225). Here, the deference given to the administration partially offsets the ambiguous guidelines of making "careful and deliberate" decisions that are not "arbitrary or capricious." Generally, and supporting the discussion of deference discussed previously, if a decision is made based on specific facts and looking to the student's performance in light of those facts, the court will support the decision of the institution (Ford & Strope, 1996; Gilfoyle, 2008). This may be seen if the student in question were consistently underperforming in their coursework and was given sufficient notifications and opportunities for remediation.

Due Process in Psychology

In addition to the legal standards governing due process rights of public university students, specific disciplines may also present guidance on procedures for working with TPPC. For example, Section F.5.b of the American

Counseling Association (ACA; 2005) Code of Ethics notes that remediation plans should be set for students prior to dismissal. The American Psychological Association (APA; 2015) created a publicly available remediation plan that provides additional and specific guidance for addressing problems of professional competence with students. The Association of Psychology Postdoctoral and Internship Centers has also set both requirements and recommendations for due process, which it recommends should be provided to interns at the beginning of their training (Aosved, 2017; Hollander, 1996).

Regarding remedial actions and setting expectations for TPPC, McAdams and Foster (2007) argued that plans must (a) "be clearly defined in advance of their execution," (b) "receive distinct faculty supervision and support," (c) "be regularly evaluated and reported," and (d) "be thoroughly documented" (p. 6). However, even though these are seemingly simple suggestions, Vacha-Haase and colleagues (2004) found an estimated 53% of clinical, counseling, and school psychology graduate programs accredited by the APA reported that they do not currently have a written policy for addressing TPPC.

For those programs without a specific plan in place, Lamb and colleagues (1987) set forth recommendations for training sites to follow: Provide the trainee with a written set of defined expectations, discuss the evaluation process, develop flexible yet specific evaluation guidelines, set procedures for determining problems of professional competence, engage in communication of concerns and decisions regarding trainees, institute remediation plans, provide appellate procedures to trainees, ensure trainees are given sufficient time to ameliorate any issues, thoroughly document all concerns and actions, and do so with the best interest of the student and their clients in mind. Additionally, Vacha-Haase and colleagues (2004) more recently set forth specific and detailed instructions on creating, implementing, and evaluating remediation plans for TPPC.

THE FIRST AMENDMENT

In *Wallace v. Jaffree* (1985), Justice Stevens "identified the individual's freedom of conscience as the central liberty that unifies the various Clauses in the First Amendment" (p. 50). Competency in working with diverse individuals is essential. This complexity mainly arises when trainees' personal or religious beliefs contradict a particular client's beliefs or characteristics, leading to potential First Amendment issues. As the court cases discussed below indicate, developing competencies related to diversity may not be as simple as establishing policies that trainees should work with individuals whose backgrounds and beliefs conflict with their own.

Students enrolled in public universities and programs retain their First Amendment rights; the most relevant of these to the discussion at hand are freedom of speech and freedom of religion. In their review of this topic, Hutchens and colleagues (2013) reviewed two cases in which psychology or counseling trainees argued against their dismissal on First Amendment grounds. Though the courts in each case came to seemingly divergent conclusions, each analysis provides important insight into the issue of remediation action for TPPC whose actions may reflect values-based judgments.

Ward v. Polite (2012) involved a graduate student in a counselor education program who was dismissed after she was assigned a client whose sexual orientation affected her ability to work with the client on relationship issues. Specifically, she expressed that her Christian faith prevented her from seeing clients in same-sex relationships. Faculty believed that Ward's attempts to refer the client out violated the ACA Code of Ethics (2005). She was dismissed following a hearing, during which it was determined that a remediation plan would not be possible. Ward appealed the decision through the legal system. Though the district court initially sided with the university in *Ward v. Wilbanks* (2010), the court of appeals found in *Ward v. Polite* that Ward's attempts to find a referral for her client complied with the ACA code, which allows for values-based referrals.

Believing generally that policies should be applied equally rather than selectively, the appeals court pointed to what appeared to be a contradiction in that the "school does not have a no referral policy for practicum students and adheres to an ethics code that permits values-based referrals in general" (*Ward v. Polite*, 2012, p. 730). The court noted that some types of referrals, such as those related to clients needing assistance with end-of-life decisions or requesting conversion therapy, were permitted while others were not. Even though courts generally give significant deference to universities, the appellate court in *Ward* noted that a jury could reasonably conclude that Ward was expelled because of the program's hostility toward her speech and faith, rather than her violation of any policies against referrals. As such, a jury could determine that the program's policies were selectively implemented and served as a pretense to act in a way that would violate Ward's First Amendment rights. The appellate court further stated that in attempting to make a referral, the student was trying to not impose her values on gay and lesbian clients, and therefore Ward was compliant with the respective ethics code. She was essentially avoiding a potential conflict. In coming to this conclusion, the appeals court wrote that "tolerance is a two-way street" (p. 735).

Because professional competencies in psychology include working with individuals with diverse identities, trainees in professional psychology programs should expect to do so during their training (BEA Virtual Working

Group on Restrictions Affecting Diversity Training in Graduate Education, 2015). However, training in cultural competency may not always involve actual clinical experience with select groups and populations. A trainee can still achieve cultural competence by other methods, such as in didactic settings or engaging in scholarly work that can enhance their knowledge of cultural differences and various worldviews. Cultural competence can often involve acknowledging when one is not well suited to work with a specific individual and identifying other providers/resources for that individual. However, supervisors and mentors may advise that in some circumstances, a referral may not be possible and trainees should expect that trainers may work with them regarding how to limit the impact of one's biases in order to enhance the welfare of clients.

In contrast to *Ward*, in *Keeton v. Anderson-Wiley* (2011), a master's student in a counseling program was required to complete a remediation program following declarations to professors and peers that she would be unable to work with LGBTQ populations outside of attempting to use the clinical relationship to convert their sexual preferences to heterosexuality. Unlike in *Ward*, there were observable indications that Keeton would actively attempt to impose her values on her clients. Faculty found that Keeton's statements (which expressed a desire to change her future clients' sexual orientations to fit her religious beliefs) were in violation of the ACA Code of Ethics, including, but not limited to, promoting the welfare of clients, not imposing one's own values that are inconsistent with counseling goals, gaining knowledge and awareness pertinent to working with diverse clients, and not engaging in discrimination. While Keeton's statements were more overt, other trainees' motives during treatment may be less obvious but equally a problem with professional competence. In general, training programs should strive to create an environment where trainees gain insight and acknowledge their biases and possible prejudices. Potential issues with cultural competence, perhaps less extreme than Keeton's, might be easier to remediate in such an environment.

Keeton was offered, and refused, a remediation plan pursuant to the university student handbook. She alleged that participation in such a program violated her First Amendment rights to free speech and free exercise of religion. Keeton filed suit in response to the remediation plan; however, the court upheld the university's decision to expel her from the program, citing the content of the remediation plan, which included the behavioral target of developing competencies regarding ethical counseling of LGBTQ clients. The court noted that the remediation plan was imposed due to her intent of imposing her religious views on clients, rather than her general views regarding the LGBTQ population.

Hutchens and colleagues (2013) and Behnke (2012) distilled the essential lessons learned from these two cases. Hutchens and colleagues argued that *Ward* and *Keeton* recognize the ability of programs to "impose ethical mandates on students requiring them to work in an affirming way with clients in relation to their sexual orientation," even if this means eventually referring the client to a different provider (p. 91). Similarly, Behnke noted that schools can adopt and implement policies prohibiting discrimination based on a profession's ethics code, and that training programs can "prohibit students from imposing their values on clients" (p. 194), such as in the *Keeton* case. In *Keeton*, it was the student's statements regarding her intentions to violate ACA standards in her potential work with LGBTQ clients, rather than her disagreement with the standards themselves, that allowed the university to take remedial action.

Hutchens and colleagues (2013) suggested that counseling programs, if they choose to implement a procedure to disallow an outcome consistent with the *Ward* decision, create specific and written "no referral" policies for their practicum students and consider blanket procedures for values-based issues that may arise in the future. Additionally, Behnke (2012) noted that a jury's role is to determine questions of fact. The relevant facts in such conscious-clause cases involve whether a policy was implemented neutrally for all trainees or used as a pretext that has implications regarding a specific student's personal beliefs. These suggested policies do not violate the students' rights to express their beliefs but instead direct how they follow standards and rules set out by programs and professions (Hutchens et al., 2013).

Wise and colleagues (2015) provided an in-depth summary of the APA Board of Educational Affairs (BEA) Virtual Working Group on Restrictions Affecting Diversity Training in Graduate Education. Going in depth with the working group's recommendations is beyond the scope of this chapter. However, their five core tenets include the following: (a) Psychology has a compelling interest in meeting the needs of a diverse client population, (b) trainers respond in a consistent manner to all trainee beliefs that conflict with competent practice, (c) trainers are responsible for education and training, (d) trainers respect trainees' developmental process and foster cognitive complexity, and (e) attaining competency to work with a diverse public is not optional. The authors go on to provide a sample program policy and recommend that these policies be approved by local legal and administrative offices.

OTHER LEGAL ISSUES

Trainees have argued against dismissal from public and private institutions on a number of other legal grounds. The purpose of the following section is not to present a complete picture of the case law surrounding these topics but rather to offer insight into other underlying legal issues in working with TPPC.

Defamation and Libel

Claims of defamation or libel may be brought against a program or educator. Generally, these issues encompass an "oral utterance (slander) or written publication (libel) of false facts or false implied facts damaging to a person's reputation" even if the person stating the facts believes them to be true (Gilfoyle, 2008 p. 205). Given the evaluative nature of graduate psychology programs, students are often evaluated by professors and supervisors. For example, in *Harris v. Blake and the Board of Trustees of the University of Northern Colorado* (1986), a student brought a defamation claim against Blake, a supervisor. Blake recommended that Harris, the student, should not be allowed to enroll in a practicum rotation because of "incompetent" and "unethical" behaviors. Blake provided definitions for each term, along with behavioral examples, such as a lack of attentive behavior, underdeveloped listening skills, and issues with warmth. The court ultimately dismissed the defamation charges against Blake and the Board of Trustees.

This evaluative analysis holds true even when the trainee is no longer a traditional student. In *Kraft v. The William Alanson White Psychiatric Foundation* (1985), the plaintiff, a licensed doctorate-level psychologist enrolled in a postgraduate continuing education program, was not awarded a certificate of completion. Kraft brought suit, claiming that faculty members made libelous and slanderous remarks about him in his student records. However, the court ruled in favor of the school, noting that Kraft was aware of the evaluative procedures, each statement made regarding his performance spoke only to his handling of patients, and communications regarding such opinions were kept among people making decisions regarding his progress.

Harris and *Kraft* highlight important considerations for working with TPPC. It is generally understood that training individuals requires some level of subjective evaluation. Typically, those engaged in evaluations for educational purposes are exempt from suit if the information is kept confidential from those not essential to decision making based on such evaluations (Gilfoyle, 2008). Faculty and other supervisors should be cautious in confining their opinions regarding trainees to performance and assessment; furthermore, these discussions should be repeated to only those who share the common goal of educating or otherwise training the individual in question.

Negligence

Negligence may be raised when the standard of care to supervise a trainee or provide reasonable care to a client is questioned (APA, 2014). Issues with negligence may be directly related to violations of various codes of conduct, whether drafted by professional organizations, such as the ACA or the APA, or by the practice sites themselves (Kaslow et al., 2007). Generally, state licensing boards have asserted that clinical supervisors are responsible for both "negligence in failing to supervise adequately [and] for the actions of supervisees" (Saccuzzo, 1997, p. 122). In one case, wherein a therapist in training engaged in inappropriate sexual conduct with their patient (*Simmons v. United States*, 1986), the courts found the supervisor responsible for the conduct of the trainee due to lack of adequate supervision. In outlining the duties of the mental health supervisor, Saccuzzo (1997) argued that each supervisor must be prepared to monitor and control the supervisory relationship, evaluate the patient, evaluate the supervisee, provide evaluative feedback, and document the supervision that occurs. If a supervisor observes or hears a report about a potential issue regarding patient care or competence problem, that issue should be well documented in their supervisory notes, and the trainee should receive the necessary supervision to correct the behavior in question.

Contract

Contract claims center on cases where students believe that they agreed to a set of terms, which were then violated by the institution or institutional actors (e.g., supervisors) when remedial or dismissive actions were taken against them. Given that most constitutional claims (such as due process violations) can be sought in litigation only against public institutions, students enrolled in programs housed at private universities typically pursue legal action under contractual claims (Gilfoyle, 2008). For these purposes, contractual agreements are presented as not typically a set document both parties agreed to but rather informal or implied terms. Courts have held that provisions in a student handbook may govern contractual relationships between trainees and institutions (*Corso v. Creighton University*, 1984). Furthermore, acceptance of a student's academic fees has been understood as a mutual agreement to abide by the terms noted in school brochures (*Steinberg v. Chicago Medical*

School, 1977) and, on the part of the institution, acknowledgment of any existing student issues known to the program at the time of admittance to said program (*Russell v. Salve Regina College*, 1986). Contractual terms have also been implied from written guidelines and oral representations from faculty members, supervisors, and administrators (Gilfoyle, 2008).

A continued and thorough review of written materials provided to the student by the university, program, or training site is essential to understanding potential contractual issues that may arise when working with TPPC. If there is any ambiguity in the terms as represented by the program, the terms in question are interpreted in a way that most advantages the party that did not draft the terms, typically the trainee (Gilfoyle, 2008). Thus, specificity of standards, expectations, and retaining the right to dismiss students who fail to meet standards and expectations after remediation are helpful to building a strong program that protects supervisors, supervisees, and clients (McAdams et al., 2007). Of note, these issues go beyond terms that are in print and can be altered by verbal agreements made between students and representatives of the program or training site.

Promissory Estoppel

Promissory estoppel, arguably a second prong of contractual considerations and an extension of procedural due process pertaining to notification, allows a plaintiff to "circumvent the program's written policies and procedures, if the court is convinced that, on the facts of the case, enforcing the terms, as a contract or otherwise, would be manifestly unfair" (Gilfoyle, 2008, p. 204). Issues of promissory estoppel typically arise when an individual in a position of authority (e.g., supervisor, faculty member) comes to an agreement with a trainee that is outside the bounds of the written policy. If the student relies on that representation of policy or procedure, which is subsequently found inaccurate, and the finding causes detriment to the student, the court may "estop" the university or program from enforcing their actual rules in favor of the representation made to the student (Gilfoyle, 2008).

In *Blank v. Board of Higher Education* (1966), a psychology student signed up for two classes with an understanding from the chair of the psychology department that the student needed only to take the final exams and not to attend the lectures. The university later cited attendance issues in these two classes as a reason the student could not matriculate. The student sued under the doctrine of promissory estoppel, and the court agreed that the student's agreement with the chair, though diverging from the university policy, constituted a promise that should have been upheld by the school.

In contrast, in *Olsson v. Board of Higher Education of the City of New York* (1980), a professor inaccurately reported the lowest passing score necessary for the completion of a master's degree. The student met the bar set by the professor, but not the accurate bar according to university policy. Here, the court ruled in favor of the university, deferring, as in *Ewing* and *Horowitz*, to the university's evaluation of Olsson's academic qualifications to obtain a master's degree and the need to retain the credibility of the credential.

Perhaps unsurprisingly, the best way to approach issues of promissory estoppel when working with TPPC is to ensure that faculty, supervisors, and administrators follow written procedures (Gilfoyle, 2008). Any deviations from the policy should be carefully considered before they are brought to the student, and any such representation should be carefully documented by both parties. These procedures will help to protect all involved from potential legal issues related to promissory estoppel.

Property Interest in Education

Property interests (i.e., a person's rights in property) are protected by the Due Process Clause as contained in the Fifth Amendment and the Fourteenth Amendment such that an individual cannot be deprived of property without due process of law. Generally, property cannot be taken away without a hearing in line with sound due process procedures. Property interests can go beyond land or tangible goods. They can be established from independent sources of law, such as statutes, regulations, or contracts. A question that could follow is whether trainees have a property interest in education. Courts have often avoided this question and instead decided claims on due process grounds.

In 1975, the Supreme Court in *Goss v. Lopez* decided that high school students have a property interest in education, given that Ohio state laws provide free education to primary students and require attendance. In a separate case heard by the Tenth Circuit Court of Appeals, *Gaspar v. Bruton* (1975), the plaintiff attended and paid tuition at a publicly owned vocational school. She was placed on probation and advised that she would be dismissed from school if her clinical deficiencies were not corrected. She was ultimately dismissed, leading her to file a lawsuit claiming that her due process rights were not met and that she was deprived of her contractual property right to her education. In *Goss*, the court noted that "the State is constrained to recognize a student's legitimate entitlement to a public education as a property interest which is protected by the Due Process Clause and which may not be taken away for misconduct without adherence to the minimum procedures required by the Clause" (p. 574). The court in *Gaspar* recognized this right and added that the student paid a fee to enroll and attend her school. Her property interest in her education served as a reason that she was entitled to due process. Ultimately, the court held that the school authorities satisfied due process prior to terminating the plaintiff.

Whether TPPC have a property interest in education, particularly at the graduate levels, has not been firmly decided by the courts. Unlike primary education, education for trainees at the university level is not required. Mott (2017) asserted that whether a property interest in education exists remains "unpredictable and varies by jurisdiction" (p. 652). He argued that courts should adopt a single approach to decide on property interest regarding education. However, the Supreme Court, in several cases, including *Horowitz* and *Ewing*, has not decided whether a property interest in education exists. For example, the court in *Horowitz* suggested that the plaintiff would have to rely on state law if she wanted to claim that a property interest existed in her case. Alternatively, the court in *Ewing* assumed that a property interest existed without analyzing the merits of that claim, and therefore created no precedent regarding property rights and education.

Mott (2017) further noted that lower courts have often simply assumed property interests in education exist and then proceeded to decide whether a student receives sufficient due process. He argued against this tactic, asserting that property interests should not be avoided "because they are a fundamental part of any due process question" (p. 667). Mott suggested that this current approach could be harmful to plaintiffs bringing claims against universities because courts do not have to decide the property interest question before deciding whether the student received due process. Traditionally, courts have deferred to the institutions in these cases, finding that universities have provided sufficient due process.

CONCLUSION

This chapter offers examples of potential legal issues that could arise during the process of working with TPPC. Laws within each jurisdiction might have their own nuances that affect how a judge or jury would view and decide specific claims. In addition to communicating clear expectations to trainees, carefully crafted policies consistent with applicable legal standards and guidance can help protect the interest of all parties involved, including training programs, trainees, and the public. Programs should continue to monitor federal and local case law and statutes relevant to training that could offer guidance when crafting relevant policies.

REFERENCES

American Counseling Association. (2005). *2005 ACA code of ethics*. https://www.counseling.org/docs/default-source/library-archives/archived-code-of-ethics/codeethics05.pdf

American Psychological Association. (2014). *Guidelines for clinical supervision in health service psychology*. https://www.apa.org/about/policy/guidelines-supervision.pdf

American Psychological Association. (2015). *Standards of accreditation for health service psychology and accreditation operating procedures* (revisions approved August 2017, June 2018, and November 2019). https://irp-cdn.multiscreensite.com/a14f9462/files/uploaded/APA-Principles-Accreditation-SoA-AOP_200116.pdf

American Psychological Association. (2017). *Ethical principles of psychologists and code of conduct* (2002, amended effective June 1, 2010, and January 1, 2017). https://www.apa.org/ethics/code/index.aspx

American With Disabilities Act of 1990, Pub. L. No. 101–336, 104 Stat. 328 (1990).

Aosved, A. C. (2017). Tips for trainers: Due process. *APPIC e-newsletter*. https://www.appic.org/Portals/0/downloads/DueProcess/2017Newsletter-DueProcess.pdf

BEA Virtual Working Group on Restrictions Affecting Diversity Training in Graduate Education. (2015). Preparing professional psychologists to serve a diverse public: A core requirement in doctoral education and training a pedagogical statement. *Training and Education in Professional Psychology*, *9*(4), 269–270. https://doi.org/10.1037/tep0000093

Behnke, S. H. (2012). Constitutional claims in the context of mental health training: Religion, sexual orientation, and tensions between the First Amendment and professional ethics. *Training and Education in Professional Psychology*, *6*(4), 189–195. https://doi.org/10.1037/a0030809

Blank v. Board of Higher Education, 273 N.Y.S. 2d 796 (Sup. Ct. 1966).

Board of Curators of the University of Missouri v. Horowitz, 435 U.S. 78 (1978).

Corso v. Creighton University, 731 F. 2d 529 (8th Cir. 1984).

Dixon v. Alabama, 294 F.2d 150 (5th Cir. 1961).

Doe v. Samuel Merritt University, 921 F. Supp. 2d 958 (2013).

Donohue v. Baker, 976 F. Supp. 136 (N.D.N.Y. 1997).

Dutile, F. N. (2001). Students and due process in higher education: Of interests and procedures. *Florida Coastal Law Journal*, *2*, 243–290.

Elman, N. S., & Forrest, L. (2007). From trainee impairment to professional competence problems: Seeking new terminology that facilitates effective action. *Professional Psychology: Research and Practice*, *38*(5), 501–509.

Esteban v. Central Missouri State College, 277 F. Supp. 649 (W.D. Mo. 1967).

Falender, C. A., Collins, C. J., & Shafranske, E. P. (2009). "Impairment" and performance issues in clinical supervision: After the 2008 ADA Amendments Act. *Training and Education in Professional Psychology*, *3*(4), 240–249. https://doi.org/10.1037/a0017153

Family Educational Rights and Privacy Act of 1974, 20 U.S.C. § 1232g (1974).

Ford, D. L., & Strope, J. L. (1996). Judicial responses to adverse academic decisions affecting public postsecondary institution students since "Horowitz" and "Ewing." *West's Education Law Reporter*, *110*, 517–542.

Forrest, L., Elman, N., Gizara, S., & Vacha-Haase, T. (1999). Trainee impairment: A review of identification, remediation, dismissal, and legal issues. *The Counseling Psychologist*, *27*(5), 627–686. https://doi.org/10.1177/0011000099275001

Forrest, L., & Elman, N. S. (2014). Trainees with problems of professional competence. In W. B. Johnson & N. J. Kaslow (Eds.), *The Oxford handbook of education and training in professional psychology* (pp. 314–335). Oxford University Press.

Gaspar v. Bruton, 513 F.2d 843 (1975).

Gilfoyle, N. (2008). The legal exosystem: Risk management in addressing student competence problems in professional psychology training. *Training and Education in Professional Psychology, 2*(4), 202–209. https://doi.org/10.1037/1931-3918.2.4.202

Goss v. Lopez, 419 U.S. 565 (1975).

Harris v. Blake and the Board of Trustees of the University of Northern Colorado, 798 F.2d 419 (10th Cir. 1986).

Health Insurance Portability and Accountability Act (HIPAA). (2004). Pub. L. No. 104–191, 110 Stat. 1936.

Hollander, P. A. (1996). Legal issues relevant to due process at APPIC internships. *APPIC Newsletter, 21*(2), 1, 34–36.

Hutchens, N., Block, J., & Young, M. (2013). Counselor educator's gatekeeping responsibilities and students' first amendment rights. *Counselor Education and Supervision, 52*(2), 82–95. https://doi.org/10.1002/j.1556-6978.2013.00030.x

Ingraham v. Wright, 430 U.S. 651 (1977).

Kaslow, N. J., Rubin, N. J., Forrest, L., Elman, N. S., Van Horne, B. A., Jacobs, S. C., Huprich, S. K., Benton, S. A., Pantesco, V. F., Dollinger, S. J., Grus, C. L., Behnke, S. H., Miller, D. S. S., Shealy, C. N., Mintz, L. B., Schwartz-Mette, R., Van Sickle, K., & Thorn, B. E. (2007). Recognizing, assessing, and intervening with problems of professional competence. *Professional Psychology: Research and Practice, 38*(5), 479–492. https://doi.org/10.1037/0735-7028.38.5.479

Keeton v. Anderson-Wiley, 664 F.3d 865 (11th Cir. 2011).

Kerl, S. B., Garcia, J. L., McCullough, S., & Maxwell, M. E. (2002). Systematic evaluation of professional performance: Legally supported procedure and process. *Counselor Education and Supervision, 41*(4), 321–332. https://doi.org/10.1002/j.1556-6978.2002.tb01294.x

Kraft v. The William Alanson White Psychiatric Foundation, 498 A.2d 1145 (1985).

Lamb, D. H., Presser, N. R., Pfost, K. S., Baum, M. C., Jackson, V. R., & Jarvis, P. A. (1987). Confronting professional impairment during the internship: Identification, due process, and remediation. *Professional Psychology: Research and Practice, 18*(6), 597–603. https://doi.org/10.1037/0735-7028.18.6.597

Legislative History of Major FERPA Provisions. (2002, June). https://www2.ed.gov/policy/gen/guid/fpco/pdf/ferpaleghistory.pdf

Martin v. Helstad, 699 F.2d 387 (7th Cir. 1983).

McAdams, C. R., III, & Foster, V. A. (2007). A guide to just and fair remediation of counseling students with professional performance deficiencies. *Counselor Education and Supervision, 47*(1), 2–13. https://doi.org/10.1002/j.1556-6978.2007.tb00034.x

McAdams, C. R., III, Foster, V. A., & Ward, T. J. (2007). Remediation and dismissal policies in counselor education: Lessons learned from a challenge in federal court. *Counselor Education and Supervision, 46*(3), 212–229. https://doi.org/10.1002/j.1556-6978.2007.tb00026.x

Medd, T. C. (2019). Due process roulette: Why public university students are not guaranteed procedural due process when facing suspension or dismissal. *Creighton Law Review, 52*(3), 375–399.

Mott, D. (2017). The Due Process Clause and students: The road to a single approach of determining property interests in education. *Kansas Law Review, 65*(3), 651–685.

Olsson v. Board of Higher Education of the City of New York, 402 N. E. 2d 1150 (1980).

Pahlavan v. Drexel University College of Medicine, 438 F. Supp. 404 (2020).

Regents of University of Michigan v. Ewing, 474 U.S. 214 (1985).

Russell v. Salve Regina College, 649 F. Supp. 391 (D. R. I. 1986).

Saccuzzo, D. P. (1997). Liability for failure to supervise adequately mental health assistants, unlicensed practitioners and students. *California Western Law Review, 34*(1), 115–152.

Schuler v. University of Minnesota, 788 F. 2d 510 (8th Cir. 1986).

Schwartz-Mette, R. (2011). Out with *impairment*, in with *professional competence problems*: Response to commentary by Collins, Falender, and Shafranske. *Ethics & Behavior, 21*(5), 431–434. https://doi.org/10.1080/10508422.2011.604551

Simmons v. United States, 805 F.2d 1363 (9th Cir. 1986).

Steinberg v. Chicago Medical School, 69 Ill. 2d 320 (1977).

U.S. Department of Education, Office for Civil Rights, Free Appropriate Public Education for Students With Disabilities: Requirements Under Section 504 of the Rehabilitation Act of 1973, Washington, D.C., 2010.

Vacha-Haase, T., Davenport, D. S., & Kerewsky, S. D. (2004). Problematic students: Gatekeeping practices of academic professional psychology programs. *Professional Psychology: Research and Practice, 35*(2), 115–122. https://doi.org/10.1037/0735-7028.35.2.115

Wallace v. Jaffree, 472 U.S. 38 (1985).

Ward v. Polite, 667 F.3d 727 (6th Cir. 2012).

Ward v. Wilbanks, 2010 WL 3026428 (E.D. Mich. July 26, 2010).

Wise, E. H., Bieschke, K. J., Forrest, L., Cohen-Filipic, J., Hathaway, W. L., & Douce, L. A. (2015). Psychology's proactive approach to conscience clause court cases and legislation. *Training and Education in Professional Psychology, 9*(4), 259–268. https://doi.org/10.1037/tep0000092

Wong v. Regents of the University of California, 192 F.3d 807 (9th Cir. 1999).

Wynne v. Tufts University School of Medicine, 932 F.2d 19 (1st Cir. 1991).

Zukle v. Regents of the University of California, 166 F.3d 1041 (9th Cir. 1999).

10
BUILDING PROGRAM POLICIES IN A COMMUNITARIAN AND MULTICULTURALLY SENSITIVE TRAINING CULTURE

JENNIFER C. VEILLEUX AND MEREDITH SCAFE

Picture two programs in health service psychology, both trying to navigate trainees with problems of professional competence (TPPC). One program is an internship with a leader who cares deeply about advancing equity and promoting multicultural sensitivity. At that internship, the trainee with problems of professional competence is included in the decision-making process, the trainers model engagement in critical self-reflection about their biases, and the trainee feels comfortable seeking advice and support from their trainers about their work and professional development. The second program is a clinical psychology doctoral training program where the director of clinical training would prefer to be doing research instead of running the program. The trainers at this doctoral training program frequently disagree about professional standards and fight over resources. Trainees who are identified as having competence problems rarely get corrective feedback but are hesitant to speak up because prior students who were vocal got negative evaluations and reduced funding.

Which of these two programs could benefit from TPPC-related program policies focused on a communitarian and multiculturally sensitive ethos?

---

https://doi.org/10.1037/0000340-011
Supporting Trainees With Competence Problems: A Practical Guide for Psychology Trainers, R. A. Schwartz-Mette, E. A. Hunter, and N. J. Kaslow (Editors)
Copyright © 2023 by the American Psychological Association. All rights reserved.

Both. Because while the policies may be crucial for *building* a strong climate in the second program that can help both prevent and assist trainers in navigating TPPC situations, codified policies can help *maintain* the habits already in place in the first program. As we detail in Table 10.1, *policies* are rules that guide future behavior, whereas *habits* represent patterns of behavior already underway. Our view is that navigating TPPC situations—while often

TABLE 10.1. Definitions of Values, Goals, Habits, and Policies With Potential Program Examples

	Definition	Program examples	TPPC identification
Value	Values are beliefs linked to emotion, and values serve as standards; values prompt goals but transcend specific behaviors (Schwartz, 2012).	Cultural humility (attention to own biases and promoting awareness of and sensitivity to multicultural topics)	The trainee does not come into the program holding the same values and thus ignores how a client's culture or background informs the client's presenting concerns.
Goal	A specific aim or desired result	The program values achievement, and thus faculty aim for grant-funding and high-impact publications; students are expected to obtain presentations and publications.	A trainee does not meet goals, because they opt out of conference presentations and coauthored manuscripts with lab members on a routine basis.
Habit	A pattern of goal-directed automatic behavior; the link between a goal and actions (Aarts & Dijksterhuis, 2000)	Program meetings focused on how to address racist comments; the program invites speakers from underrepresented groups and regularly reflects on and revises program policies related to social justice.	The trainee's behavior is inconsistent with habits; they are observed making homophobic and anti-Semitic comments toward peers during classes.
Policy	A rule representing the acceptable course of action or procedures adopted by the program	The training clinic requires business casual dress, no piercings/tattoos, and no low-cut tops for women.[a]	The trainee does not have funding to purchase new clothing and is chastised by clinic staff for being unprofessional by wearing casual clothes and sneakers to sessions.

Note. [a]This is an example of where the policy is inconsistent with communitarian and multiculturally sensitive values (Veilleux & Schwartz-Mette, 2021) and can result in a student being identified as a trainee with problems of professional competence (TPPC) erroneously.

difficult—is easier within a strong climate, and thus a goal is to build program policies that can either create or maintain strong climates (Veilleux et al., 2012). To do this, programs need to identify values consistent with communitarian and multiculturally sensitive values, figure out specific behavioral goals that align with those values, and craft policies that will allow the program to meet their articulated goals. Drawing comparisons to the American Psychological Association's (APA's; 2017) *Ethical Principles of Psychologists and Code of Conduct*, values are akin to the general principles, and policies are akin to the ethical standards; the former suggests directions and ways "to be," whereas the latter comprises specific rules to govern behavior. Programs can clarify their values, use them to develop goals, and self-assess to cultivate habits and policies consistent with their values.

In this chapter, we aim to describe the rationale for policies and descriptions of policies that—in our eyes—support a communitarian and multiculturally sensitive training climate, with a particular emphasis on navigating TPPC. Because many of the things programs (and people within programs) do are not codified into policies, we also review program-level habits we believe are associated with strong and supportive climates that help prevent TPPC and likely better navigate TPPC situations. We finally review some factors that we think may facilitate development of effective policies and habits, as well as factors that we think may serve as barriers. Throughout, we provide examples both from our program and other programs we know, with a particular eye to applications for TPPC situations. In doing so, we try to share our personal perspectives about the policies and habits from both a trainer and a trainee lens because ultimately these policies may have different implications for different stakeholders.

PURPOSE OF PROGRAM POLICIES

Policies serve two principal functions. First, they outline rules that aim to ensure department members engage in appropriate and ethical behavior. Policies aim to *protect*. Second, policies *guide behavior* because they describe procedures for program members to follow. By establishing policies, program members are aware of expectations and know what will occur if they fail to meet them. When a policy is not in place, individuals (including but not limited to TPPC) might engage in inappropriate or ineffective actions not out of malice but because there are no rules or procedures to guide behavior. For example, consider a training clinic run by a clinical psychology doctoral program, where a client dies by suicide. Very likely, this program has clear guidelines for responding to client risk, but it probably does not have policies on how to navigate a client death. How do we know? This was the exact situation that occurred in our program several years ago, where the relevant trainers (supervisor, clinic director) had good intentions, but the lack of policies created confusion and lack of coordination that ultimately failed to adequately attend to the needs of the grieving clinician trainee. Thankfully, in this case, the lack of policy was a catalyst for creating a guideline for client death postvention, which is now in place should another unfortunate incident like this occur again (Veilleux & Bilsky, 2016). For example, if a client suicide were to occur with a trainee with problems of professional competence who failed to adequately assess risk, the postvention policy would provide guidance on how and when to address the risk management competence problem while also providing the trainee time and support to process their loss.

POLICIES INFORMED BY A SYSTEMS PERSPECTIVE

In our view, the very best policies—both general and TPPC specific—that support communitarian and multiculturally sensitive values will take a systems approach (Forrest et al., 2008). That is, programs are tasked with recognizing and balancing the needs of multiple stakeholders (e.g., trainers, trainees, staff) at the individual level, program level, and/or department level. For example, a pregnant trainee might request exceptions from the typical trainee sequence for postpartum recovery (e.g., lower course load, release from practicum); preemptively asking for these exceptions may help prevent drops in competence that could occur if the trainee pushes herself beyond her physical and/or mental limits. However, exclusive attention to individual needs could be problematic if perceived as unfair ("Why did she get time off and I did not?"), and a systems approach attends to factors at all levels. Moreover, health service psychology programs are situated within different institutions that each have their own values and norms, and these programs generally serve (and are gateways into) the overall field of psychology. Thus, programs are gatekeepers and must take the norms of the field into account as well as the ethical mandate to protect the public. While often complementary, these different systems can certainly clash. Essentially, our view is that the best policies are crafted with consideration of the myriad of individuals and systems affected by policy decisions (Forrest et al., 2008, 2021; Gilfoyle, 2008), and are particularly important when working with TPPC to best balance the needs of all relevant stakeholders.

PROGRAM POLICIES THAT PROMOTE COMMUNITARIAN AND MULTICULTURAL VALUES

In the sections that follow, we describe a few examples of existing policies that we believe promote strong climates. We emphasize overarching policies, rather than TPPC-specific policies, due to our belief that program climates that are aligned with communitarian and culturally sensitive values will facilitate programs and trainers effectively helping TPPC. We also describe strategies to consider for effective policy implementation, with some attention to TPPC-specific situations.

Policies Regarding Eliciting Trainee Perspectives

In higher education, eliciting students' opinions is considered crucial for gaining insight into trainees' perspectives about program policies, including the curriculum (Seale, 2010). Regularly eliciting trainees' perspectives is a potent way for departments to learn about and understand their students' experiences and concerns. When trying to either prevent or remediate TPPC, eliciting trainee perspectives is particularly important to ensure due process (Gilfoyle, 2008).

The specifics of *how* a program elicits trainee perspectives can be built into a policy. For example, a department might have a policy about conducting regular (e.g., annual or biannual) anonymous climate surveys (see Veilleux et al., 2012, for a validated climate measure) or anonymous trainer evaluations. These methods protect trainee confidentiality, making trainees feel more comfortable sharing their real experiences (Fluit et al., 2013). Notably, trainees can participate in some program-related decisions (e.g., having a seat on committees, faculty job searches) but not others (e.g., crafting remediation plans for peer TPPC). When trainee voices are included, they can share the student perspectives with trainers, advocate for trainee issues, communicate program information to peers, and potentially vote on issues (Seale, 2010). For example, trainees could be consulted on how training clinics revise their dress codes (see the Table 10.1 example under "Policy") to facilitate multiculturally sensitive policies and enhance discussions of professionalism (Veilleux & Schwartz-Mette, 2021) to prevent trainees from being erroneously identified as TPPC. In general, including trainee voices in policy decisions can minimize power dynamics between trainers and trainees, further supporting communitarian values.

Fair Evaluation Procedures

In addition to promoting research and cultivating professional values (similar to other kinds of graduate programs), trainers in health service psychology programs also want to cultivate competent and effective practitioners. Evaluations must thus focus on knowledge acquisition *and* skill application. Considering the anxiety students often feel about evaluations (McKibben et al., 2019), programs that aspire to communitarian and multiculturally sensitive climates can construct evaluation policies that follow evaluation best practices for feedback: Evaluations should be transparent, frequent (though not *too* frequent), specific, and balanced (Heckman-Stone, 2004; James, 2015).

Crafting clear policies on summative feedback is particularly important for TPPC because summative feedback (i.e., end of semester or internship rotation, end of practicum, yearly) tends to be saved in the trainee's file and thus has a greater impact on trainee progress than formative (i.e., ongoing) feedback. Consider a trainee (Ophelia) who is suffering from significant mental health issues and struggling with attending advising/lab meetings and completing assessment reports. With transparent policies, this trainee with problems of professional competence knows when the yearly evaluations will take place, has seen the practicum evaluation form, and knows the domains they will be evaluated on, both of which may provide the trainee with a time frame for improving performance or at least an understanding of when critical feedback may be coming.

The frequency of feedback also matters, particularly for TPPC. Summative feedback given too frequently (i.e., multiple times per semester) is likely overkill for most trainees and a burden on trainers. For TPPC, excessive summative feedback may actually increase shame about poor performance and not give sufficient time to demonstrate growth. In addition, feedback should be behaviorally specific and balanced, with a mix of both positive and negative comments. Most trainees *want* critical feedback to facilitate growth (Heckman-Stone, 2004), but for TPPC in particular, a sole focus on critical feedback can feel demoralizing, both for trainees who are aware of their competency deficits and for those who feel attacked and discredited in an unexpected way. Both positive and negative feedback should be specific. For example, critical feedback of "You're unprofessional" given to Ophelia, the student with mental health issues, is unhelpful because it does not articulate what exactly the trainee is doing that is unprofessional (i.e., skipping lab meetings, canceling advising meetings 10 minutes before the scheduled time), nor whether there are actions that could result in improvement (i.e., "Please complete the first draft of an assessment report within 2 weeks of the testing session").

Policies can help trainers adhere to these principles of effective evaluation. See Exhibit 10.1 for an example of a policy regarding a yearly summative evaluation within a doctoral training program. This multidomain competency

EXHIBIT 10.1. Example of a Yearly Evaluation Procedure: Competency Evaluations With Proctors

At the University of Arkansas, we developed a comprehensive proctor system for conducting yearly competence evaluations for our trainees. About 1 month prior to our annual evaluations, each trainee completes an extensive self-evaluation form detailing their accomplishments and experiences in the prior year, along with their self-assessment. Then, each trainee is assigned to a proctor, a trainer (faculty member) who is *not* the trainee's research advisor and *not* someone who was a primary clinical supervisor in the prior year. The proctor is thus someone who synthesizes and organizes feedback from other trainers. During the evaluation meetings, the proctor completes an extensive competency-based rating form that has specific behavioral anchors where expectations for performance grow as the trainee moves through the program. Finally, the proctor schedules a one-on-one meeting with the trainee to review their feedback. In this meeting, the trainee is given the opportunity to respond to (and/or refute) the written feedback.

Trainer's impression	Trainee's impression
Cons: This system is incredibly time consuming; it typically takes a minimum of 30 minutes per trainee and easily over an hour if there are competency issues or lack of concordance between trainers.	*Cons:* This system is very intensive and can be intimidating because as a trainee you receive feedback across multiple domains and are evaluated by all of the faculty within the department. Furthermore, it can take several months before you receive your feedback.
Pros: Discussing each trainee so extensively and obtaining multiple perspectives feels respectful and idiographic. Being the proctor also allows me to get to know students I haven't worked closely with, which I appreciate.	*Pros:* The feedback allows you to address any areas of concern identified by the faculty. Furthermore, the faculty often highlight your strengths and accomplishments, which is rewarding.

evaluation occurs with input from the entire clinical training faculty and adds to summative practicum evaluations submitted by each clinical supervisor from each semester. Completing this evaluation allows for early identification of competence issues in trainees and provides clear guidelines for trainers on feedback.

In addition to clear policies about the evaluation process itself, there should be details on the potential consequences of the evaluation procedure. New trainees who are unfamiliar with program norms may not recognize areas of competence deficits. Or TPPC who recognize they are struggling may be incredibly anxious about the possibility of being "kicked out" of the program as a result of a summative evaluation. Annual evaluation policies thus should provide feedback on all competency domains, as well as explicitly connect to policies on remediation (Vacha-Haase et al., 2019) and dismissal.

Finally, programs that truly wish to adhere to communitarian and multiculturally sensitive values can craft policies for evaluating trainers (clinical supervisors, program administrators, and/or research mentors) that promote the value of bidirectional feedback, thus attempting to balance the hierarchical power structure of training programs. Policies developed to evaluate trainers should be constructed to emphasize trainee safety. For example, if a supervisor supervises only one trainee in a given year, even an anonymous evaluation would be identifiable. Rolling evaluations (e.g., collecting evaluation data yearly but disseminating to trainers every 3–5 years) or spaced evaluations (e.g., collecting data only every 3 years) could help trainees provide honest feedback and protect them from potential retaliation. This is particularly important for TPPC, because sometimes the competence issue—even if identified by a trainer—is actually a problem of trainer incompetence (January et al., 2014) or even harmful supervision (Ellis, 2017). For example, consider Ila, who is identified as a trainee with problems of professional competence by her mentor for repeatedly missing deadlines. However, if multiple trainees subsequently complain about that mentor as having poor time management skills with constantly shifting deadlines, the program may learn that the issue is actually best conceptualized as a trainer issue, rather than Ila's.

Equity-Related Policies

Effective program policies attend to both equity and individuality. On the equity side, both trainers and trainees need to feel that policies are consistent and that resources are distributed fairly. For example, an internship program might have a policy that all trainees work 40-hour weeks with consistent hours. However, individuals may have unique needs that deserve reasonable accommodations, such as a trainee with a documented physical disability who requests to work 30 hours per week with an extended training year. This example highlights the need to balance *equality* and *equity* (Espinoza, 2007), whereby policies attempt to ensure equality of opportunities for trainees that can also flexibly adapt to individuals' needs.

The need to balance equality and equity is particularly important when navigating TPPC situations. TPPC may need accommodations, remediation, and extra attention to achieve competence. For example, consider Len, a trainee who started a doctoral program in clinical psychology after completing a terminal masters at a different institution. Len requested to get credit for his empirical master's thesis, and the program granted it. However, a year later, Len was identified as having competence problems in the research domain, which initially went undetected as he bypassed some of the initial research training offered by the program due to the assumption that completing an empirical thesis conveyed competence. The program had no policy in place to assess critical thinking or data analytic skills of students coming in with a master's degree to ensure equity with students completing their master's thesis as a part of the doctoral program due to the assumption of equality.

Attending to the broader context of health service psychology training programs is also important because programs are typically situated within larger departments (e.g., graduate departments may also have experimental psychology; psychiatry departments may manage both psychology interns and medical residents). Thus, departmental policies must also consider issues of equity and individuality for trainees and trainers across different programs. We recommend programs—and departments—adopt a framework of "flexible equity" where policies attend to balancing a fair distribution of resources based on needs, with wiggle room for individual exceptions.

HABITS THAT PROMOTE COMMUNITARIAN AND MULTICULTURAL VALUES

In addition to written program policies, most health service psychology programs also have habits (see Table 10.1). Habits are patterns of behavior that are consistent with values held within the department; however, habits do not necessarily reflect codified policies. Habits are *norms* cultivated by program and department leaders, which are a major determinant of program climate (Veilleux et al., 2012). Importantly, while the habits of all program members contribute to the climate, because the trainers and administration wield more power and tend to be a part of the program for longer than trainees, the habits of trainers are particularly important in setting program norms. Habits are important to understand for TPPC situations because at worst, bad habits of trainers can create a breeding ground that could create competence problems in trainees or model poor professional behavior. In addition, ineffective habits can exacerbate stress for both trainers and trainees, whereas effective habits can prevent TPPC from feeling demoralized.

Transparent Communication

Transparent communication among program members promotes a strong program climate because individuals are informed and can openly share their views. Transparency breeds trust (Norman et al., 2010) and, in our view, transparent communication should be regular, respectful, and clear. *Regular* communication demonstrates that individuals are actively considering one another, whereas less frequent communication might suggest individuals are not interested in or concerned about others within the program. Furthermore, communication should be *respectful* because how individuals communicate information influences how individuals perceive and respond (Reitman & Jurbergs, 2002). Finally, communication should be *clear*, so individuals do not misunderstand or misinterpret information (Brown, 2018). Lack of frequent, respectful, and/or clear communication habits can contribute to struggles in TPPC situations. For example, if trainees do not know about changes in policies or upcoming deadlines, they could be identified as TPPC without the opportunity to preemptively course correct. When trainees are accurately identified as TPPC, clear and regular communication (e.g., weekly check-ins, email updates about tasks) can help everyone stay informed about both progress and any barriers that arise.

Moreover, transparent communication means individuals at different levels within a program should be able to openly express their individual perspectives without fearing criticism or judgment. To promote such communication, program leaders can model open and respectful communication and encourage trainees to do the same. The psychotherapy literature provides guidance about effective communication skills that could be used among program members (Reitman & Jurbergs, 2002), such as using "I" statements and describing feelings clearly. Beyond just transparency in communication, attention to interpersonal effectiveness skills, which aim to increase assertiveness, attend to relationships, and resolve conflicts with others (Linehan, 1993, 2015), are likely hallmarks of strong communication habits. While these attributes are important for all programs, and are consistent with communitarian values (Forrest et al., 2008), they are particularly important when supporting TPPC. Trainers are often frustrated with TPPC due to the time and energy that TPPC can consume, and they may be tempted to speak *at* TPPC to give advice or suggestions rather than listening *to* TPPC with an ear to understanding what may be happening and how the program—or the trainer—could be contributing to the problem.

Reflection and Growth

Programs that prioritize communitarian values also prioritize reflection and growth, consistent with the concept of *humility* (Paine et al., 2015; Watkins et al., 2019). Humility is particularly valuable in promoting multicultural sensitivity due to the emphasis on asking questions rather than making assumptions, using self-reflection to identify and address cultural biases, and using openness to repair cultural ruptures (Mosher et al., 2017).

Practically speaking, an emphasis on reflection and growth can involve many behaviors at the individual, program, and/or department levels. One crucial habit regarding reflection and growth is that it must happen at all levels to truly adhere to communitarian values. Programs that ask trainees to self-assess but do not demonstrate individual trainer self-assessment or program review (other than when required for APA accreditation) are likewise not demonstrating the openness, reflectiveness, and curiosity consistent with clinical humility. Programs, supervisors, and instructors can find creative ways to obtain feedback from trainees in a safe way (see Exhibit 10.2). Program and trainer habits of self-reflection can go a long way toward modeling humility and pave the way for trainees who may be struggling to actively seek help, ideally before a competence problem becomes severe.

EXHIBIT 10.2. Example Program Assessment: Group Assessment

My (JCV) internship program used a group assessment to obtain feedback about the internship year. We were given a day off and asked to spend it together (my cohort played miniature golf and bumper boats and then relaxed by a pool for the afternoon). We were given a list of questions to complete as a group and submitted one overall response document that integrated everyone's perspectives. When I started at the University of Arkansas as faculty, I adopted a similar approach to obtain feedback on my supervision practices. Once per semester, typically in the middle of the semester, I ask the group of trainees I'm currently supervising (typically four to eight trainees) to meet without me. We turn off the camera in the clinic room so I cannot listen in. I provide a list of questions for them about their impression of my teaching and individual supervision, which they answer as a group. After they all read the group response and approve it, they email it to me and I look through it for feedback.

Trainer's impression	Trainee's impression
This has been an invaluable way of collecting feedback, and it is really not identifiable—I cannot tell who says what. They write things like "Some of us think X, while others think Y" to show differences, and "All of us agree that . . ." for similarities. I keep the things they like and carefully consider the things they don't. For example, one cohort expressed concerns that the workload was too heavy, leaving them less time for other obligations, and I cut back on assignments. Some of their suggestions are not things I can easily change, but in these cases I come back to them and tell them why I won't make a particular change, but I do make changes based on their feedback when I can. I look forward to seeing this group feedback document every semester!	I liked that students' feedback was elicited in a group format because it allowed me to check in with my peers about their perspectives and experiences. This was powerful because we were able to discuss our thoughts collectively and be validated by others in the group. Conversely, in instances where we disagreed, this method allowed me to consider why my perspective might be different from my peers. Overall, I think this process allowed us to give our instructor balanced feedback because we were able to draw from each other's experiences to reach a consensus about specific strengths and weaknesses to include in her feedback. I believe this process also encourages students to provide honest feedback because the group format increased our individual anonymity.

Valuing Human Relationships

Supportive relationships are powerful and can promote numerous positive physical and mental health outcomes (Umberson & Montez, 2016). These findings should not go unnoticed by health service psychology programs because research also shows that students who have strong relationships with their peers and trainers are more likely to have positive academic outcomes (Brouwer et al., 2016). In health service psychology programs, relationships between trainers and trainees are frequently formally established, with the aim of trainers overseeing trainees' clinical work, research, and/or coursework. Beyond these formal roles, however, trainers can serve as *mentors*, which differs from advising or supervision in that mentoring is positive, is proactive, and helps trainees achieve their professional goals *and* provides trainees psychosocial support as they face life stressors (Cobb et al., 2018). Research suggests that effective relationships between faculty mentors and graduate students can promote students' developmental and academic trajectories, while negative advising relationships are potentially harmful and may contribute to competence problems (Cobb et al., 2018; Tuma et al., 2021). Good mentors treat their trainees ideographically and identify their unique strengths and weaknesses (e.g., allow trainees to prioritize different aspects of their training), provide emotional support and validation (e.g., ask about well-being, provide resources for help), model professionalism, and attend to cultural humility (Cobb et al., 2018).

Good relationships between trainees can also promote well-being and success (Brouwer et al., 2016). Peers can promote other trainees' learning and be sources of support via study partners/groups, peer-to-peer mentoring, or tutoring (Palmer et al., 2014). Peer relationships are helpful for TPPC because peers are often the first to learn about competence problems, and they turn to each other for support and advice (Jacobs et al., 2011). Trainees who are disconnected from their peers are likely to think they alone are struggling, perpetuating a cycle of shame and withdrawal. Alternatively, trainees with interpersonal or professionalism-related competence problems (Veilleux et al., 2012) may enact their competence deficits with their peers in a manner that is visible within the program.

Health service psychology programs can benefit from cultivating clear habits regarding peer support. For example, they establish a tradition of matching incoming trainees with more advanced trainees as a formal peer–mentor. Programs can also promote trainee relationships more informally within program settings by encouraging collaboration in classes, research projects, or clinical work, or by assigning students to interdisciplinary offices. As one additional example, trainees in our program form a social committee annually that promotes social gatherings outside the professional context (e.g., trainee kickball games).

BARRIERS AND FACILITATORS

Although codifying habits into policies can help communicate a program's explicit values, programs that already have good habits tend to have norms consistent with communitarian principles. They either implicitly or explicitly select trainees and hire trainers with similar attitudes and acculturate new people into the system by demonstrating program norms. A more difficult situation is when a program does *not* have a communitarian climate but wants to adopt one. What might be factors that facilitate or hinder the development of communitarian policies, and how do these apply to TPPC situations?

Leadership

Leaders in health service psychology programs play a predominant role in shaping the program's broader climate (Amey, 2006). As such, leadership can function as either a facilitator or a barrier to the sustainment of culturally sensitive and communitarian program values. For instance, if a program values diversity and inclusion, leaders will likely promote policies and habits that protect these values (e.g., regular diversity training) and also actively oppose policies and habits that jeopardize these values (e.g., maintaining a curriculum that is not multiculturally sensitive). Good leaders will not shy away from tackling TPPC situations or talking with staff or trainers who may be engaging in problematic behavior (January et al., 2014). Additionally, good leaders recognize and fill important gaps in their programs. For instance, our generalist clinical psychology program had few trainers who focused on child intervention despite significant trainee interest. Therefore, our program leaders intentionally recruited a clinical child psychologist to create more opportunities for child work. Essentially, strong leaders craft value-consistent goals, habits, and policies.

On the other hand, poor leadership might act as a barrier. Some program leaders might not share values that promote a strong program climate (e.g., they may wish to foster competition rather than cooperation). Moreover, there is the possibility that program leaders hold communitarian values but do not engage in behaviors consistent with these values. For example, consider a program that recognizes increased stress and burnout is common for graduate students (Rummell, 2015) and wants to promote trainee mental health wellness. The leader—and the other trainers—state verbally that they care about addressing trainee mental health. However, if the leader is unsure of *how* to help, has some sort of skill deficit that prevents them from enacting any change, or is afraid of what might be revealed by addressing mental health directly, then nothing will happen and trainees will continue to struggle, perhaps increasing the number of students with competence problems. The importance of policies here is that policies provide the framework for action even if leadership is poor. By "baking in" practices across trainers and leaders, the likelihood increases that shared program values will be implemented, regardless of any changes in leadership.

Considering that leaders are instrumental in crafting policies and cultivating habits, selection of leadership is critical. Sometimes leaders are selected based on pragmatics (e.g., who is willing) rather than on who will either best sustain the program's current values and mission or shift the program's values in the desired direction. Most trainers did not seek out faculty positions to become administrators, so finding good leaders can be a real challenge. This is particularly important with respect to TPPC, because leaders must approach (rather than avoid) TPPC directly and compassionately. Leaders who are conflict averse are likely to struggle with TPPC. For those who are thrust into a leadership role, carefully assessing the program's values and self-assessing willingness to approach conflict can be useful proactive steps prior to launching new initiatives and prior to the first inevitable TPPC situation.

Trainer Collegiality

One potential facilitator of enabling communitarian values is trainer collegiality, which means the inverse is also relevant—a *lack* of collegiality in trainers may serve as a barrier to enacting policies and habits that cultivate a strong climate. Likewise, a poor climate may either be a vulnerability for or exacerbate TPPC situations.

A strong climate cannot be built without buy-in from the trainers, who likewise serve as models for how people interact with each other within the program. When trainers like and respect each other as humans, and demonstrate collegiality and the ability to separate professional disagreements from personal grudges, the program is better off. We wish to reiterate this last point: Trainers are almost certainly going to disagree with one another about policies, curriculum, preferences, and so forth. They may disagree about how to best handle TPPC. Trainers may stem from different theoretical orientations, have different attitudes or experiences with research, and may even come from different training models (e.g., clinical vs. counseling vs. school, PhD vs. PsyD). Disagreeing is not inherently problematic. What becomes toxic is when trainers assume malintent and make the disagreement about the person (e.g., "He is an idiot") rather than the perspective or behavior (e.g., "I prefer Z approach, because . . .").

Most faculty know whether their program has a cohesive and functional training group, or whether there are problems with trainer collegiality. We have heard of programs that are mostly functional but with one "bad apple" who refuses to do their share of work or exhibits the tendency to take everything personally. Indeed, there are instances where the bad apple may be at the root of a TPPC situation. For example, consider Reina, a multiracial student who was identified as a trainee with problems of professional competence by her supervisor, Dr. Peterson, who stated that Reina was deficient in conducting psychotherapy and assessment, and put her on a remediation plan. Ultimately, it was revealed that Dr. Peterson—a White woman—made repeated microaggressions at Reina, overlooked her in classes, took other students out to lunch, and placed her under undue and unfair scrutiny to the point that Reina developed an autoimmune disease and significant imposter-related anxiety. Although this example sounds far-fetched, this is a true story of harmful supervision (Ellis, 2017, Narrative 1). (Although this article did not provide names, we added some here for clarity.)

Strong leadership and/or communitarian approaches are crucial in cultivating trainer collegiality and trainer accountability, where leaders need to document problems and colleagues can directly address concerns. Inversely, diffusion of responsibility and fears of confrontation can allow problems to fester indefinitely.

Funding

One barrier to enacting communitarian values is practical: funding. While on the surface funding may not be directly applicable to TPPC, it likely is relevant from a systems perspective.

People who have stable and adequate funding are likely better able to pay attention to some of the "higher-order" communitarian practices, consistent with Maslow's hierarchy of needs (Maslow, 1948). Lack of funding often leads to identifying TPPC due to a mismatch (Wright, 2021) between program expectations (e.g., working more hours than a full-time job for very little money and taking on additional debt) and living expectations (e.g., money for food, shelter, leisure, and for atypical expenses such as car repairs and medical bills). Financial insecurity could create the type of stress that would then prompt impaired competence, whether a result of anxiety about money or taking an additional job that stretches them so thin they cannot perform competently. In addition, when funding is unstable, uncertain, or awarded without attention to equity, contempt and resentment are likely outcomes. Unfortunately, funding is often not in the program's control, though we have heard of some programs using creative fundraising solutions (e.g., community raffles to increase revenue for a training clinic).

Inertia and Resistance to Change

Inertia is the tendency of an organism to stay in the same state until force is exerted from an outside influence. It is far easier to keep doing the same thing, or to do nothing, than to put forth significant efforts to enact new policies and/or habits (Anderson, 2003). Someone (or a group) has to take the initiative to make changes, which is an effort many busy trainers simply do not have time for.

It is tempting to say that an additional barrier is "resistance to change," which could take the form of leaders, trainers, or trainees expressing skepticism or outright refusal to make changes. However, the concept of a global *resistance to change* has been challenged (Dent & Goldberg, 1999) because the phrase tends to implicitly blame those with less power and does not identify what would specifically be lost if change occurred. Thus, it may be better to reframe to trying to understand specific concerns in response to specific *elements* of change. Are the trainees worried that provision of equal funding to all students might result in losing status? Are the trainers concerned that adopting trainer evaluations will result in complaints and negative performance evaluations? Those interested in promoting change need to solicit feedback on the specific critiques of each change they are trying to make. In many ways, this advice echoes dialectical behavior therapy (Linehan, 1993), which suggests that people are all capable of change, but the context has to facilitate change effectively. Trainers and leaders who want to promote change need to embark on a mission to understand the contexts that will support the changes they want to make. With regard to TPPC, this means planning for the inevitable trainee who will struggle to achieve (or maintain) competence. No program is immune to TPPC. Unfortunately, some TPPC situations are so unique that they feel impossible to plan for (Veilleux & Bilsky, 2016), and thus it is easier to be reactive (e.g., handling situations when they arise) instead of proactive. However, anticipating change (because of changes in trainee characteristics, cultural norms, or expectations within the field) should be incorporated into programs so that good habits and strong policies can be set that are flexible enough to allow for change but also preempt and plan for TPPC situations.

Policies With No Teeth

Although policies that promote culturally sensitive and communitarian values have the potential to facilitate a positive program climate, the benefits of these policies will likely not come to fruition if programs do not uphold them. It is one thing to write a policy down in a program handbook, but it is another for trainers to enforce policies fairly and consistently. Program policies need to be flexible; however, if policies are too flexible, are they effective? From an operant conditioning perspective, one might hypothesize that individuals will not follow the policy when it is not consistently reinforced. One method to increase adherence to policies could involve providing rewards or incentives to those who follow the rules (e.g., positive feedback, formal recognition for dedication to policy) and/or consequences to those who do not (e.g., remediation plan, critical performance review). Program leaders must consider how to address trainers, trainees, and staff who do not adhere to policies. In addition, as alluded to above, leaders must also be accountable to program policies and demonstrate a willingness to provide the "teeth" to the policy when necessary, even though these actions may be uncomfortable or difficult (Jacobs et al., 2011). If programs do not enforce policies, then the standards and values of a department are in jeopardy. Furthermore, lack of policy enforcement could contribute negatively to the program climate, as program members might become frustrated with individuals who are not held accountable for ignoring or breaking policies.

These are particularly difficult issues in the TPPC realm, due to confidentiality concerns. For example, consider Toni, a trainee who was identified as having a competence concern for violating client confidentiality by talking about clients in a public space. This is both an ethical violation and a policy violation in Toni's clinic. However, Toni's peers may not *know* if Toni is undergoing remediation or even if the program has identified the problem because the remediation plan is confidential. Trainees (and trainers) need to have faith that the program will enact policies fairly (attending to both equity and equality), even if the enactment is not always publicly visible.

CONCLUSION

Building—and maintaining—policies that reflect communitarian and multiculturally sensitive training climates are important for cultivating the type of environments that people want to work in. These are climates where trainees can learn the knowledge and application of health service psychology and feel safe, heard, and nurtured. These are climates that support trainees struggling with competence problems. These are the environments that everyone at all levels (trainees, trainers, leadership) is proud to be a part of.

Policies and habits within programs (and departments) can both reflect the values of a program and be used to create new values and norms within a program. Programs that already have habits consistent with communitarian and multiculturally sensitive values can develop policies to codify their habits to ensure that any changes in leadership will not dilute their already-strong training climate. Programs that do not have these habits may need to carefully craft explicit policies that align with these values and monitor their effectiveness while trying to nurture the development of a sensitive training climate consistent with their values.

Is the process of building communitarian and multiculturally sensitive policies easy? Often, no. Is it worth it? Yes. Graduate training in health service psychology is often hard (Rummell, 2015), and a career as a trainer (e.g., faculty advisor, supervisor) is not easy either. But building a system that encourages bidirectional feedback, clear evaluation procedures, transparent communication, attention to equity, and an emphasis on growth provides a sustainable framework for building (and remediating, when necessary) competencies for current and future health service psychologists.

REFERENCES

Aarts, H., & Dijksterhuis, A. (2000). Habits as knowledge structures: Automaticity in goal-directed behavior. *Journal of Personality and Social Psychology, 78*(1), 53–63. https://doi.org/10.1037/0022-3514.78.1.53

American Psychological Association. (2017). *Ethical principles of psychologists and code of conduct* (2002, amended effective June 1, 2010, and January 1, 2017). https://www.apa.org/ethics/code/index.aspx

Amey, M. J. (2006). Leadership in higher education. *Change, 38*(6), 55–58. https://doi.org/10.3200/CHNG.38.6.55-58

Anderson, C. J. (2003). The psychology of doing nothing: Forms of decision avoidance result from reason and emotion. *Psychological Bulletin, 129*(1), 139–167. https://doi.org/10.1037/0033-2909.129.1.139

Brouwer, J., Jansen, E., Flache, A., & Hofman, A. (2016). The impact of social capital on self-efficacy and study success among first-year university students. *Learning and Individual Differences, 52*, 109–118. https://doi.org/10.1016/j.lindif.2016.09.016

Brown, B. (2018). *Dare to lead: Brave work. Tough conversations. Whole hearts.* Random House.

Cobb, C. L., Zamboanga, B. L., Xie, D., Schwartz, S. J., Meca, A., & Sanders, G. L. (2018). From advising to mentoring: Toward proactive mentoring in health service psychology doctoral training programs. *Training and Education in Professional Psychology, 12*(1), 38–45. https://doi.org/10.1037/tep0000187

Dent, E. B., & Goldberg, S. G. (1999). Challenging "resistance to change." *The Journal of Applied Behavioral Science, 35*(1), 25–41. https://doi.org/10.1177/0021886399351003

Ellis, M. V. (2017). Narratives of harmful clinical supervision. *The Clinical Supervisor, 36*(1), 20–87. https://doi.org/10.1080/07325223.2017.1297752

Espinoza, O. (2007). Solving the equity–equality conceptual dilemma: A new model for analysis of the educational process. *Educational Research, 49*(4), 343–363. https://doi.org/10.1080/00131880701717198

Fluit, C. V., Bolhuis, S., Klaassen, T., DE Visser, M., Grol, R., Laan, R., & Wensing, M. (2013). Residents provide feedback to their clinical teachers: Reflection through dialogue. *Medical Teacher, 35*(9), e1485–e1492. https://doi.org/10.3109/0142159X.2013.785631

Forrest, L., Elman, N. S., Bodner, K. E., & Kaslow, N. J. (2021). Trainee confidentiality: Confusions, complexities, consequences, and possibilities. *Training and Education in Professional Psychology*. Advance online publication. https://doi.org/10.1037/tep0000364

Forrest, L., Shen-Miller, D. S., & Elman, N. S. (2008). Psychology trainees with competence problems: From individual to ecological conceptualizations. *Training and Education in Professional Psychology, 2*(4), 183–192. https://doi.org/10.1037/1931-3918.2.4.183

Gilfoyle, N. (2008). The legal exosystem: Risk management in addressing student competence problems in professional psychology training. *Training and Education in Professional Psychology, 2*(4), 202–209. https://doi.org/10.1037/1931-3918.2.4.202

Heckman-Stone, C. (2004). Trainee preferences for feedback and evaluation in clinical supervision. *The Clinical Supervisor, 22*(1), 21–33. https://doi.org/10.1300/J001v22n01_03

Jacobs, S. C., Huprich, S. K., Grus, C. L., Cage, E. A., Elman, N. S., Forrest, L., Schwartz-Mette, R., Shen-Miller, D. S., Van Sickle, K. S., & Kaslow, N. J. (2011). Trainees with professional competency problems: Preparing trainers for difficult but necessary conversations. *Training and Education in Professional Psychology, 5*(3), 175–184. https://doi.org/10.1037/a0024656

James, I. A. (2015). The rightful demise of the sh*t sandwich: Providing effective feedback. *Behavioural and Cognitive Psychotherapy, 43*(6), 759–766. https://doi.org/10.1017/S1352465814000113

January, A. M., Meyerson, D. A., Reddy, L. F., Docherty, A. R., & Klonoff, E. A. (2014). Impressions of misconduct: Graduate students' perception of faculty ethical violations in scientist-practitioner clinical psychology programs. *Training and Education in Professional Psychology, 8*(4), 261–268. https://doi.org/10.1037/tep0000059

Linehan, M. M. (1993). *Cognitive behavioral therapy of borderline personality disorders*. Guilford Press.

Linehan, M. M. (2015). *DBT skills training manual* (2nd ed.). Guilford Press.

Maslow, A. H. (1948). Higher and lower needs. *The Journal of Psychology, 25*(2), 433–436. https://doi.org/10.1080/00223980.1948.9917386

McKibben, W. B., Borders, L. D. A., & Wahesh, E. (2019). Factors influencing supervisee perceptions of critical feedback validity. *Counselor Education and Supervision, 58*(4), 242–256. https://doi.org/10.1002/ceas.12155

Mosher, D. K., Hook, J. N., Captari, L. E., Davis, D. E., DeBlaere, C., & Owen, J. (2017). Cultural humility: A therapeutic framework for engaging diverse clients. *Practice Innovations, 2*(4), 221–233. https://doi.org/10.1037/pri0000055

Norman, S. M., Avolio, B. J., & Luthans, F. (2010). The impact of positivity and transparency on trust in leaders and their perceived effectiveness. *The Leadership Quarterly, 21*(3), 350–364. https://doi.org/10.1016/j.leaqua.2010.03.002

Paine, D. R., Sandage, S. J., Rupert, D., Devor, N. G., & Bronstein, M. (2015). Humility as a psychotherapeutic virtue: Spiritual, philosophical, and psychological foundations. *Journal of Spirituality in Mental Health, 17*(1), 3–25. https://doi.org/10.1080/19349637.2015.957611

Palmer, R. T., Wood, J. L., Dancy, T. E., & Strayhorn, T. L. (2014). *Black male collegians: Increasing access, retention, and persistence in higher education*. John Wiley & Sons.

Reitman, D., & Jurbergs, N. (2002). Communication skills training. In M. Hersen & W. Sledge (Eds.), *Encyclopedia of psychotherapy* (pp. 469–473). Academic Press. https://doi.org/10.1016/B0-12-343010-0/00052-0

Rummell, C. M. (2015). An exploratory study of psychology graduate student workload, health, and program satisfaction. *Professional Psychology: Research and Practice, 46*(6), 391–399. https://doi.org/10.1037/pro0000056

Schwartz, S. H. (2012). An overview of the Schwartz theory of basic values. *Online Readings in Psychology and Culture, 2*(1), 1–20. https://doi.org/10.9707/2307-0919.1116

Seale, J. (2010). Doing student voice work in higher education: An exploration of the value of participatory methods. *British Educational Research Journal, 36*(6), 995–1015. https://doi.org/10.1080/01411920903342038

Tuma, T. T., Adams, J. D., Hultquist, B. C., & Dolan, E. L. (2021). The dark side of development: A systems characterization of the negative mentoring experiences of doctoral students. *CBE Life Sciences Education, 20*(2), 1–21. https://doi.org/10.1187/cbe.20-10-0231

Umberson, D., & Montez, J. K. (2016). Social relationships and health: A flashpoint for health policy. *Journal of Health, 51*(Suppl.), S54–S66. https://doi.org/10.1177/0022146510383501

Vacha-Haase, T., Elman, N. S., Forrest, L., Kallaugher, J., Lease, S. H., Veilleux, J. C., & Kaslow, N. J. (2019). Remediation plans for trainees with problems of professional competence. *Training and Education in Professional Psychology, 13*(4), 239–246. https://doi.org/10.1037/tep0000221

Veilleux, J. C., & Bilsky, S. A. (2016). After a client death: Suicide postvention recommendations for training programs and clinics. *Training and Education in Professional Psychology, 10*(4), 214–222. https://doi.org/10.1037/tep0000127

Veilleux, J. C., January, A. M., VanderVeen, J. W., Reddy, L. F., & Klonoff, E. A. (2012). Perceptions of climate in clinical psychology doctoral programs: Development and initial validation of the Graduate Program Climate Scale. *Training and Education in Professional Psychology, 6*(4), 211–219. https://doi.org/10.1037/a0030303

Veilleux, J. C., & Schwartz-Mette, R. A. (2021). Pink hair, don't care? Unpacking the concept of professional appearance for modern therapists. *Behavior Therapist, 44*(2), 80–84.

Watkins, C. E., Hook, J. N., Mosher, D. K., & Callahan, J. L. (2019). Humility in clinical supervision: Fundamental, foundational, and transformational. *The Clinical Supervisor, 38*(1), 58–78. https://doi.org/10.1080/07325223.2018.1487355

Wright, A. J. (2021). Deliberate context-driven conceptualization in psychological assessment. *Journal of Personality Assessment*. Advance online publication. https://doi.org/10.1080/00223891.2021.1942024

11 TROUBLESHOOTING COMMON PITFALLS

EVELYN A. HUNTER AND REBECCA A. SCHWARTZ-METTE

The following hypothetical vignettes are intended to illustrate brief examples of some of the potential trainee competence issues that trainers may encounter. Each is followed by a summary discussion, highlighting policy/procedural, legal, ethical, and remediation considerations, along with considerations for approaching each situation from a communitarian and multicultural perspective. We also attempt to highlight common reactions from trainees and trainers as a way to help prepare trainers for the process as well as content variables that may present themselves in these or similar situations.

These vignettes and subsequent discussions are not meant to be exhaustive descriptions of all the aspects of a certain case or all the considerations and actions that could or should be taken. Nor are they intended to serve as direct guidance (legal or otherwise), no matter how similar they may be to real situations programs may be currently navigating. We hope, instead, that these vignettes serve as a starting point for proactive reflection and discussion, in the hopes that doing so better prepares you and your system for supporting students who are struggling with competence problems. Finally, each vignette—including names, identities, descriptions, and actions—is fictional.

https://doi.org/10.1037/0000340-012
Supporting Trainees With Competence Problems: A Practical Guide for Psychology Trainers, R. A. Schwartz-Mette, E. A. Hunter, and N. J. Kaslow (Editors)
Copyright © 2023 by the American Psychological Association. All rights reserved.

Details of each case have been integrated from multiple sources: the literature, consultation, and the deidentified training experiences of several authors in this volume. Any similarity to actual trainees, trainers, their characteristics, or competence issues is unintended and should not be inferred.

VIGNETTE 1: "HE'S JUST NOT PROFESSIONAL"

During a faculty meeting, Dr. Lewis, the director of clinical training (White; he/him) in a doctoral training program, details his concerns about Riley (Indigenous; they/them), a second-year trainee just starting their clinical work. He mentioned that he often observes Riley in the training clinic wearing plain, short-, or long-sleeved tops made of what appears to be T-shirt material and cargo-type pants with heavy work boots. The training director elaborates that he believes clients won't take Riley seriously, given their attire, and adds that Riley has long hair worn in a "messy" bun or ponytail and a medium-length beard. "He's just not professional," the training director says.

Dr. Bing (White; she/her), Riley's primary graduate advisor, sits uncomfortably during this discussion. She knows that Riley identifies as gender fluid and uses they/them pronouns in their meetings, but she is unaware of who else in the department may know. She also believes that Riley may have limited financial resources, as they are a primary caretaker of an aging parent with a disability. Dr. Bing disagrees with the training director's assessment of Riley's appearance as unprofessional but chalks this up to the fact that she and Dr. Lewis were trained in different eras and frequently have different perspectives on student behavior. Having recently expressed her disagreement with Dr. Lewis on a separate student issue in a previous faculty meeting, Dr. Bing chooses not to share her perspective at this time.

Following the faculty meeting, the director of clinical training prepares a letter on behalf of the faculty detailing concerns about Riley's professionalism. The letter is careful to say that the program is not asking Riley to engage with a specific remediation plan at this time; rather, they expect Riley will immediately consult the clinic's dress code in the program handbook and make appropriate changes to adopt a more professional appearance ahead of their next scheduled sessions in the clinic, or else remediation will follow.

Although this vignette does not involve direct remediation, it is a good example of a problematic trainer conceptualization of competence issues that, if pursued further, may result in harm to the trainee and liability to the program. In this scenario, a training director has taken issue with a trainee's appearance and conflates their appearance with the competency of professionalism. Standard definitions and assessments of professional competencies (see Chapter 2, this volume) are necessarily behavioral in nature (see Chapter 6, "Remediation, Counseling Out, and Dismissal") and the behavioral descriptions of professionalism as a competency are no exception. In other words, there is nothing in the "Competency Benchmarks" document that prescribes what professionalism looks like in terms of clothing, hairstyle, or other aesthetic.

Scholars have discussed the myriad problems inherent in prescribing specific aspects of professional appearance, including that most dress codes emphasize and reward a Western, White, male, traditional/conservative, and resourced view of what "looks professional" (Veilleux & Schwartz-Mette, 2021). Riley's appearance in this vignette simply does not conform to Dr. Lewis's view of what a therapist should look like, and this, in combination with Dr. Lewis's fears about clients' perceptions, has been used as the sole basis to determine that Riley is exhibiting competence problems. What is more, the program directs Riley to consult the clinic's dress code and to immediately conform to these standards to avoid remediation. This action likely leaves Riley feeling alienated and unclear about whether they can safely express their identities in the program, not to mention the undue financial burden required to immediately procure new work clothes.

A second set of issues is illuminated in the response (or lack thereof) of Riley's graduate mentor, Dr. Bing. Dr. Bing's discomfort with the discussion about Riley's appearance is indicative of her awareness that Dr. Lewis's views on this situation are potentially discriminatory. Her emotional response also may reflect her past experiences discussing her differing perspectives with Dr. Lewis. Perhaps these conversations have not resolved well, perhaps she didn't feel heard, or perhaps Dr. Lewis is on her peer committee for tenure. Regardless, she may be in a one-down power position and feel conflicted about what she can and should do to support Riley. So, what could improve this situation for Riley?

Regarding whether Riley has truly exhibited problems of professional competence, there is no clear evidence that Riley has violated anything, apart from Dr. Lewis's expectations. We would argue that a program in this situation should first take a critical look at its dress code, whether it is articulated formally or informally. Many dress codes indeed prescribe traditional attire, hairstyles, and presentations that follow largely from a dominant cultural gaze and are not inclusive of multiple identities. For example, many prescriptions against tight clothing, showing cleavage, or revealing too much skin on the arms or legs reflect an undue burden on cisgender women to manage heterosexual men's attention and desires. Some dress codes prohibit visible tattoos or piercings; others may prescribe "acceptable" hair colors, lengths, coverings, styles, or placement (e.g., minimal facial hair). Each of these restrictions may intersect with important aspects of a trainee's identity, leaving them feeling rejected and potentially unsafe. Moreover, dress codes typically prioritize more expensive clothing and shoes, as these have traditionally been viewed as "more professional." Many trainees face financial hardships and may view this requirement as burdensome. This particular program may benefit from adopting a more flexible dress code that allows freedom of individual expression within the constraints of the job to be done.

Moreover, because appearance does not constitute any aspect of widely accepted, behavioral definitions of professionalism, members of a program may find themselves on unsteady ground in prescribing certain aspects of appearance, particularly if they remediate a student for their clothing choices. As discussed throughout this volume, a program must assess competency in behavioral terms, linking any problems of professional competence to benchmarks and professional standards. Even if remediation could proceed under these circumstances, remediation targets must be clear. It is interesting to ponder what types of remediation targets could emerge from this situation. "Look more professional" is certainly not clear enough, and "spend more money on clinic clothes" is obviously unwise. All in all, this scenario appears to reflect a problem not in competence but potentially with program culture and policy.

Relatedly, a yet unarticulated aspect of this vignette is the potential for conscious or unconscious bias against Riley's identity and/or identity expression on the part of Dr. Lewis and the program faculty. Whether Dr. Lewis is aware of Riley's preferred pronouns or not, he does not use them. Dr. Bing, who has more information about Riley's identity, is wise to use caution in the faculty meeting with regard to pronouns and disclosure of information. However, Dr. Bing seems to be the only faculty member aware of these issues of potential bias, and without addressing this unverbalized issue, the problems are unlikely to resolve themselves. It seems Dr. Bing could have addressed the conceptualization of Riley's appearance as unprofessional in the initial faculty meeting, questioning the utility and fairness of the program's dress code and the choice to threaten remediation if Riley's appearance did not change. This could be done without revealing yet undisclosed information about Riley's identity. If Dr. Bing felt that the power differential between Dr. Lewis and her was too great, she could have first consulted with a trusted colleague, prior to sharing her concerns with Dr. Lewis and the rest of the faculty. Dr. Bing may be in a power-down position, but she is not the one with the least power in this situation. She has an ethical obligation to protect and support the safety of her trainee, and speaking up on behalf of Riley (and perhaps other students in the program who may also feel unsafe) to question the program's dress code is a requirement of her role.

VIGNETTE 2: HOW DID WE END UP HERE?

Angela (Black; she/her), who holds multiple diverse identities and a documented disability, is an intern at a VA hospital training site. Dr. Rey (Asian; he/him), Angela's supervisor, began to observe that Angela lacked some basic competence in psychological assessment. Because this is not altogether uncommon for new interns in this setting, Dr. Rey decided to informally support Angela's acquisition of assessment knowledge, skills, and attitudes in the first months of her internship by encouraging Angela to shadow various staff psychologists and by providing more intensive supervision for Angela's assessment cases than initially planned. Angela then requested accommodations from the training program for her disability, which she felt was contributing to the observed difficulties in assessment. The internship site was unable to provide reasonable accommodations for Angela until 8 weeks later. During that period, Dr. Rey observed two instances of Angela crossing boundaries with other trainees in the program and one instance of Angela lying about her role in failing to protect the confidentiality of a client. Angela also continued to experience difficulties with assessment, due to the lack of accommodations.

The internship training staff met to discuss how best to support Angela. A remediation plan was created in collaboration with Angela, with targets of improving her competence in assessment, holding better boundaries with colleagues, and sufficiently protecting client confidentiality. Meetings were held with Angela's graduate training program to establish reciprocal communication about the competence issues, remediation plan, and progress toward remediation goals. As weeks went on, Angela continued to struggle with her performance in the assessment competency domain, despite accommodations in place, and she subsequently withdrew from the internship and her graduate program. Upon learning that Angela left the program, the other interns staged a protest in which they outlined instances of racism in the program and called for Dr. Rey's resignation.

In this scenario, we have a trainee exhibiting several types of competence problems. First, from the vignette, we learn that at least some of Angela's challenges with assessment in the early days of her internship are linked with a documented disability, for which she is able to request accommodations.

Given the delay in obtaining reasonable accommodations, her competence issues in assessment worsened, and she is placed on remediation. In a separate arena, she appears to be struggling with interpersonal interactions (boundaries) and ethics (confidentiality), two challenges for which she was also placed on remediation. Even after reasonable accommodations were in place, she continued to struggle with meeting the competency expectations related to the assessment domain, and eventually, she withdrew from her training. At this point, her departure is public, and fallout among other interns ensued, with claims of racism in the program and a particular vendetta against Dr. Rey. How did this snowball so quickly, and what could have been done?

Angela and Dr. Rey appear to have taken a reasonable course, at least at first. Dr. Rey communicates his concerns about Angela's assessment competencies, contextualizes them as not altogether unusual in this internship context, and offers additional training support. Angela advocates for herself in this situation by bravely disclosing her documented disability and the need for accommodation, which presumably will improve the assessment issues. The first hiccup is the delay in obtaining reasonable accommodations. Clearly, it is ideal if accommodations can be in place as soon as possible, to reduce the time a trainee is performing under unsupported conditions (for extended discussion, see Pearlstein et al., 2021; Wilbur et al., 2019). However, this is not always possible. The real issue is that her performance without accommodation after her disability was disclosed was used as evidence that formal remediation for assessment was required. The program should have waited until accommodations were in place and Angela had sufficient time to adjust accordingly before evaluating whether she should be placed on a remediation plan related to the assessment competency.

The second set of competence issues does not, at least immediately, appear to be directly linked with her disability and/or the lag in obtaining accommodations in the workplace. It seems reasonable that the program placed her on a remediation plan for these difficulties, given that the behavior rose to the threshold of remediation at that time. However, again, her issues with assessment should not have been linked with this particular remediation plan, given the need to allow Angela to adjust to the accommodations. The fact that her problems with assessment persisted, even under conditions of reasonable accommodation and remediation, may reflect accumulated stress from her situation (e.g., that she was remediated prematurely). This stress may have ultimately led her to withdraw from the program and, sadly, may have been avoidable if she had been offered time to get her assessment skills up to speed.

Separate from the details of Angela's remediation and the unfortunate impact of the situation of her training is that of the broader intern and program cultures. On the one hand, the interns staging the protest may have misinterpreted the situation, particularly if they were not privy to complete and accurate information. Indeed, trainee confidentiality, although intended to protect the trainee, can have unintended consequences for program culture, such as elevated levels of trainee paranoia and stress (see Chapter 6, "Remediation, Counseling Out, and Dismissal"; see also Chapter 7, "Trainee Confidentiality"). Dr. Rey, in particular, may find himself at the center of trainees' ire, as the face of Angela's remediation efforts, and may need members of his competent community constellation to make themselves available for support and consultation. Forrest and Elman (Chapter 7) have advocated for a proactive approach to program-level communication about competence issues that may help to reduce secret-keeping and unnecessary program stress. We recognize that this approach may be challenging under certain circumstances and that it may not be a good fit for all competence problem situations.

On the other hand, the interns may have valuable information about the program and bias that may indeed be present. Their reasons for protesting may have been building over time, and their distress only catalyzed by Angela's departure. It would be important for this internship program to take seriously any claims of discrimination or bias and to not immediately dismiss trainees' concerns because they are linked with a remediation situation. The program could work to allow all trainees to have a voice about these issues, support trainees in distress, hear trainee concerns and suggestions for improvement, and/or secure an outside audit of program culture and climate to identify additional avenues for correcting issues that may be present. The institution's Office of Equal Opportunity or a departmental ombudsperson may also be helpful in supporting students' voices.

VIGNETTE 3: THE LAST STOP

Simon (White; he/him) is a fourth-year graduate student in a research-focused, cognitive psychology PhD program. He successfully progressed through the first two major milestones in the program: a second-year thesis project and the third-year comprehensive exams. Despite this, Simon began struggling to keep up with his research laboratory responsibilities early in his fourth year and failed to fully develop an idea for his dissertation. The proposal of his dissertation project was expected by the end of the fourth year, as it is for all students, but Simon was unable to meet this goal. The program handbook outlines that students who do not successfully propose their dissertation by the end of the fourth year are placed on probation, and a remediation plan is implemented. Simon's research advisor, in collaboration with Simon and the program faculty, developed a remediation plan, with clear articulation that, as detailed in the handbook, the final deadline for the successful proposal of the dissertation must occur by the end of the fifth year.

In the context of program supports, Simon made some progress toward developing a dissertation project and preparing a proposal document in the spring of the fifth year. However, even with support from his advisor and consulting faculty, Simon did not complete the proposal by the end of the academic year. The program subsequently provided Simon with a letter detailing that, given his failure to meet the first and final deadlines and in accordance with articulated program policies, he would be dismissed from the program. In response, Simon submitted a complaint to the university and secured outside legal representation to challenge the program's decision to dismiss him.

This vignette offers an opportunity to grapple with a situation involving nonclinical and noninterpersonal competencies, which we believe may occur as often but may not receive as much attention as those situations that involve harm or the potential for harm to others. What is more, a situation like this involves the stalled progress of an otherwise (or at least heretofore) competent trainee vis-à-vis concrete policies that may lead to their dismissal. On the one hand, having clear policies may help trainers and trainees alike to be prepared for what may come; on the other hand, the time invested by students and their trainers in these situations may pull either or both of them to resist following program policies until the situation has become unmanageable. From the vignette, it appears that program policies were articulated and followed, including those related to due process and the opportunity to remediate. Below, we discuss considerations for how the program could work to support the student in this situation, while still adhering to program policy.

One potential source of conflict in this situation is the investment of the trainers and the trainee in the trainee's development thus far. Mentoring trainees in research is a full-time endeavor, particularly for those trainees who wish to be successful in the competitive, academic job market. As such, the farther a trainee/trainer mentorship pair gets in their journey to graduation, the harder it may be to change course. Trainers may feel pulled to stay the course, give one more chance, and veer from program policy in an effort to avoid a negative outcome for the student. Trainees are also likely motivated to avoid dismissal, given their investment in the program to date and the potential career limitations that may ensue from unsuccessful completion of the degree.

In this vignette, the program did well to follow its policies. If the program had not followed its policies and retained the student at this time, they may have avoided complaint from Simon at this juncture but may have kicked the can down the road, so to speak. That is, the program could have ended up in a similar situation at a later point if the student failed to make progress yet again and a dismissal decision felt more comfortable. At that point, the program ironically may be subjecting itself to increased liability because it had not followed its own policies (see Chapter 9, "Legal Issues in Working With Trainees With Problems of Professional Competence"). Moreover, even if Simon did make progress following one more chance, the program's future decisions about other students may be called into question. Future students for whom policy was accurately enforced could certainly attempt to challenge program decisions if they were aware that, in other cases, the program bent the rules. Thus, even if Simon files a complaint, the program is best protected by following its policies, provided they are appropriate.

Liability of the program is not the only concern, of course. In this situation, any potential emotional and career damage to the trainee may be minimized by engaging in a collaborative and supportive "counseling out" process. Counseling out can be part of the process for students who leave training programs by choice and for those students who are dismissed. We would argue that it should be part of both. The program should meet frequently with Simon during this process to discuss his goals and to brainstorm all possible next steps, including transferring to another program within or outside of the university, identifying jobs Simon could take given his qualifications, or other avenues. The program also could support any face-saving strategies Simon wished to employ, such as discussing with peers that he is leaving the program to pursue other goals.

VIGNETTE 4: JUST "DUE" IT

Dr. Peck (Latina; she/her) is the training director at a university counseling center, where she directs a predoctoral internship program. One of the staff psychologists, Dr. Toby (White; he/him), supervises Dan (White; he/him), an intern from a prestigious doctoral program. Dan's letters of recommendation noted many strengths and impressive experiences, and the staff at the counseling center had been eager when Dan matched at their site.

Early in the fall, Dr. Toby began to notice that Dan's client files were missing several notes, and his review of Dan's recorded sessions revealed that Dan was frequently ending sessions early. Dr. Toby felt nervous about approaching Dan about his behavior. He decided to give Dan feedback in a cautious, yet warm, way in order to protect their growing rapport. In supervision, Dan appeared dismissive of Dr. Toby's concerns, becoming defensive and argumentative. Dr. Toby decided to continue to monitor Dan's behavior before taking other steps.

Over the next few months, many of Dan's clients no-showed their appointments, and several terminated treatment earlier than planned or expected. When Dr. Toby reviewed a recording of a session with one of these clients, he observed Dan looking visibly annoyed and verbally expressing his frustration with the client due to lack of progress. Dr. Toby felt that Dan's behavior at this point was clearly inappropriate and met with Dr. Peck to discuss his concerns. Dr. Peck strongly recommended that Dr. Toby directly address Dan's behavior. In the next supervision meeting where this feedback was given, Dan shouted at Dr. Toby and abruptly left the room when confronted with feedback about his behavior. Concerns about Dan's competencies across a variety of domains were subsequently documented in his midyear evaluation. The staff of the counseling center agreed they would continue to support Dan and assigned him to be supervised by Dr. Peck, in the hopes that a change in supervisory relationship would benefit Dan. In the late spring, a month before the internship was set to end, Dan missed several days of work and became visibly agitated when Dr. Peck confronted him with questions about his absence. Dan's documentation in client files was again observed to be insufficient, and he failed to engage fully and openly in his supervision meetings with Dr. Peck. In a difficult end-of-year meeting, the staff of the counseling center decided that, given accumulated concerns, Dan would not successfully complete his internship, a decision that Dr. Peck then communicated to Dan and the training director of Dan's graduate program.

This vignette illustrates the relevance of due process for protecting students and training programs. In this challenging situation, we have a supervisor (Dr. Toby) who is hesitant to directly confront a trainee (Dan) early in the process of observing competency problems. The supervisor provides some feedback once a problem is established, but the feedback is not direct and does not result in improved behavior. Following a clear display of unprofessional behavior in a second feedback meeting, the trainee is then reassigned to a new supervisor (Dr. Peck), who observes new competence issues, in addition to recurrent problems with chart documentation. It is unclear whether the problems have been sufficiently documented or communicated to the trainee, and no remediation has yet been offered. Supervisors may have felt that, because the trainee came so highly recommended or because problems were initially attributed to a problematic supervisory relationship, the problems would resolve themselves in time on their own. The staff then finds themselves at a point of no return, where they decide they cannot approve the trainee's completion of internship.

There are several problems with this hypothetical situation, including poor communication and documentation of competence problems, no remediation plan, and no due process. In effect, the trainers at this site have identified competence problems but have failed to adequately document each, communicate the problems to the trainee, or offer an opportunity for the trainee to remediate before making a decision that will, effectively, prevent this trainee from graduating and becoming a psychologist. Now both the trainee and the program are in jeopardy. The trainee is facing the potential of being unable to realize their professional goals, and the program is liable to legal challenges by the trainee because they did not provide sufficient due process. So, what could have happened instead? We will explore considerations at the trainer and program policy levels.

Besides the trainee competence issues themselves, one of the first signs of trouble here is the hesitancy Dr. Toby feels at confronting Dan in supervision with feedback about his behavior. Such hesitancy is common, particularly in supervisors who wish to preserve the professional relationship and motivate trainees to engage in the process of improving their behavior. Yet in a communitarian framework, seeking consultation and professional support is normalized and has the potential to help mitigate collateral damage in the process of supporting students with competence problems (see Chapter 1, "Creating a Communitarian, Multiculturally Sensitive, and Socially Just Training Culture"). Upon recognizing his hesitation to provide direct feedback, Dr. Toby should have consulted with a colleague about his concerns and brainstormed the best ways to deliver the feedback, given his emotional reaction to this process. If Dr. Toby did not recognize in himself the need for consultation before the initial feedback session, he could have met with a colleague after the fact, to process how best to proceed given Dan's response. Instead, Dr. Toby finds himself in an isolated holding pattern in which he, alone, is aware of Dan's struggles and has not yet been able to have productive interactions with Dan regarding ways to improve. The problem becomes public only when Dan's unprofessional behavior cannot be ignored.

At this point, Dr. Toby may be ready and willing to take more drastic steps than the other trainers, who are only first learning of Dan's struggles. This potential splitting among the staff poses another challenge to the program responding to Dan as a unified whole. Questions could be raised about whether this is just an unfortunate interpersonal pairing between Dan and Dr. Toby or an actual competence issue that needs immediate attention. The decision to switch Dan to be supervised by Dr. Peck suggests the former perspective and that the staff as a whole was relying on the hope that Dan's struggles would resolve themselves. In this situation, Dr. Peck would have better supported Dr. Toby following their first meeting, taking their concerns about Dan's competence to the larger training staff, for additional consultation. It may be that other staff, at this point, had relevant observations (even concerns) about Dan to share, and at the very least, group communication would have brought all staff up to speed and helped to ward off any splitting that may have occurred.

Finally, with regard to the last decision by the staff to terminate Dan from the internship program, it could be that the passing of Dan from supervisor to supervisor until his issues were unignorable put the rest of the staff in a bind. Here they are, looking at an array of clearly problematic behavior near the end of the internship and tasked with gatekeeping responsibilities. With little time to remediate, many from the larger group could have felt pressure to act quickly and without consideration of alternatives, which could have been avoided with earlier and more frequent communication about Dan's performance.

In addition to actions taken by individual trainers in this situation, there are clear problems with program policy, implementation of program policy, or both. It is unclear whether program policies regarding competence, remediation, and dismissal existed at all or whether existing policies simply were not implemented according to plan. In any event, the concerns about Dan's behavior should have been corroborated by assessment of Dan's competencies and clearly documented and communicated to the student in both verbal and written form (see Chapter 5, "Identification and Assessment of Problems of Professional Competence"). If the initial concerns rose to the threshold of remediation, then a remediation plan should have been articulated at that point, and the student should have had the opportunity to acquire and demonstrate the various competencies in question (see Chapter 6, "Remediation, Counseling Out, and Dismissal"). From the information available in this vignette, it seems reasonable that remediation activities be offered to Dan at the first point of concern, given his training stage. However, if the program decided not to remediate formally, concerns still should have been properly documented with plans for addressing the concerns with formal remediation should they continue. Moreover, as competency concerns were communicated to the student, the internship staff should have also communicated their concerns back to the training program, so that there were no surprises.

Although the staff of the counseling center attempted to act in their capacity as gatekeepers by preventing an incompetent trainee from passing the internship, their decision was not made on the basis of sufficiently documented evidence that a competence problem was present and that, following an opportunity to remediate, the trainee did not successfully demonstrate mastery of the competencies in question. Additionally, given the stakes of this training stage, the program would benefit from having clearly articulated policies about due process and standards for dismissal. Because there was insufficient due process in this case, the trainee then has grounds to challenge the internship's decision and could likely be successful in this endeavor (see Chapter 9, "Legal Issues in Working With Trainees With Problems of Professional Competence").

VIGNETTE 5: TIK, TIK . . . BOOM

Dr. Causey is the training director at the Midland County Community Health Center. Dr. Causey receives a text message from a clinical staff member that contains a TikTok video link and immediately opens the link (the staff frequently share funny social media content). In the TikTok video, Rodolfo (Italian; he/him), a second-year practicum student at the training site, has a video titled "Things That SUCK About Practicum." The post includes Rodolfo describing inadequate supervision (especially regarding working with people of color), poor site management, and a quote that he "would never let his family seek treatment there." Though Rodolfo does not indicate the training site in the video, he has named the site in a comment response to another trainee, who asks: "Where is this so I can avoid the site?" At the next meeting, the staff make it clear that they expect Dr. Causey to remediate Rodolfo for the social media post, as well as contact the home training program to inform them of the issue.

Preventatively, training programs/sites benefit when they have clear and consistent policies relevant to professional behavior, including online behavior (see Chapter 10, "Building Program Policies in a Communitarian and Multiculturally Sensitive Training Culture"). Additionally, these policies should be proactively communicated to trainees early and often in the training program/site. Policies should directly indicate expected/allowed and prohibited online behaviors. Policies should also cover trainer engagement (e.g., whether trainers are allowed to "follow" on social media and to search posts). Trainees should receive clarity early on about how they are expected to engage on social media and what they should expect from trainers regarding social media engagement. Additionally, policy documents should differentiate between the types of social media engagement covered by each policy, including personal accounts (limited to private use), business accounts (intended for advertising/promotion), and influencer accounts (intended to disseminate psychological information). For instance, policies regarding sharing private clinical information should cover all three types of social media accounts. However, policies regarding professional use of the training site's name or online drug/alcohol depictions may cover only social media that is intended to be accessible to the public (i.e., business or influencer accounts). For a more thorough discussion of ethical social media engagement, see Smith et al. (2021) and the American Psychological Association's (APA's; 2021) *Guidelines for the Optimal Use of Social Media*.

With regard to this vignette, there are several issues to explore. We will examine potential responses to the trainee and training site culture. First, Dr. Causey must identify any problems of professional competence concerns that may exist. As noted in this volume, Dr. Causey might rely on the "Competency Benchmarks" to identify the professional competencies in question (see Chapter 5, "Identification and Assessment of Problems of Professional Competence"). For instance, professionalism competencies (e.g., professional values and ethical and legal standards) and relational competencies might be relevant to explore. Dr. Causey's assessment should also take into account broader information collected in the form of past formative or summative evaluations of the trainee. Primarily, Dr. Causey must answer whether the online behavior demonstrates a deficit in competencies given the trainee's developmental level (i.e., does it violate program policy or compromise clinical care?). Dr. Causey might also consider whether cultural perspectives are influencing their lens on this particular concern. For example, are there generational differences between trainers and trainees with regard to the use of social media? If so, the trainee's choice to engage may be rooted in these cultural differences rather than true competency concerns. (Note that clear social media policies would mitigate these differences by clarifying expected behaviors with regard to the training site.) Additionally, are there aspects of Rodolfo's message that may invoke defensiveness in trainers? Again, aligning the behavior with benchmark competencies may help to mitigate the tendency for trainers to respond from a defensive position. Finally, Dr. Causey should consider the response that would promote and/or maintain a communitarian training culture (see Chapter 1, "Creating a Communitarian, Multiculturally Sensitive, and Socially Just Training Culture"). In the absence of a clear social media policy, a direct threat to clinical care of patients, and a history of evaluation (formative and summative) with similar competency concerns, Dr. Causey might opt to engage in a formative discussion with Rodolfo concerning the behavior. This discussion might identify the concerns, allow space for Dr. Causey and Rodolfo to engage in self-reflective practice, and identify a collaborative solution that can be documented and shared with the training staff. Dr. Causey and Rodolfo might also choose to share collaborative strategies developed with the home training program as a means of fostering communication. Finally, Dr. Causey might take the opportunity to acknowledge areas of misstep within the training site, including the access and sharing of Rodolfo's social media and the lack of policy related to social media use (if that is the case).

There are a number of issues related to the training program that Dr. Causey should also consider. First, the content of Rodolfo's message suggested deficits in supervision, especially related to working with people of color. Just as Dr. Causey would consider potential harm to clients from Rodolfo's message, Dr. Causey might also consider potential harm if the issues raised regarding supervision are true. Investigation of this concern, in the context of a communitarian training culture, should include open reflection with training staff and engaging plans to strengthen supervision competencies of training staff. Additionally, Dr. Causey should explore staff policies on searching, viewing, and sharing social media of trainees. APA guidelines suggest balancing the risks of online searches with the reasons to search social media (APA, 2021). It is likely that in this case, Rodolfo's right to privacy and self-determination (to share concerns with the training site) were violated. It would benefit the training culture to address boundaries that better protect trainee autonomy.

VIGNETTE 6: ADAPTING TO CHRONIC PAIN

Lune (Latinx; they/them) is a fifth-year student currently on internship in a small community hospital setting. They are a strong clinician with a budding specialization in health psychology, specifically related to the psychological treatment of chronic pain. Lune's interest in chronic pain began in their third year of graduate school. That year, they were involved in a significant motor vehicle accident and began experiencing chronic pain. After a year of tests that failed to identify a source of the chronic pain, Lune was diagnosed with somatic symptom disorder (with predominant pain) and began working with a therapist to manage the symptoms. The pain subsided after a few months in therapy. Lune's chronic pain difficulties in the third year caused them to miss a significant number of classes and practicum hours as they navigated regular doctors' visits. Most notably, Lune missed almost 50% of their practicum hours that year. However, Lune's training director wanted to be supportive as their chronic pain difficulties were ongoing. As opposed to requiring the traditional hours in the practicum course, they allowed Lune to complete papers on intervention to substitute for the missed hours. Lune passed the practicum and continued to move through the program.

During the internship, Lune has been struggling with a resurgence of chronic pain difficulties that have caused them to miss 1 to 2 days of internship each week. Most recently, Lune failed to properly cancel an evaluation they missed in the electronic health system, which led to the patient and insurance company receiving charges for services that had not been rendered. As a result, the internship site is considering dismissing Lune for competency issues and has requested to meet with Lune's program-based training director.

There are a number of competency issues alongside critical complexities to explore in this case. As an intern, Lune made a mistake that led to a fraudulent insurance claim and billing to a patient. This issue is both ethically and legally risky. Additionally, Lune's mistake seems to be one consequence of significant absences related to the complications of Lune's chronic illness and/or somatic symptom disorder. Systemically, there are a number of factors to consider. First, considerations for Lune's physical and mental health challenges, and whether Lune might be eligible for reasonable accommodations (per the Americans With Disabilities Act [ADA]), are warranted. Studies suggest that chronic pain is often misdiagnosed (estimates of 40%–80% of patients; Hendler, 2016). Additionally, experiences of pain are more often underestimated and less likely to be treated for patients with diverse identities, including racial/ethnic diversity, gender diversity, and low socioeconomic status patients (e.g., Samulowitz et al., 2018; Summers et al., 2021; Trawalter et al., 2016). Given this, it is possible that Lune's pain challenges have been misdiagnosed and/or undertreated in conjunction with or as opposed to being psychosomatic. This is a critical consideration in the systemic context of approach to this competency concern.

The internship site is tasked with determining what, if any, competency issues may be relevant in the decision to dismiss Lune from the internship. For instance, competencies related to maintaining complete and accurate record keeping (i.e., administrative) are likely relevant to this case. However, the internship site should consider (a) the developmental level of the trainee as it relates to expected competencies, (b) relevant remediation opportunities, (c) policies related to the competency issue, and (d) due process concerns.

First, it is important to consider the developmental level of the trainee in context. At this stage, it is reasonable to assume that Lune understands policies related to accurate record keeping but may still be developing the skill to navigate these policies in the context of their own disruption of work. It is possible that a remediation opportunity exists to better develop Lune's competence in this pertinent competency domain. It is also important to differentiate the source of the potential competency concern in determining potential remediations. For instance, remediating a shortfall in learning how to manage record keeping appropriately may necessitate education-based training, whereas remediating a competency issue rooted largely in the impact of a physical/mental health condition necessitates support-based efforts. For instance, at the outset of the resurgence of chronic pain, both Lune and the internship site may have benefited from developing a supportive remediation plan that considers Lune's need for increased absenteeism and navigating various aspects of the internship requirements in the new context (e.g., fewer clients, hours dedicated to navigating documentation, a staff member to support coordination during last-minute absenteeism).

Consultation between the internship site and the home training program is also an important and valuable opportunity in this case. It is important that both sites and training programs clearly articulate in policy documents when and how they may communicate about trainees. Consultation may help the internship site balance supporting the trainee (and following relevant ADA laws) and navigating their gatekeeping function by ensuring competencies are met. This case requires a both/and approach. Given this has been an ongoing challenge for Lune in the context of their physical/mental health, the training program and the internship site may consider "counseling in." As opposed to counseling out of the profession (see Chapter 6, "Remediation, Counseling Out, and Dismissal"), counseling in relates to helping a trainee or psychologist reflect on the areas of practice they are best suited to pursue, alongside the important considerations and support mechanisms they will need to put into place to ensure success as they navigate across settings and career span. For Lune, the internship site and the training program may use the counseling-in process within the supportive remediation plan to help Lune apply the supports that have been helpful to new contexts.

Finally, policies that clearly outline documentation and attendance requirements should help guide the internship site in its decision making at this stage. Any exceptions made to policy (e.g., given Lune's chronic pain difficulties) should be well documented within the supportive remediation plan. In the best-case scenario, the ethical/legal issue would be avoided. In the worst-case scenario, the internship site would properly attend to due process concerns that will likely arise should they attempt to outright dismiss Lune.

REFERENCES

American Psychological Association (APA). (2021). *Guidelines for the optimal use of social media in professional psychological practice*. APA Committee on Professional Practice and Standards. https://www.apa.org/about/policy/guidelines-optimal-use-social-media.pdf

Hendler, N. (2016). Why chronic pain patients are misdiagnosed 40 to 80% of the time? *Journal on Recent Advances in Pain, 2*(3), 94–98.

Pearlstein, J. G., Schmidt, A. T., Lund, E. M., Khazem, L. R., & Liu, N. H. (2021). Guidelines to address barriers in clinical training for trainees with sensory disabilities. *Training and Education in Professional Psychology*. Advance online publication. https://doi.org/10.1037/tep0000367

Samulowitz, A., Gremyr, I., Eriksson, E., & Hensing, G. (2018). "Brave men" and "emotional women": A theory-guided literature review on gender bias in health care and gendered norms towards patients with chronic pain. *Pain Research & Management, 2018*, 1–14. https://doi.org/10.1155/2018/6358624

Smith, K. M., Jones, A., & Hunter, E. A. (2021). Navigating the multidimensionality of social media presence: Ethical considerations and recommendations for psychologists. *Ethics & Behavior*. Advance online publication. https://doi.org/10.1080/10508422.2021.1977935

Summers, K. M., Deska, J. C., Almaraz, S. M., Hugenberg, K., & Lloyd, E. P. (2021). Poverty and pain: Low-SES people are believed to be insensitive to pain. *Journal of Experimental Social Psychology, 95*, Article 104116. https://doi.org/10.1016/j.jesp.2021.104116

Trawalter, S., Hoffman, K. M., & Waytz, A. (2016). Correction: Racial bias in perceptions of others' pain. *PLOS ONE, 11*(3), e0152334. https://doi.org/10.1371/journal.pone.0152334

Veilleux, J. C., & Schwartz-Mette, R. A. (2021). Pink hair, don't care? Unpacking the concept of professional appearance for modern therapists. *Behavior Therapist, 44*(2), 80–84.

Wilbur, R. C., Kuemmel, A. M., & Lackner, R. J. (2019). Who's on first? Supervising psychology trainees with disabilities and establishing accommodations. *Training and Education in Professional Psychology, 13*(2), 111–118. https://doi.org/10.1037/tep0000231

Appendix A

KEY TERMS

Antiracist: One who supports an antiracist policy through their actions or expressing an antiracist idea (Kendi, 2019); in other words, to actively fight against racism rather than be passive in claiming to be nonracist.

Chronosystem: "Changes (and continuities) over time in the environment" in which a trainee is developing (Bronfenbrenner, 1986, p. 724).

Communitarianism: Communal insight and responsibility related to each individual psychologist's competence (Johnson et al., 2014).

Communitarian training culture: This culture infuses communitarian values (e.g., humility, reflective practice, compassion, self-care) and collegial engagement (e.g., mentorship, consultation, collaboration, mutual support, collegial assertiveness) to address training within health service psychology, including problems with professional competence (Johnson et al., 2012).

Competence: The intentional coordination and application of professional skills, attitudes, values, judgment, reasoning, reflection, and emotion in the practice of psychology (see Barnett et al., 2007; Epstein & Hundert, 2002); "a dynamic set of skills and attributes that are context specific, ever evolving and embedded in being connected to a community of others" (Wise & Reuman, 2019, p. 130).

Competencies: Components of performance; the knowledge, skills, and attitudes and their integration that comprise competence (Kaslow et al., 2009);

the building blocks that when integrated cogently and intentionally, compose competence (Ridley et al., 2011).

Competent: "Generally understood to mean that a professional is qualified, capable, and able to understand and do certain things in an appropriate and effective manner. Simply having knowledge or skill is insufficient for someone to be considered competent. Rather, there is the implication that competency requires action and in some public way verification of what is achieved by that action. Moreover, appropriate and effective action requires judgment, critical thinking, and decision-making. In a profession, competency also connotes that behaviors are carried out in a manner consistent with standards and guidelines of peer review, ethical principles, and values of the profession, especially those that protect and otherwise benefit the public" (Rodolfa et al., 2005, p. 348).

Counseling in: A process that helps a trainee (or psychologist) reflect on the areas of practice they are best suited to pursue, alongside the important considerations and support mechanisms they will need to put into place to ensure success as they navigate across settings and span their career.

Counseling out: A collaborative process between program and trainee involving support and identification of alternate training programs and/or professional paths for trainees unable or unwilling to continue in their current training program.

Cultural humility: The "ability to maintain an interpersonal stance that is other-oriented (or open to the other) in relation to aspects of cultural identity that are most important to the client [or supervisee]" (Hook et al., 2013, p. 354).

Decolonization: Naming and dismantling the hidden presumptions of colonial mentality from policy, curriculum, and guidelines of Western psychology (Zetzer, 2021).

Exosystem: "Refers to one or more settings that do not involve the developing person [trainee] as an active participant, but in which events occur that affect, or are affected by, what happens in the setting containing the developing person" (Bronfenbrenner, 1979, p. 25).

Formative evaluation: Ongoing, often informal feedback that is provided to a trainee who is in the process of learning. Formative evaluation assists with identifying what is yet to be learned and to provide a trainee with information about their already developed skills and abilities, as well as those in need of further development.

Foundational competencies: Building blocks needed for effective practice across all areas of professional functioning (Rodolfa et al., 2005).

Functional competencies: Requisite knowledge, skills, and attitudes to conduct the typical domains of professional practice of a psychologist (Rodolfa et al., 2005).

Gatekeeper function: The ethical obligation not to graduate—or pass through to the next level of training—a trainee who has not demonstrated sufficient mastery of the competencies commensurate with that level of training.

General ethical principles: Foundational and aspirational ethical/moral commitments that guide professional behavior and undergird the enforceable ethical standards.

Liberation psychology: Centers on the development of a critical consciousness of the struggle of oppressed individuals and the importance of liberating them from oppressive forces (French et al., 2020).

Macrosystem: "Consistencies, in the form and content of lower-order systems (micro-, meso-, and exo-) that exist, or could exist, at the level of the subculture or the culture as a whole, along with any belief systems or ideology underlying such consistencies" (Bronfenbrenner, 1979, p. 26).

Mesosystem: "Comprises the interrelations among two or more settings in which the developing person [trainee] actively participates" (Bronfenbrenner, 1979, p. 25).

Microaggressions: Subtle or unintentional discrimination toward marginalized people (Sue et al., 2009).

Microsystem: "A pattern of activities, roles, and interpersonal relations experienced by the developing person [trainee] in a given setting with particular and material characteristics" (Bronfenbrenner, 1979, p. 22).

Multicultural: "The coexistence of diverse cultures that reflect varying reference group identities. Multicultural can embody the coexistence of cultures within an individual, family, group, or organization" (American Psychological Association, 2017, p. 167).

Problem of professional competence: A term used to indicate when a trainee is not performing at the developmentally expected level for a defined area of competence.

Summative evaluation: This evaluation occurs at the end of a learning experience and provides a summary of a trainee's current skills and abilities.

Often formalized through a written form, the evaluation can be thought of as the outcomes of the learning experience at a particular point in time.

Trainees with problems of professional competence: Those students/trainees identified by their educators/trainers/peers "whose performance, behaviors, and/or attitudes do not meet ethical or professional standards . . . expected given their stage of training" (Shen-Miller et al., 2011, p. 113), grounded in the Benchmarks Competencies (see Fouad et al., 2009; Hatcher et al., 2013).

REFERENCES

American Psychological Association. (2017). *Multicultural guidelines: An ecological approach to context, identity, and intersectionality, 2017.* https://www.apa.org/about/policy/multicultural-guidelines.pdf

Barnett, J. E., Doll, B., Younggren, J. N., & Rubin, N. J. (2007). Clinical competence for practicing psychologists: Clearly a work in progress. *Professional Psychology: Research and Practice, 38*(5), 510–517. https://doi.org/10.1037/0735-7028.38.5.510

Bronfenbrenner, U. (1979). *The ecology of human development.* Harvard University Press.

Bronfenbrenner, U. (1986). Ecology of the family as a context for human development: Research perspectives. *Developmental Psychology, 22*(6), 723–742. https://doi.org/10.1037/0012-1649.22.6.723

Epstein, R., & Hundert, E. (2002). Defining and assessing professional competence. *Journal of the American Medical Association, 287*(2), 226–235. https://doi.org/10.1001/jama.287.2.226

Fouad, N. A., Grus, C. L., Hatcher, R. L., Kaslow, N. J., Hutchings, P. S., Madson, M. B., Collins, F. L., Jr., & Crossman, R. E. (2009). Competency benchmarks: A model for understanding and measuring competence in professional psychology across training levels. *Training and Education in Professional Psychology, 3*(4S), S5–S26. https://doi.org/10.1037/a0015832

French, B. H., Lewis, J. A., Mosley, D. V., Adams, H. Y., Chavez-Dueñas, N. Y., Chen, G. A., & Neville, H. A. (2020). Toward a psychological framework of radical healing in communities of color. *The Counseling Psychologist, 48*(1), 14–46. https://doi.org/10.1177/0011000019843506

Hatcher, R., Fouad, N., Grus., C., Campbell, L., McCutcheon., S., & Leahy, K. (2013) Competency benchmarks: Practical steps toward a culture of competence. *Training and Education in Professional Psychology, 7*(2), 84–91. https://doi.org/10.1037/a0029401

Hook, J. N., Davis, D. E., Owen, J., Worthington, E. L., Jr., & Utsey, S. O. (2013). Cultural humility: Measuring openness to culturally diverse clients. *Journal of Counseling Psychology, 60*(3) 353–366. https://doi.org/10.1037/a0032595

Johnson, W. B., Barnett, J. E., Elman, N. S., Forrest, L., & Kaslow, N. J. (2012). The competent community: Toward a vital reformulation of professional ethics. *American Psychologist, 67,* 557–569. https://doi.org/10.1037/a0027206

Johnson, W. B., Barnett, J. E., Elman, N. S., Forrest, L., Schwartz-Mette, R., & Kaslow, N. J. (2014). Preparing trainees for lifelong competence: Creating a communitarian training culture. *Training and Education in Professional Psychology, 8*(4), 211–220. https://doi.org/10.1037/tep0000048

Kaslow, N. J., Grus, C. L., Campbell, L. F., Fouad, N. A., Hatcher, R. L., & Rodolfa, E. R. (2009). Competency Assessment Toolkit for professional psychology. *Training and Education in Professional Psychology, 3*(4, Suppl.), S27–S45. https://doi.org/10.1037/a0015833

Kendi, I. X. (2019). *How to be an antiracist*. One World.

Ridley, C. R., Mollen, D., & Kelly, S. M. (2011). Beyond microskills: Toward a model of counseling competence. *The Counseling Psychologist, 39*(6), 825–864. https://doi.org/10.1177/0011000010378440

Rodolfa, E., Bent, R., Eisman, E., Nelson, P., Rehm, L., & Ritchie, P. (2005). A cube model for competency development: Implications for psychology educators and regulators. *Professional Psychology: Research and Practice, 36*(4), 347–354. https://doi.org/10.1037/0735-7028.36.4.347

Shen-Miller, D. S., Grus, C. L., Van Sickle, K., Schwartz-Mette, R., Cage, E., Elman, N. S., Jacobs, S. C., & Kaslow, N. J. (2011). Trainees' experiences with peers having competence problems: A national survey. *Training and Education in Professional Psychology, 5*(2), 112–121. https://doi.org/10.1037/a0023824

Sue, D. W., Lin, A. I., Torino, G. C., Capodilupo, C. M., & Rivera, D. P. (2009). Racial microaggressions and difficult dialogues on race in the classroom. *Cultural Diversity and Ethnic Minority Psychology, 15*(2), 183–190. https://doi.org/10.1037/a0014191

Wise, E. H., & Reuman, L. (2019). Promoting competent and flourishing life-long practice for psychologists: A communitarian perspective. *Professional Psychology: Research and Practice, 50*(2), 129–135. https://doi.org/10.1037/pro0000226

Zetzer, H. A. (2021, Winter/Spring). Decolonizing the curriculum in health service psychology. *APTC Bulletin: Practicum Education & Training*, pp. 20–22. https://aptc.org/images/File/newsletter/APTC_Bulletin_PET_2021_Spring%20FINAL.pdf

Appendix B

CUBE MODEL FOR COMPETENCY DEVELOPMENT

TABLE B.1. Definitions of Functional Competency and Foundational Competency Domains

Domain	Definition
Functional competency	
Assessment–diagnosis–case conceptualization	Assessment and diagnosis of problems and issues associated with individuals, groups, and/or organizations.
Intervention	Interventions designed to alleviate suffering and to promote health and well-being of individuals, groups, and/or organizations. Understanding of empirically supported treatments.
Consultation	The ability to provide expert guidance or professional assistance in response to a client's needs or goals.
Research–evaluation	The generation of research that contributes to the professional knowledge base and/or evaluates the effectiveness of various professional activities.
Supervision–teaching	Supervision and training of the professional knowledge base and/or evaluates the effectiveness of various professional activities.
Management–administration	Managing the practice of mental health services and/or the administration of health organizations, programs, and agencies.

TABLE B.1. Definitions of Functional Competency and Foundational Competency Domains (*Continued*)

Domain	Definition
Foundational competency	
Reflective practice–self-assessment	Practice conducted within the boundaries of competencies, commitment to lifelong learning, engagement with scholarship, critical thinking, and a commitment to the development of the profession.
Scientific knowledge–methods	The ability to understand research, research methodology and a respect for scientifically derived knowledge, techniques of data collection and analysis, biological bases of behavior, cognitive-affective bases of behavior, and lifespan human development.
Relationships	Capacity to relate effectively and meaningfully with individuals, groups, and/or communities.
Ethical–legal standards–policy	Application of ethical concepts and awareness of legal issues regarding professional activities with individuals, groups, and organizations. Advocating for the profession.
Individual–cultural diversity	Awareness and sensitivity in working professionally with diverse individuals, groups, and communities who represent various cultural and personal background and characteristics.
Interdisciplinary systems	Identification and involvement with one's colleagues and peers. Knowledge of key issues and concepts in related disciplines and the ability to interact with professionals in them.

Note. Definitions are based on the Council of Credentialing Organizations in Professional Psychology (CCOPP) 2004 document titled *A Conceptual Framework for Specialization in the Health Service Domain of Professional Psychology*. CCOPP used the 2002 Competencies Conference specialties and proficiencies work group cube model in their document and expanded the definitions initially developed by the work group. Adapted from "A Cube Model for Competency Development: Implications for Psychology Educators and Regulators," by E. Rodolfa, R. Bent, E. Eisman, P. Nelson, L. Rehm, & P. Ritchie, 2005, *Professional Psychology: Research and Practice*, *36*(4), p. 350 (https://doi.org/10.1037/0735-7028.36.4.347). Copyright 2005 by the American Psychological Association.

Appendix C

COMPETENCY REMEDIATION PLAN

Date of Competency Remediation Plan Meeting:
Name of Trainee:
Primary Supervisor/Advisor:
Names of All Persons Present at the Meeting:
All Additional Pertinent Supervisors/Faculty:
Date for Follow-up Meeting(s):

Circle all competency domains in which the trainee's performance does not meet the benchmark:

Foundational Competencies: Professionalism, Reflective Practice/Self-Assessment/Self-care, Scientific Knowledge and Methods, Relationships, Individual and Cultural Diversity, Ethical Legal Standards and Policy, Interdisciplinary Systems

Functional Competencies: Assessment, Intervention, Consultation, Research–Evaluation, Supervision, Teaching, Management–Administration, Advocacy

Description of the problem(s) in each competency domain circled above:

Date(s) the problem(s) was brought to the trainee's attention and by whom:

Steps already taken by the trainee to rectify the problem(s) that was identified:

Competency domain/ essential components	Problem behaviors	Expectations for acceptable performance	Trainee's responsibilities/ actions	Supervisors'/ faculty responsibilities/ actions	Time Frame acceptable performance	Assessment methods	Dates of evaluation	Consequences for unsuccessful remediation

Steps already taken by the supervisor(s)/faculty to address the problem(s):

Competency Remediation Plan

I, _____, have reviewed the above competency remediation plan with my primary supervisor/advisor, any additional supervisors/faculty, and the director of training. My signature below indicates that I fully understand the above. I agree/disagree with the above decision (please circle one). My comments, if any, are below (*PLEASE NOTE: If trainee disagrees, comments, including a detailed description of the trainee's rationale for disagreement, are REQUIRED*).

Trainee Name	Date	Training Director	Date

Trainee's comments (Feel free to use additional pages):

All supervisors/faculty with responsibilities or actions described in the above competency remediation plan agree to participate in the plan as outlined above. Please sign and date below to indicate your agreement with the plan.

Competency Remediation Plan Continued

242 • Appendix C

SUMMATIVE EVALUATION OF COMPETENCY REMEDIATION PLAN

Follow-up Meeting(s):
Date (s):
In Attendance:

Competency domain/ essential components	Expectations for acceptable performance	Outcomes related to expected benchmarks (met, partially met, not met)	Next steps (e.g., remediation concluded, remediation continued and plan modified, next stage in due process procedures)	Next evaluation date (if needed)

I, _____, have reviewed the above summative evaluation of my competency remediation plan with my primary supervisor(s)/ faculty, any additional supervisors/faculty, and the director of training. My signature below indicates that I fully understand the above. I agree/disagree with the above outcome assessments and next steps (please circle one). My comments, if any, are below. (*PLEASE NOTE: If trainee disagrees with the outcomes and next steps, comments, including a detailed description of the trainee's rationale for disagreement, are REQUIRED*).

_____ _____   _____ _____
Trainee Name   Date   Training Director   Date

Trainee's comments (Feel free to use additional pages):

Appendix D

ADDITIONAL RESOURCES FOR READERS

After Skool. (2019, October 1). *The Dunning–Kruger effect—Cognitive bias: Why incompetent people think they are competent* [Video]. YouTube. https://www.youtube.com/watch?v=y50i1bI2uN4

American Psychological Association. (2012). *Benchmarks Evaluation System.* https://www.apa.org/ed/graduate/benchmarks-evaluation-system

American Psychological Association. (2012). *Revised competency benchmarks in professional psychology.* https://www.apa.org/ed/graduate/benchmarks-evaluation-system

American Psychological Association. (2013). Professional psychologist competencies to serve a diverse public. https://www.apa.org/ed/graduate/diversity-preparation?tab=2

American Psychological Association. (2015). *Competency remediation plan.* https://www.apa.org/ed/graduate/competency-resources

American Psychological Association. (2015). *Resources related to trainees competence.* https://www.apa.org/ed/graduate/competency

American Psychological Association. (2015). *Resources related to trainees with problems of professional competence.* https://www.apa.org/ed/graduate/competency-resources

American Psychological Association, Commission on Accreditation. (2019). *Standards of accreditation for health service psychology and accreditation operating procedures.* https://www.apa.org/ed/accreditation/about/policies/standards-of-accreditation.pdf

ANU TV. (2020, October 19). *Cecil Gibb research seminar: The psychology of secrecy* [Video]. YouTube. https://www.youtube.com/watch?v=GzdjI95uBSQ

Aosvad, A. (2017. May). Tips for trainers: Due process. https://www.appic.org/Portals/0/downloads/DueProcess/2017Newsletter-DueProcess.pdf

Association of Psychology Postdoctoral and Internship Centers. (n.d.). *Elements to consider in developing due process and grievance policy.* https://www.appic.org/Portals/0/downloads/ElementsOfDueProcess.pdf

Association of Psychology Postdoctoral and Internship Centers. (2022). APPIC Informal Problem Consultation. https://www.appic.org/Forms/APPIC-Informal-Problem-Consultation

Association of State and Provincial Psychology Boards. (n.d.). *2017 ASPPB competencies expected of psychologists at the point of licensure.* https://cdn.ymaws.com/www.asppb.net/resource/resmgr/eppp_2/2017_asppb_competencies_exp.pdf

Council of Chairs of Training Councils. (2020). *CCTC 2020: Social Responsiveness in Health Service Psychology Education and Training Toolkit.* https://www.appic.org/Portals/0/downloads/TrainingDocs/CCTC_Socially-Responsive-HSP-Ed-Training.pdf

Falender, C. (2021, May). *Decolonizing clinical supervision* [Slides]. https://www.tc.columbia.edu/media/conferences/decolonizing-psychology/pdfs/Decolonizing-Clinical-Supervision-Slides.pdf

Kahlmann, J.-P. (n.d.). *What if healthcare embraces just culture?* [Video]. TEDx. https://www.ted.com/talks/jean_pierre_kahlmann_what_if_healthcare_embraces_just_culture

Kellogg School of Management. (2018, January 31). *Why transparency is critical to creating trust in an organization* [Video]. YouTube. https://www.youtube.com/watch?v=do6e1UE4ruI

Life Noggin. (2019, July 11). *Why keeping a big secret is worse than you think* [Video]. YouTube. https://www.youtube.com/watch?v=B32JRmYBaho

National Council of Schools & Programs of Professional Psychology. (2019). *NCSPP model of training.* https://www.ncspp.net/training-model/ncspp-model-of-training/

sidneydekker. (2015, December 2). *Just Culture Short Course 1* [Video]. YouTube. https://www.youtube.com/watch?v=PVWjgqDANWA

sidneydekker. (2015, December 2). *Just Culture Short Course 2* [Video]. YouTube. https://www.youtube.com/watch?v=7_4b3hU03lk

sidneydekker. (2015, December 2). *Just Culture Short Course 3* [Video]. YouTube. https://www.youtube.com/watch?v=loNyaKM1-Ls

sidneydekker. (2015, December 2). *Just Culture Short Course 4* [Video]. YouTube. https://www.youtube.com/watch?v=2BsHmwAFPKs

VA Section Division 18. (2021, March 10). *Diversity dialogues in supervision* [Video]. YouTube. https://www.youtube.com/watch?v=5rgB-8vEqGc

WTCSystem. (2020, May 26). *Understanding microaggressions* [Video]. YouTube. https://www.youtube.com/watch?v=e4N50b76cZc

Index

A

ACA (American Counseling Association) Code of Ethics, 179–180
Academic dismissals, 115
Accountability, 49, 165
Accreditation, 36
    Commission on Accreditation, 26, 33
    Standards of Accreditation, 26, 88, 91, 155, 156
Accuracy in Teaching (Standard 7.03), 157–158
Action, in multicultural perspective, 39
ADA Amendments Act of 2008, 173
ADA (Americans With Disabilities Act) of 1990, 44, 172–176
ADDRESSING model, 16
Addressing problems of professional competence, 50–53, 80
Ad Hoc Working Group on Trainees With Competence Problems, 106
Advising
    mentoring vs., 204
    transactional, 161
Advocacy
    cultural, 20–21
    culturally adaptive, 13
    gatekeeping-advocacy tension, 161–162
    in multicultural perspective, 39
American Counseling Association (ACA) Code of Ethics, 179–180
American Psychological Association (APA)
    BEA Virtual Working Group on Restrictions Affecting Diversity Training in Graduate Education, 183
    Commission on Accreditation, 26, 33
    Competencies Conference, 28
    Ethics Code of. *See Ethical Principles of Psychologists and Code of Conduct*
    Guidelines for Clinical Supervision in Health Service Psychology, 17
    Guidelines for the Optimal Use of Social Media, 226
    Multicultural Guidelines: An Ecological Approach to Context, Identity, and Intersectionality, 12–13, 22
    remediation plan available from, 180
    Standards of Accreditation, 26, 88, 91, 155, 156
Americans With Disabilities Act (ADA) of 1990, 44, 172–176
Antiracist (term), 231
APA. *See* American Psychological Association
APA Ethics Code. *See Ethical Principles of Psychologists and Code of Conduct*
Appearance, professional, 92, 214–217
APPIC (Association of Psychology Postdoctoral and Internship Centers), 28, 105
Articulation of competencies, 27–28
Aspirational ethics, 152–153
ASPPB (Association of State and Provincial Psychology Boards), 26, 34
Assessing Student and Supervisee Performance (Standard 7.06), 159, 160, 163
Assessment. *See also* Evaluation(s)
    applying models of racial and ethnic development to, 67

245

of competence, 30–36
of competencies, 93
Competency Assessment Toolkit for Professional Psychology, 82–83
context for, 93–94
culturally appropriate and informed, 13
defined, 80
direct vs. indirect, 160
ethical issues in, 160–161, 163
in evaluating success of remediation activities, 110–111
of female trainees, 152
formative, 82, 84, 89–92
group program assessment, 203
of one's own competence, 64
self-assessment of functioning, 36, 37
summative, 84, 89, 91
system perspective related to. *See* System perspective related to assessment
vignette of trainees lacking competence in, 217–219
as way to identify problems of professional competence, 80. *See also* Identification and assessment of problems of professional competence
Assessment of Competency Benchmark Workgroup, 88
Assessments
formal, 82–84, 90–92
informal, 83–84, 90–92
Assistance, multisource network for, 20
Association of Psychology Postdoctoral and Internship Centers (APPIC), 28, 105
Association of State and Provincial Psychology Boards (ASPPB), 26, 34
Attendance policies, 229
Attire, professional, 92, 214–217
Attitudes, 38–39
Avoidance of False or Deceptive Statements (Standard 5.01), 155–156
Avoiding Harm (Standard 3.04), 156, 159, 164

B

Balancing competing goals, 6
Barnett, J. E., 63
Basterfield, C., 36
Behavior(s)
assessing competency in terms of, 216
clear and consistent policies relevant to, 225–226
online, 225–227
policies guiding, 195–196
for reflection and growth, 202–203
unprofessional, vignette of trainee exhibiting, 221–225
Behavioral indicators of PPC, 50–51, 101
Behavior problems
egregious, 53
as source of problems of professional competence, 46–48
Behnke, S. H., 165, 183
Beliefs, 38–39, 51–52
Benchmark evaluation system, 88
Benchmarks, 88
Benchmarks model, 32–34, 45
Benchmarks system, 88
Beneficence and Nonmaleficence (Principle A), 151
Bernard, J. M., 159–160
Biaggio, M. K., 53
Bias(es), 13
in assessments of female trainees, 152
cognitive, 36
cultural and institutional, 18
due to lack of cultural competence, 65–68
fear of, 52
against identity and/or identity expression, 216–217
implicit, 19
in self-assessment of abilities, 64
Biosocialcultural context, 13
Birchall, C., 135
Blank v. Board of Higher Education, 186
Board of Curators of the University of Missouri v. Horowitz, 178, 179, 188
Boundaries, struggles with, 217–219
Boundaries of Competence (Standard 2.01[a]), 63, 154
Bronfenbrenner, U., 80
Brown-Rice, K., 52, 56

C

Capacity building, 74
CCTC. *See* Council of Chairs of Training Councils
Change
for creating a just culture, 136
difficulty of, 19
elements of, 208
resistance to, 208
Chronic pain, trainee adapting to, 227–229

Index • 247

Chronosystem, 81, 90
  defined, 231
  in identifying and addressing problems of professional competence, 90–91
Clear communication, 202
Clinical documentation, 86
Clinical humility, 203
CoA (Commission on Accreditation), 26, 33
Cognitive bias, 36
Collegiality, among trainers, 206–207
Colonial ways of thinking, 13–14
Commission on Accreditation (CoA), 26, 33
Communication
  in communitarian training culture, 155–157
  of competence problem to trainee, 100–102
  effective skills for, 202
  frequency of, 201
  in identifying/assessing problems of professional competence, 95
  of informal assessments, 83
  between program and practicum/internship sites, 85–86, 130–131
  role of, 13
  transparent, 201–202
  vignette of problems with, 221–225
Communitarian, multiculturally sensitive, and socially just training culture, 9–22. *See also specific topics*
  challenges in building, 18–19
  communitarian training, 10–11
  decolonizing supervision, 13–18
  multiculturally sensitive and socially just training, 12–13
  and professional missteps, 21–22
  solutions to and recommendations for addressing challenges of, 19–21
Communitarian and culturally humble supervision, 16
Communitarianism
  assertions in, 37
  defined, 231
  living/modeling of, 154
  working toward, 4
Communitarian perspective
  on competency, 36–38
  and freedom to share information, 87
  incorporation of, 12
  on trainee confidentiality, 131–132
Communitarian training culture, 10–11, 49, 152–158. *See also* Communitarian, multiculturally

sensitive, and socially just training culture
  absence of, 153
  best practices for, 166–167
  in building competent communities, 87
  challenge in building, 18–19
  communication in, 155–157
  creating, 153–155
  defined, 231
  focus in, 132
  gatekeeper role in, 162–163
  information sharing in, 155–157
  normalization of consultation and professional support in, 223
  to prevent ethical issues, 152–158
  training contract in, 157–158
Communitarian values
  in APA Ethics Code, 11
  emancipatory, 74
  feedback in context of, 84
  funding as barrier to enacting, 207–208
  habits promoting, 201–205
  program policies promoting, 197–201. *See also* Program policies
  in training culture, 4, 49
Competence
  across areas of professional functioning, 150
  across training stages, 5. *See also individual areas*
  articulating barriers to, 101–102
  assessment of, 30–36
  conceptualization and application of, 63–64
  cultural variance in, 67
  culture of, 88
  defined, 25, 39, 231
  importance of, 62–63
  multicultural, 18–19, 68–69
  need for, 25
  of supervisors, 17
Competence (Standard 2), 164
Competence constellation model, 10–11, 37
Competence problems. *See also* Problems of professional competence (PPC); Trainees with problems of professional competence (TPPC)
  communication of, 100–102, 221–225
  diverse backgrounds and judgments about, 128–129
  documentation of, 221–225
  ecological approach to, 11
  multiple, 217–219

248 • Index

pitfalls in handling. *See* Troubleshooting common pitfalls
supportive culture for addressing, 3–7
terminology and description of, 44–46
trainers' conceptualization of, 214–217
in training and in providing services, 48
Competencies Conferences, 28, 29, 88
Competency(-ies), 25–40
  in addressing problems of professional competence, 130
  articulation of, 27–28
  assessing, 31–32
  from communitarian perspective, 36–38
  competency cube, 29–31
  conversations about concerns with, 17
  current models of, 33–35
  defined, 39, 231–232
  defining, 28, 31
  development over time of, 45
  egregious violations of, 52–53
  establishing standards of, 25
  foundational and functional, 28–36
  insight for, 39
  modeling struggles with, 22
  from multicultural perspective, 38–39
  nonclinical and noninterpersonal, 219–221
  practical side of, 27
  professional, 25
  and professional values, 26–27
  program-specific, 34–36
  standards of, 28–36
  supervisory, 17
Competency Assessment Toolkit, 88, 89
Competency Assessment Toolkit for Professional Psychology, 82–83
Competency-based supervision, 17
Competency-based training, 31–32
Competency Benchmark Evaluation System, 92
Competency Benchmarks
  behavioral examples of, 47, 52
  developmental benchmarks of, 45
  iterations of, 63–64
  and professional appearance, 215
Competency benchmarks model, 101
Competency cube, 29–31, 33, 34, 45
Competency frameworks, 28
Competency movement, 87–88
Competent (term), 232
Competing goals, 6
Confidentiality. *See also* Trainee confidentiality (TC)
  common concerns about, 95
  ethical issues with, 165–166
  in personal psychotherapy, 139
  right to privacy vs., 126
  secrecy implied by, 132
  vignette of trainee who struggles with, 217–219
Conflict of Interest (Standard 3.06), 161, 164
Constantine, M. G., 68
Consultation
  culturally appropriate and informed, 13
  between internship site and home training program, 229
Contextualization
  of problems of professional competence, 46–49
  of remediation as supportive intervention, 99–100
Contract claims, 185–186
Council of Chairs of Training Councils (CCTC), 19, 21, 132, 142
Counseling in, 232
Counseling out, 114–115
  defined, 232
  to minimize potential damage to trainee, 221
  taking stock following, 118
  trainer self-care during, 118–119
Cultural competence
  achieving, 182
  and biased evaluations, 65–68
Cultural humility
  defined, 39, 232
  in forming competent action and learning, 39
  lack of, 19
  in supervision, 14–15
  for trainer–trainee understanding, 93
Culturally adaptive interventions and advocacy, 13
Cultural responsiveness, 65
Culture
  of competence, 88
  dominant, training culture affected by, 18
  just, 135–136
  organizational, confidentiality and, 135–137
  processes embedded in, 80
  professional, 12, 26–27
  and trainee–trainer relationship, 130
  of training programs, 90. *See also* Training culture

D

Decolonization
 defined, 232
 need for, 12
 of supervision, 13–18
 of supervisory and power-inflected relationships, 12
Decolonizing supervision, 13–18
Defamation, 117, 184–185
Delegation of Work to Others (Standard 2.05), 159
Demyan, A. L., 70
Departmental policies, 201
Deportment, 92
Descriptions of Education and Training Programs (Standard 7.02), 155, 156
Design of Education and Training Programs (Standard 7.01), 154–155
Developmental problems, as source of problems of professional competence, 46–48
Developmental stages
 in competency cube, 29–31, 45
 of trainee, considering, 229
Disability
 Americans With Disabilities Act, 172–176
 defined, 173
 legal definitions of, 47
 reasonable accommodations for, 173–175, 217–219, 228
Disciplinary dismissals, 115
Disclosures (Standard 4.05), 164
Discussing the Limits of Confidentiality (Standard 4.02), 164
Dismissal of trainees, 115–117
 due process rights in, 177
 for ethical violations, 53
 legal issues with, 115–117, 181, 183, 185–186
 nonlegal advice for, 117
 for significant competency concerns, 103
 taking stock following, 118
 trainer self-care during, 118–119
 vignettes of pitfalls with, 219–225, 228
Diversity
 and addressing of trainees with problems of professional competence, 65–66
 faculty conflicts around, 52
 intersection of problems of professional competence and, 51–52
 and judgments about competence problems, 128–129
 legal issues regarding, 181–183
Diversity training statement, 73
Documentation
 clinical, 86
 in dismissal process, 117
 ethical standard for, 163
 policies for, 229
 at program level, 102
 of remediation plans, 165
 vignette of problems with, 221–225
Documentation of Professional and Scientific Work and Maintenance of Records (Standard 6.01), 163, 165
Doe v. Samuel Merritt University, 175
Dress codes, 215–216
Due process, 115–117, 177–180
 procedural, 116, 177–179
 property interests, 187–188
 for protecting students and training programs, 221–225
 in psychology, 179–180
 substantive, 116, 177, 179
Dunning–Kruger effect, 64

E

Ecological conceptualization of trainees with competence problems, 11
Ecological model, 49, 80–81
Education, property interest in, 187–188
Education records, access to, 176–177
Egregious problems of professional competence, 52–53
Electronic health care records, 86
Elman, N. S., 44, 49, 64–65, 173
Emancipatory communitarian model, 73–74
Emancipatory communitarian values, 74
Emotion regulation difficulties, 50
Engagement with trainees, 14
Entrenched problems of professional competence, 47–49
Epstein, R. M., 25, 63
Equality, balancing equity and, 200–201
Equity-related program policies, 200–201
Ethical and Legal Standards competency, 91
Ethical issues, 6, 149–167
 and APA Ethics Code General Principles, 150–152
 assessment, evaluation, and feedback, 160–161

competence, 63
confidentiality, 165–166
creating communitarian culture to prevent, 152–158
feedback and remediation, 162–165
gatekeeper functions and obligations, 158–166
general ethical principles, 233
multiple relationships and gatekeeping-advocacy tension, 161–162
with nonbehavioral descriptions of problems, 101
with problems of professional competence, 53–55
recommendations for preventing, 166–167
with remediation process, 113–114
and systemic effect of trainees with problems of professional competence, 53–54
violation of ethical standards, 52–53
Ethical Principles of Psychologists and Code of Conduct (APA Ethics Code; American Psychological Association), 11
competence language in, 63
competency obligation under, 26
Ethical Standards, 152, 195. *See also* Ethical issues; *individual standards*
General Principles, 27, 150–152, 155–157, 195
trainee confidentiality, 138
Evaluation(s). *See also* Assessment
advocacy–evaluation tension, 162
biased, 65
competency evaluations with proctors, 199
cultural contexts in, 65–66
culturally appropriate and informed, 13
ethical issues in, 160–161
fair procedures for, 197–200
formal, 82
formative, 102, 232
and marginalized trainees' cultural contexts, 67
microaggressions' impact on, 68–69
multisource network for, 20
policies for, 198, 199
of remediation plans, 109–111
rolling, 199–200
subjectivity in, 50
summative, 101, 198, 199, 233–234
trainee discomfort with, 84–85, 94
of trainers, 199–200
Evaluation system, 89–90

Examination for Professional Practice Part 2–Skills, 34
Exosystem
defined, 232
in ecological conceptualization, 11, 49, 80
practicum and internship exosystem, 86
Exploitative Relationships (Standard 3.08), 156

F

Faculty
conflicts around diversity among, 52
informal resolution of concerns by, 158
keeping of trainees' secrets by, 134
perceptions of multicultural values among, 67
trainees' perceptions of multicultural competence of, 68–69
Fair evaluation procedures, program policies for, 197–200
Falender, C. A., 14, 44
Family Educational Rights and Privacy Act of 1974 (FERPA), 104, 114, 176–177
Feedback
concerning competencies, 93
ethical issues with, 160–165
formative, 85
frequency of, 198
hesitancy in giving, 223
informal, 102
from informal assessments, 83–84
multisource network for, 20
negative self-efficacy effects of, 56
proximal, 102–103
in remediation process, 102–103, 111–112
summative, 198, 199
from summative review process, 82
trainers' challenges with, 159
verbal and written, 95, 111–112
willingness to accept, 84
Feminist–multicultural theory, 73
Feminist supervision, 15
FERPA. *See* Family Educational Rights and Privacy Act of 1974
Fidelity and Responsibility (Principle B), 151, 157
First Amendment rights, 180–183
Flexible equity, 201
Formal assessments, 82–84, 90–92
Formative assessment, 82, 84, 89–92
Formative evaluation, 102, 232

Forrest, L., 11, 44, 49, 64–65, 70–71, 80, 89, 95, 113, 118, 173
Forward feeding, 54
Foster, V. A., 180
Fouad, N. A., 33
Foundational competencies
  in benchmark system, 88
  in competency cube, 29–31, 45
  core, 28–36
  defined, 233
  problems with, 45
  remediation plan for, 107
France, C., 35–36
Functional competencies
  in benchmark system, 88
  in competency cube, 29–31, 45
  core, 28–36
  defined, 233
  in multicultural perspective, 39
  problems with, 45
  remediation plan for, 107–108
Funding, program policies and, 207–208
Furr, S., 52, 56

G

Gaspar v. Bruton, 187, 188
Gatekeeper functions, 154, 158–166
  assessment, evaluation, and feedback, 160–161
  in communitarian training culture, 162–163
  confidentiality, 165–166
  defined, 233
  ethical considerations for, 54–55
  failure to perform, 225
  feedback and remediation, 162–165
  and limit on trainee confidentiality, 126
  and multiple relationships, 161–162
  and problems of professional competence, 44
  of programs, 196
  trainer unease with, 82
Gatekeeping-advocacy tension, 161–162
Gateslipping, 54–55
Gaubatz, M. D., 54
Gaughen, S., 48
General ethical principles
  APA Ethics Code General Principles, 27, 150–152, 155–157
  defined, 233
Gilfoyle, N., 54–55, 186

Gizara, S. S., 70–71, 113, 118
Goals
  aligned with values, 195
  competing, 6
  defined, 194
  linking problem behaviors to, 101
  program examples of, 194
  of remediation, 100, 164
  of trainees, 194
Goodrich, K. M., 52
Goodyear, R. K., 159–160
Goss v. Lopez, 187–188
Graduate training programs
  barriers for marginalized students in, 66
  lack of cultural responsiveness in, 65
  relative separation between internships and, 54
Grice, T., 134–135
Growth, program prioritization of, 202–203
Guidelines for Clinical Supervision in Health Service Psychology (APA), 17
Guidelines for the Optimal Use of Social Media (APA), 226

H

Habit(s)
  defined, 194, 201
  of mind, competencies dependent of, 27–28
  program examples of, 194
  for reflection and growth, 202–203
  that promote communitarian and multicultural values, 201–205
  and trainee behavior, 194
  of transparent communication, 201–202
  of valuing human relationships, 204–205
Handelsman, M. M., 152
Harris v. Blake and the Board of Trustees of the University of Northern Colorado, 184
Hatcher, R., 33, 34
Health Insurance Portability and Accountability Act (HIPAA), 176
Health service psychology (HSP)
  competency standards in, 25, 28
  core values of, 26
  creating competent communities in, 86–87
  growth of, 36
  Social Responsiveness in Health Service Psychology Education and Training Toolkit, 19–21
  specialty practice within, 35–36
  training programs in, 33

Hensley, L. G., 50
Hidden curriculum, 83
HIPAA (Health Insurance Portability and Accountability Act), 176
HSP. *See* Health service psychology
Human relationships, valuing, 204–205
Humility
  clinical, 203
  cultural. *See* Cultural humility
  value of, 202–203
Hundert, E. M., 25, 63
Hunsley, J., 34
Hutchens, N., 181, 183

I

ICD (individual and cultural diversity), 51–52
Identification and assessment of problems of professional competence, 79–96
  and chronosystem, 90
  defined, 80
  key considerations in, 93–95
  and practicum and internship exosystem, 86
  and professional community macrosystem, 86–87
  and professionalism, 92–93
  and professional training macrosystem, 87–90
  and program–practicum/internship site mesosystem, 85
  system perspective related to assessment, 80–91
  and trainee–practicum microsystem, 84–85
  and trainee–training program microsystem, 81–84
Identifying and addressing problems of professional competence, 50–53, 80
Identities
  cultural, 66
  fluidity of, 12
  intersecting, 12, 16
  and perceptions of others, 51
  sharing and discussing, 16–17
  of trainers and trainees, 9
  troubleshooting pitfalls involving, 216–219
Identity-based assumptions, 65–66
Identity-based bias, 216–219
Impairment, 44, 64, 173
Implicit bias, 19
Imposter syndrome, 68
Inconsistent policies, 225–227

Individual and cultural diversity (ICD), 51–52
Inequity, maintaining systems of, 20–21
Inertia, policy enactment and, 208
Informal assessments, 83–84, 90–92
Informal formative feedback, 102
Informal Resolution of Ethical Violations (Standard 1.04), 157–158
Information sharing
  in communitarian training culture, 155–157
  providing mechanism for, 163
Informed Consent (Standard 3.10), 157, 160, 164, 165
Informed consent process, 157
Ingraham v. Wright, 178
Insight, 39
Integrity (Principle C), 151
International professional context, 13
Internships
  conflict between academic training programs and, 130–131
  practicum and internship exosystem, 86
  program–practicum/internship site mesosystem, 85
  relative separation between graduate programs and, 54
  vignettes of pitfalls with, 217–219, 227–229
Interpersonal effectiveness skills, 202
Interpersonal functioning
  competency problems in, 45
  problems of professional competence related to, 50–51
Interpretation, culturally appropriate and informed, 13
Intersectionality in training situations, 9
Interventions
  culturally adaptive, 13
  tailored, 163–164. *See also* Remediation plans
Intrapersonal functioning, problems of professional competence related to, 50–51

J

Jacobs, S. C., 71, 94, 113
Johnson, W. B., 10, 37, 49, 87, 94, 153, 159
Jones, J., 38
Just culture, 135–136
Justice (Principle D), 151

K

Kallaugher, J., 70, 112
Kaslow, N. J., 45–47, 82–83
Keeton v. Anderson-Wiley, 182, 183
Kerl, S. B., 177
Kissil, K., 68–69
Kitchener, K. S., 159
Knowledge
  competency problems in, 45
  in multiculturalism, 39
Knowledge, skill, and attitude (KSA), 87–88, 140
Koch, J. M., 64, 68
Kraft v. The William Alanson White Psychiatric Foundation, 184
KSA (knowledge, skill, and attitude), 87–88, 140

L

"Lacking capacity," 48
Lamb, D. H., 180
Language
  in conceptualizing trainees with problems of professional competence, 64–65
  regarding competence in APA Ethics Code, 63
  role of, 13
  trainee's preferred pronouns, 216–217
Leadership
  in cultivating trainer collegiality, 207
  policy enforcement by, 209
  in shaping program policies, 205–206
Legal issues, 6, 171–188
  ADA of 1990 and Section 504 of Rehabilitation Act, 172–176
  contract claims, 185–186
  defamation and libel, 184–185
  disability, 47
  dismissals, 115–117
  dismissal without remediation, 103
  due process, 115, 177–180
  Family Educational Rights and Privacy Act, 176–177
  First Amendment, 180–183
  Health Insurance Portability and Accountability Act, 176
  impairment, 44
  negligence, 185
  with problems of professional competence, 53–55
  promissory estoppel, 186–187

property interest in education, 187–188
release of remediation information, 104–105
remediation plans, 105
with remediation process, 113–114
and systemic effect of trainees with problems of professional competence, 53–55
in vignette of trainee adapting to chronic pain, 228
violation of legal standards, 52
Libel, 184–185
Liberation psychology, 12, 233
Licensure, 34
Lichtenberg, J. W., 162
Lilienfield, S., 36

M

Macrosystem
  confidentiality and secrets in, 142
  defined, 233
  in ecological conceptualization, 11, 49, 80
  professional community, 86–87
  professional training, 87–90
Maintaining Confidentiality (Standard 4.01), 165
Mandatory Individual or Group Therapy (Standard 7.05), 164
Maslow, A. H., 207
McAdams, C. R., III, 180
McCutcheon, S., 53, 54
McWhirter, B. T., 73–74
McWhirter, E. H., 73–74
Mentoring
  advising or supervising vs., 204
  investment in, 220–221
  transformational, 161–162
Mesosystem
  communicating assessment results in, 83
  defined, 233
  in ecological conceptualization, 11, 49, 80
  opportunities for change in, 89
  program–practicum/internship site, 85
Microaggressions
  defined, 233
  in evaluations of trainees with problems of professional competence, 68–69
  and mentorship approaches, 74
Microsystem
  defined, 233
  in ecological conceptualization, 11, 49, 80
  opportunities for change in, 89

trainee–practicum, 84–85
trainee–training program, 81–84
Minimal levels of achievement (MLA), 90
Minimizing Intrusions on Privacy (Standard 4.04), 165
Mintz, L. B., 73
Misgendering, 21–22, 68
Missteps, professional, 21–22
MLA (minimal levels of achievement), 90
Model rating forms, 88
Models of competencies, 33–35, 64
Molinari, V., 36
Mollen, D., 70, 112
"Motherhood penalty," 152
Mott, D., 188
Multicultural (term), 233
Multicultural competence
   of faculty, trainees' perceptions of, 68–69
   lack of, 19
   supervisor–supervisee mismatch in, 18–19
Multicultural feminist supervision, 15
Multicultural Guidelines: An Ecological Approach to Context, Identity, and Intersectionality (APA Multicultural Guidelines; APA), 12–13, 22
Multiculturalism
   abstract nature of, 38
   beliefs and attitudes component of, 38–39
   defined, 4
   working toward, 4
Multiculturally sensitive training, 12–13, 195. *See also* Communitarian, multiculturally sensitive, and socially just training culture
Multicultural perspective
   on competency, 38–39
   in supervision, 15
Multicultural values
   faculty's perceptions of, 67
   habits promoting, 201–205
   program policies promoting, 197–201
   in training culture, 4
Multiple relationships, 161–162
Multiple Relationships (Standard 3.05), 160–161, 164

N

National Council of Schools and Programs of Professional Psychology, 87
Negligence, 185
Ng, K., 67–68
Nicholson Perry, K., 64

Nonclinical competencies, 219–221
Nondisclosure, in absence of communitarian training culture, 153
Nonpersonal competencies, 219–221
Norms
   habits as, 201. *See also* Habit(s)
   professional, 92–93

O

Olkin, R., 48
Olsson v. Board of Higher Education of the City of New York, 187
Oppression
   awareness of, 14
   experiences with, 13
   maintaining systems of, 20–21
Organizational behavior and culture, trainee confidentiality and, 135–137
Orientation process, 156
Othermothering, 74

P

Pahlavan v. Drexel University College of Medicine, 174, 175
Peer support networks, 38
Peer trainees
   effects of trainees with problems of professional competence on, 55–56
   experiences with other trainees with competence problems, 69–70
   impact of remediation plans on, 113
   responses to trainees with problems of professional competence by, 128
   supportive relationships among, 204–205
   tensions between trainers and, 129–130
   and trainee confidentiality, 126–129
Personal Problems and Conflicts (Standard 2.06), 164
Personal psychotherapy
   ethical standard for, 164
   limits of confidentiality in, 139
   as remediation strategy, 108–109
Persutte-Manning, S., 129
Physical environments, 13
Pitfalls in handling competency problems. *See* Troubleshooting common pitfalls
Policies
   defined, 194
   departmental, 201
   program examples of, 194

trainees impacted by, 194
of training programs. *See* Program policies
Positive ethics, 152–153
Power
  experiences with, 13
  links of ecological levels with, 80
Power differential, 9, 18, 74
  avoiding abuse of, 162
  and trainee–trainer relationship, 130
Power dynamics
  in addressing trainees with problems of professional competence, 66
  in supervisory relationship and, 14
PPC. *See* Problems of professional competence
Practicums
  deportment in, 92
  practicum and internship exosystem, 86
  program–practicum/internship site mesosystem, 85
  trainees' microsystems in, 84
Preventative training evaluation, 73–74
Prilletensky, I., 73–74
Privacy
  right to, 126, 165
  secrecy vs., 132
Privacy and Confidentiality (Section 4), 160
Privilege
  awareness of, 14
  experiences with, 13
  unconscious desire to hold on to, 18
Problems of professional competence (PPC), 43–57. *See also* Trainees with problems of professional competence (TPPC)
  broad effects of, 53–56
  clarifying and communicating to trainee, 100–102
  competency in addressing, 130
  contextualizing, 46–49
  defined, 43, 233
  developmental vs. entrenched, 47–49
  egregious, 52–53
  ethical issues with, 53–55
  identifying and addressing, 50–53, 80. *See also* Identification and assessment of problems of professional competence
  intersection of diversity and, 51–52
  legal issues with, 53–55
  other trainers and trainees affected by, 55–56
  pitfalls in dealing with. *See* Troubleshooting common pitfalls
  potential sources of, 46–47

related to interpersonal and intrapersonal functioning, 50–51
  stakeholders impacted by, 5
  systems-oriented conceptualizations of, 49
  terminology and describing of, 44–45
  trajectory of, 43–44
Procedural due process, 116, 177–179
Professional care team, 20
Professional community macrosystem, 86–87
Professional competence/competency
  defined, 25
  problems of. *See* Problems of professional competence (PPC)
Professional context, international, 13
Professional culture, of psychology, 12, 26–27
Professional development stages, 29–31, 150
Professional ecosystem, 142
Professionalism, 92–93
  competency problems in, 45
  defined, 92
  Eurocentric ideals of, 68, 69
  vignette of trainee's lack of, 214–217
Professional missteps, 21–22
Professional responsibilities, competing demands of beliefs and, 51–52
Professional training macrosystem, 87–90
Professional values, competencies and, 26–27
Professional Values and Attitudes competency, 91, 92
Profession-wide competency (PWC), 28, 33–36
Program letter, 103
Program policies, 193–210
  advance disclosure of, 140–141
  barriers and facilitators in codifying, 205–209
  consistent with communitarian training culture, 155–156
  for documentation and attendance requirements, 229
  for eliciting trainee perspectives, 197
  enforcement of, 209
  equity-related, 200–201
  for fair evaluation procedures, 197–200
  and funding, 207–208
  and habits promoting communitarian and multicultural values, 201–205
  importance of following, 221
  inconsistent, 225–227

and inertia/resistance to change, 208
informed by systems perspective, 196
leadership in shaping, 205–206
problems with, 224–227
and promissory estoppel, 186–187
to promote communitarian and multicultural values, 197–201
purpose of, 195–196
questioning of, 73
social media, 225–227
for trainee confidentiality, 138–140
and trainer collegiality, 206–207
Program–practicum/internship site mesosystem, 85
Program-specific competencies (PSC), 34–36
Promissory estoppel, 116–117, 186–187
Property interest in education, 187–188
Protection
  due process for, 221–225
  program policies for, 195
Proximal feedback, in remediation process, 102–103
PSC (program-specific competencies), 34–36
Psychological problems, as source of problems of professional competence, 46
Psychotherapy, personal. See Personal psychotherapy
PWC (profession-wide competency), 28, 33–36

R

Racial microaggressions, 68
Racism
  institutional, 128–129
  in learning environment, 14
  systemic, 18
  and trainee–trainer relationship, 130
Rating forms, 88
Reasonable accommodations, 173–175, 217–219, 228
Reciprocity, 86–87
Reflection
  about belief systems, 51
  concerning professionalism, 93
  for identifying/assessing problems of professional competence, 91
  on maintaining systems of oppression and inequity, 20–21
  program prioritization of, 202–203
  of student, in creating remediation plan, 104

Reframing of trainees with problems of professional competence issue, 74
Regents of University of Michigan v. Ewing, 178, 179, 188
Rehabilitation Act, Section 504 of, 172–176
Relational cultural supervision, 15–16
Relationships, supportive, 204–205
Release of information, in remediation process, 104–105
Remediation, 99–119
  appropriateness of, 48
  clarifying and communicating problem to trainee in, 100–102
  contextualized as supportive intervention, 99–100
  cultural contexts in, 65, 66
  designing effective plan for, 105–106. *See also* Remediation plans
  emotions triggered by, 99–100
  ethical issues in, 162–165
  for ethical violations, 53
  evaluating plans for, 109–111
  goals of, 100, 164
  negative self-efficacy effects of, 56
  of problems in functional competencies, 45
  program letter in, 103
  providing feedback throughout, 111–112
  proximal feedback in, 102–103
  releases of information in, 104–105
  selecting and implementing activities for, 106–109
  suggestions for, 71
  systemic context of, 112–114
  taking stock following, 118
  thresholds for, 102–103
  and trainee confidentiality, 126
  trainee response to, 103–104
  and trainee–trainer relationship, 129–130
  trainer self-care during, 118–119
  unsuccessful, 114–117
Remediation plans
  designing, 105–106
  documenting, 165
  evaluating, 109–111
  legal issues with, 177, 180–183, 185–186
  and success of remediation, 100
  trainee feedback used in creating, 104
  vignettes of difficulties with, 217–221, 224, 229
Research, culturally appropriate and informed, 13

Resistance to change, 208
Resources, 6
　for addressing problems of professional competence, 55
　professional care team, 20
Respect for People's Rights and Dignity (Principle E), 151
Respectful communication, 202
Reuman, L., 25, 37
Right to privacy, 126, 165
Rodolfa, E., 29, 34–36, 64
Rolling evaluations, 199–200
Rose, J. S., 129

S

Saccuzzo, D. P., 185
Schaffer, J., 36, 64
Schwartz-Mette, R. A., 46, 47
Secrets and secrecy
　in absence of communitarian training culture, 153
　impact on systems of, 132–135
　and organizational behavior and culture, 135–137
Section 504 of Rehabilitation Act, 172–176
Self-assessment
　of functioning, 36, 37
　of problems of professional competence, 91
Self-reflection
　about belief systems, 51
　concerning professionalism, 93
　habits of, 202–203
　for identifying/assessing problems of professional competence, 91
Sexism
　institutional, 129
　and trainee–trainer relationship, 130
Shen-Miller, D. S., 43, 52, 65–67, 70, 128
Shin, R. Q., 52
Simmons v. United States, 185
Situational stressors, as source of problems of professional competence, 46
Skills
　competency problems in, 45
　for handling remediation/dismissal actions, 118–119
　synergy of knowledge, attitude, and, 87–88, 140
Smith, B., 83
Smith, K. M., 225
Smith, S. D., 67–68

SoA. *See* Standards of Accreditation
Social contract, 44
Social-ecological theory, 73
Social environments, of others, 13
Social-justice-focused approach, 73–74
Socially just training, 12–13. *See also* Communitarian, multiculturally sensitive, and socially just training culture
Social media policy, 225–227
Social Responsiveness in Health Service Psychology Education and Training Toolkit, 19–21, 132
Sources of problems of professional competence, 46–47
Stakeholders
　in creating remediation plan, 105
　"hot potato game" played by, 94
　impact of problems of professional competence on, 5
　recognizing and balancing needs of, 196
　understanding of ethical principles among, 156–157
Stalled progress, trainee with, 219–221
Standards
　ethical, 63, 149, 152
　for professional competence, 52
　of professionalism, 92–93
Standards of Accreditation (SoA; APA), 26, 88, 91, 155, 156
Strengths-based approaches, 13, 74
Student Disclosure of Personal Information (Standard 7.04), 162
Substantive due process, 116, 177, 179
Sue, D. W., 68
Summative assessment, 84, 89, 91
Summative evaluation, 101
　defined, 233–234
　feedback from, 198, 199
Summative reviews, 81–82
Supervision
　allegations of deficits in, 225–227
　communitarian and culturally humble, 16
　competency-based, 17
　cultural humility in, 14–15
　culturally appropriate and informed, 13
　decolonization of, 13–18
　feminist, 15
　legal issues with, 185
　mentoring vs., 204
　relational cultural, 15–16
　transactional, 161

258 • Index

Supervision contract, 157
Supervisors
  keeping of trainees' secrets by, 134
  monthly meetings of, 84
  on remediation process, 113
  trainers vs., 5
Supportive culture, 3–7
Supportive relationships, 204–205
Systemic context of remediation, 112–114
Systemic perspectives, on trainee confidentiality, 131–137
Systemic perspectives on trainees with problems of professional competence, 51, 61–74
  case vignette, 61–62, 72–73
  challenges for trainees, 67–69
  challenges for trainers, 66–67
  conceptualization and application of competence, 63–64
  diversity issues, 65–66
  importance of competence, 62–63
  peers' experiences, 69–70
  recommendations for establishing TPPC procedures, 73–74
  trainers' experiences, 70–73
System perspective related to assessment, 80–91
  chronosystem, 90
  practicum and internship exosystem, 86
  professional community macrosystem, 86–87
  professional training macrosystem, 87–90
  program–practicum/internship site mesosystem, 85
  trainee–practicum microsystem, 84–85
  trainee–training program microsystem, 81–84
Systems
  effects of trainees with problems of professional competence on, 53–56
  impact of secrets in, 132–135
Systems-oriented conceptualizations of problems of professional competence, 49
Systems perspective
  on competency, 4–5
  program policies informed by, 196

T

TC. *See* Trainee confidentiality
Teaching, culturally appropriate and informed, 13

Terminology for problems of professional competence, 44–45
Thresholds for remediation, 102–103
TPPC. *See* Trainees with problems of professional competence
Trainee(s)
  challenges for, 67–69
  diverse, recruiting and retaining, 18
  due process for protecting, 221–225
  feedback on observed competency problems from, 103–104
  identities of, 9
  with nonclinical and noninterpersonal competencies and stalled progress, 219–221
  orientation process for, 156
  policies for eliciting perspectives of, 197
  preparing, for confidentiality, 140–142
  with problems of professional competence. *See* Trainees with problems of professional competence (TPPC)
  tensions between trainers and, 129–130
  use of term, 5
  who are adapting to chronic pain, 227–229
  who are exhibiting several types of competence problems, 217–219
Trainee confidentiality (TC), 125–143
  communitarian perspective on, 131–132
  continuum of, 136–137
  and impact of secrets in systems, 132–135
  limits to, 126–127
  and national training system changes, 142–143
  and organizational behavior and culture, 135–137
  preparing programs and trainers for, 138–140
  preparing trainees for, 140–142
  recommendations for, 138–142
  systemic perspectives on, 131–137
  and tensions among peer trainees, 127–129
  and tensions among trainers, 130–131
  and tensions between trainees and trainers, 129–130
  training environment impact of, 127–131
Trainee–practicum microsystem, 84–85
Trainees with problems of professional competence (TPPC), 64–65. *See also*

Problems of professional competence (PPC)
broad effects of, 44, 53–56
challenges in supporting, 9
confidentiality issues with. *See* Trainee confidentiality (TC)
definitions of, 44, 63, 65, 233–234
ecological conceptualization of, 11
ethical and legal considerations with, 53–55. *See also* Ethical issues; Legal issues
factors in failure to disclose issues of, 134
long-term effects of, 44
other trainers and trainees affected by, 55–56
over- or underidentification of, 67
peers' experiences with. *See* Peer trainees
pitfalls in dealing with. *See* Troubleshooting common pitfalls
recommendations for establishing procedures for, 73–74
supportive culture for, 3–7
systemic perspectives on. *See* Systemic perspectives on trainees with problems of professional competence
as term, 44, 64–65
trainers' challenges in addressing, 159
Trainee–training program microsystem, 81–84
Trainers
challenges for, 66–67, 159
collegiality among, 206–207
conceptualization of competence issues by, 214–217
conceptualization of competency problems by, 12–13
discomfort with evaluation in, 94–95
diverse, recruiting and retaining, 18
effects of trainees with problems of professional competence on, 55, 56
in establishing communitarian training culture, 153–154
ethical obligations of, 152
experiences with trainees with competence problems, 69–73
forward feeding by, 54
identities of, 9
impact of remediation plans on, 113
individual and cultural diversity competence of, 52
informal resolution of concerns by, 158
keeping of trainees' secrets by, 134
legal issues with dismissals for, 116–117
policies for evaluating, 199–200
preparing, for trainee confidentiality, 138–140
as role models, 20
self-care during remediation process, 118–119
supervisors vs., 5
tensions among, 130–131
tensions between trainees and, 129–130
and trainee confidentiality, 126
Training contract, 157–158, 185–186
Training culture, 90
collectivistic and intersectional, 12
communitarian, 10–11. *See also* Communitarian training culture
competitive and individualistic, 153
current, 12
of ethics and care, 17
impact of remediation plans on, 113–114
supportive, 3–7
values of multiculturalism and communitarianism in, 4. *See also* Communitarian, multiculturally sensitive, and socially just training culture
Training environment
creating communitarian culture within, 152–158
effects of trainees with problems of professional competence on peers in, 55–56
and gateslipping, 54–55
hierarchy in, 9
impact of trainee confidentiality on, 127–131
racism in, 14
safe and healthy, 114
Training models
competency-based, 31–32
hierarchical, top-down, 4
Training programs
culture of, 90. *See also* Training culture
due process for protecting, 221–225
ethical obligations of, 149
forms used by, 85
graduate, 54, 65, 66
in health service psychology, 33
high-stakes consequences for, 171–172
policies of. *See* Program policies
preparing, for trainee confidentiality, 138–140

in professional ecosystem, 142
and program–practicum/internship site mesosystem, 85
qualities of family systems in, 135
tools used by, 89
trainee confidentiality issues in, 125
and trainee–training program microsystem, 81–84
Transactional advising/supervision, 161
Transformational mentoring, 161–162
Transparency
about curriculum aspects, 83
in communication, 201–202
in dismissal process, 117
of feedback, 198
in identifying remediation activities, 106–107
and limit on trainee confidentiality, 126
in training program elements, 51
Troubleshooting common pitfalls, 213–229
with due process for protecting students and training programs, 221–225
with inconsistent policies, 225–227
with trainees adapting to chronic pain, 227–229
with trainees exhibiting several types of competence problems, 217–219
with trainees having nonclinical and noninterpersonal competencies and stalled progress, 219–221
with trainer conceptualization of competence issues, 214–217

U

"Unsuitable" students, 48

V

Vacha-Haase, T., 17–18, 56, 71, 106, 156, 163, 179, 180
Values
communitarian. *See* Communitarian values
defined, 194
identified in programs, 195
of leaders, 205
multicultural. *See* Multicultural values
policies and habits reflecting, 210
professional, 26–27
program examples of, 194
of trainees, 194
Valuing human relationships, 204–205
Vasquez, M. J. T., 9
Veilleux, J. C., 47, 56
Vera, E. M., 54
Virtual Working Group on Restrictions Affecting Diversity Training in Graduate Education (APA Board of Educational Affairs), 183

W

Wallace v. Jaffree, 180
Ward v. Polite, 181, 183
Ward v. Wilbanks, 181
Wise, E. H., 25, 37, 183
Wong v. Regents of the University of California, 174, 175

About the Editors

Rebecca A. Schwartz-Mette, PhD, is a licensed psychologist and associate professor at the University of Maine. Her research examines (a) the interpersonal context of adolescent psychopathology and (b) competency and well-being in health care professionals, with a particular focus on working with trainees with competence problems. Dr. Schwartz-Mette maintains a private clinical practice and mentors doctoral students in ethics, research, and clinical practice. She is a member of the American Psychological Association's (APA) Board of Educational Affairs' Workgroup on Trainees With Problems of Professional Competence, past cochair of the APA Advisory Committee on Colleague Assistance, and past chair of the APA Ethics Committee. She regularly provides training workshops and consultation on the topic of trainees with competence problems.

Evelyn A. Hunter, PhD, is a licensed psychologist and associate professor at Auburn University. Her research investigates the pathways by which multicultural and diversity characteristics intersect with mental health, behavioral, and training constructs. This work has followed two directions: (a) the development of psychology trainee competencies and (b) disparities in mental health and physical health correlates (e.g., multiple sclerosis). She is engaged in the development and training of doctoral level supervisees in an American Psychological Association (APA)–accredited counseling psychology program, with a particular focus on ethics and professional issues training. She is co-owner of Auburn Psychological Wellness Center, a multidisciplinary group practice that provides therapy, assessment, and psychiatric services. Dr. Hunter is the incoming (2023) chair of the APA Ethics Committee, a member of the APA Board of Educational Affairs' Workgroup on Trainees With Problems of Professional Competence, and the current vice president of scientific affairs for the Society of Counseling Psychology.

Nadine J. Kaslow, PhD, ABPP, is a professor and vice chair for faculty development, diversity, equity, and inclusion, Emory University School of Medicine, Department of Psychiatry and Behavioral Sciences; chief psychologist, Grady Health System; and director of postdoctoral residency training, Emory University School of Medicine. A licensed psychologist, she is board certified through the American Board of Professional Psychology. The 2014 president of the American Psychological Association (APA), Dr. Kaslow is past president/chair of four APA divisions, the American Board of Professional Psychology, and the Association of Psychology Postdoctoral and Internship Centers. She has received numerous national awards for her roles as educator, supervisor, and mentor. The recipient of multiple federal and foundation grants, she has published over 350 articles and four books, including the *Oxford Handbook of Education and Training in Professional Psychology*. The chair of the APA Board of Educational Affairs' Workgroup on Trainees With Problems of Professional Competence, she is one of the authors of APA's *Guidelines for Clinical Supervision in Health Service Psychology* (2015). Dr. Kaslow has given countless local, regional, national, and international workshops on psychology education, training, and supervision with a multicultural and communitarian focus.